Audacity

ALSO BY JONATHAN CHAIT

The Big Con

Audacity

How Barack Obama
Defied His Critics
and Created a Legacy
That Will Prevail

Jonathan Chait

HARPER LUXE

An Imprint of HarperCollinsPublishers

FIRST HARPERLUXE EDITION

ISBN: 978-0-06-249669-0

HarperLuxe™ is a trademark of HarperCollins Publishers.

Library of Congress Cataloging-in-Publication Data is available upon request.

17 18 19 20 21   ID/LSC   10 9 8 7 6 5 4 3 2 1

To my families—first, Mom, Dad and Daniel, and now Robin, Joanna and Benjy. They have given me a life of boundless joy.

Contents

Introduction

On January 21, 2009, Barack Hussein Obama delivered his inaugural address as president of the United States. Thirty-four days later, he appeared before a joint session of Congress to lay out his agenda for the coming session. Between those two speeches—the poetry of the historic inaugural address, and the prose of his more detailed speech a month later—the young president identified a series of core priorities: fiscal stimulus to prevent the economy from spiraling into depression, health care reform, new regulation of the financial industry, steps to begin transitioning the energy industry to renewable power, an overhaul of schools to make them accountable for results, and a refashioning of America's moral standing in the world.

The merits of the agenda already provoked bitter dispute. That Obama had set out for himself an astonishingly ambitious agenda was a rare point of universal agreement. The left-wing *Guardian* newspaper hailed his "radical new agenda"; David Gergen, a fixture of the Washington establishment who had worked for several Republican administrations as well as Bill Clinton's, announced, "This was the most ambitious president we've heard in this chamber in decades." Conservatives, naturally, reacted to this sweeping new program with terror. Charles Krauthammer, the Fox News commentator and *Washington Post* columnist whose views were deemed so influential that a *National Review* cover story declared him the leader of the opposition to Obama, warned, "An ambitious president intends to enact the most radical agenda of social transformation seen in our lifetime." *Commentary* columnist Jennifer Rubin feared Obama's program "would permanently refashion the role of the federal government in the lives of every American." For good or for ill, Obama had proposed change on a massive, historic scale. Neither friend nor foe denied the new president's audacity.

This book makes the case that Obama succeeded. He accomplished nearly everything he set out to do, and he set out to do an enormous amount. Some of his success was partial rather than complete. And a great deal of it is subject to attack by a Republican government led by Donald Trump. Gleeful Republicans hailed their victory as a rejection of the leader they were never able to defeat themselves. "The election outcome is a clear repudiation of President Obama, his policies, his vision, how those policies will be implemented," Eric Cantor, the former House Republican majority leader, told the *New York Times*, "and frankly, I think it reflects the fact that most Americans think he failed."

This was a complete inversion of reality. Obama had the approval of a clear majority of Americans. If not for the Twenty-Second Amendment to the Constitution, which limits presidents to two full terms in office, he very likely could have won a third term easily, with the benefit of a much less popular opponent and a much healthier economy than he faced when he won reelection in 2012. In contrast to the popular Obama, polls registered sweeping disapproval of the Republican Congress. (Unlike Obama, who won both his campaigns decisively, Cantor himself actually *was* repudiated by his constituents, who voted him out of office in 2014.)

Obama's would-be successor, Hillary Clinton, did face a far more skeptical electorate, whose views of her were shaped by a second-tier scandal over a private email server. Whatever its basis in fact, distrust of Clinton was intensely personal. She lost despite, not because of, her association with the popular sitting president. And even her loss itself reflected the unusual construction of the Electoral College rather than the expressed preference of the voting majority. Trump's aging supporters were disproportionately clustered in battleground states, allowing him to prevail despite her clear win in the national vote.

The myth of repudiation had a clear purpose: to make it appear both fair and inevitable that the conquering Republican government would destroy Obama's legacy. The conclusion even had natural appeal to despairing liberals. But, as we will see, the fatalistic conclusion that Trump can erase Obama's achievements is overstated—perhaps even completely false.

Obama's reactionary opponents are determined to destroy his legacy not because it changed little, but because it changed so much. Any large-scale reordering of power and resources in American life will inevitably face resistance, sometimes for decades. After Lincoln managed to ban slavery, Southern states launched a violent terrorist counterattack, disenfranchising their African-American citizens, subjecting them to constant physical terror, and forcing them into exploitative labor arrangements almost tantamount to slavery. Conservatives never gave up their hatred for Franklin Roosevelt's reforms, and the war against New Deal programs has never ended. (In 2005, when freshly reelected George W. Bush set out to privatize Social Security, *National Review* splashed a smiling Roosevelt on its cover, under the headline, "Wipe That Grin Off Your Face," reflecting the right's confidence his signature social insurance program would soon be phased out.) Sweeping reforms create powerful enemies who do not disappear.

And Obama's reforms have worked. The evidence of their success lies not only in laws but in concrete and measurable results. Obama's program has already reshaped the economy, health care, energy, finance, and education in quantifiable ways. Its imprint has gone beyond the realm of theoretical promise and into observable results.

Faced with the enactment of such ambitious reforms, the conservative opposition responded in the expected partisan fashion. After their initial overwrought and frequently hysterical claims that Obama would destroy all that was good about America, they shifted the terms of their critique when their predictions of doom failed to materialize. Instead the very same conservatives who had quaked in terror at the breadth of his ambition began to emphasize that Obama had simply not done much of anything. Krauthammer, once frenzied at Obama's revolutionary ambitions, sniffed five years later that he "will be seen as a parenthesis in American political history." Rubin, hopefully anticipating a court ruling to overturn Obamacare that did not come, gloated in 2014 that he "will end his presidency with no significant accomplishment . . . putting him in the running for the most unsuccessful president in history."

More curious than the dismissal by the partisan opposition is how many Americans who did *not* oppose Obama's agenda came to believe something not much different. Obama's supporters spent most of his presidency in a state ranging from resignation to despair. In the *New York Times,* journalist Robert Draper identified "the central critique" of the Obama presidency as being "far better versed in hopey-changey atmospherics and cutting-edge campaign tactics than in actual governing." Veteran reporter Howard Fineman, writing in the *Huffington Post* in 2014, attempting to provide a sympathetic answer to the question, "Remember The Fresh Promise Of Barack Obama? What Happened To That Guy?"

This was not an idiosyncratic complaint, nor the expression of closeted hostility. The notion that Obama had largely failed to live up to his promise attained the status of conventional wisdom, so widely held that it often required no defense. It was more common to find Obama's defenders excusing his failure to deliver transformational change—it was the economy, or George W. Bush, or the partisanship of the Republicans in Congress that had thwarted him—than to hear them affirm that he had indeed delivered that change. This book records many important thought leaders expressing versions of this conviction, because it is worth placing them in a time capsule now—in the not very distant future, it will be hard to believe people predisposed to agree with Obama thought this way.

Audacity is not a history of the Obama administration. Nor is it a real-time repository of juicy inside accounts. It is a book that makes an argument. I am not making this argument like a lawyer, who brushes aside any inconvenient facts that might damn his client, but as an opinion journalist who takes intellectual standards seriously. That is to say, my conclusion, while strongly favorable, is not entirely so. Obama, like any elected official, made mistakes and endured setbacks. This is not an "official" account of the administration, members of which disagree with parts of it, and none of them participated in it. It builds its case from information that was available to the public—yet that information, hiding in plain sight, often failed to be understood or appreciated. (I know because I spent eight years trying to make the case in *The New Republic* and *New York* magazine, developing many of the arguments which this book synthesizes.) The evidence that Obama succeeded in changing America in the major ways he set out to do is so strong that an explanation is required for why so many of us failed to see what was there all along.

A full understanding of what Obama accomplished, and of the immensity of the opposition he overcame in order to do so, is not only a matter of correct history. It is a vital question—maybe *the* vital question—at the heart of the political struggle of this era. How was a black president able to win two elections in a country where vile retrograde attitudes still enjoy wide acceptance? How can sensible progressive reforms be designed and enacted in the face of fanatical opposition on the right? Obama's presidency is a model of what pragmatic and liberal Americans ought to believe in, how they can achieve it, and a standard around which they can rally in the dark years that lie ahead.

Barack Hussein Obama was introduced to America as a youthful, magnetic Illinois state senator representing a portion of Chicago's South Side who had burst suddenly and somewhat mysteriously on the scene. An electrifying keynote address he delivered at the 2004 Democratic National Convention, despite having yet to win election to the United States Senate, let alone serve in national politics, propelled an ascent that turned into a presidential campaign three years later. But the head-spinning rapidity of Obama's rise also burdened him. The initial image—superficially appealing yet weightless—followed Obama throughout his primary campaign, when Hillary Clinton cast him as an inspirational Martin Luther King–esque speechmaker as opposed to a viable president, and the general election, when John McCain scathingly labeled him a "celebrity," appealing but vacuous. It has clung to him as well over the course of his presidency. A remarkably substantial number of critics and saddened supporters alike have described Obama and his era as a time of unfulfilled promise, poetry without prose.

And yet, the lived reality of Obama's presidency has unfolded as almost the precise opposite of the now-calcified trope. He amassed a record of substantial accomplishment far deeper than even many of his supporters give him credit for. It is his poetic qualities that have been found wanting.

Over and over, Obama's agenda would collide with the cultural assumptions of the Washington establishment. American politics had a long tradition of bipartisanship, shaped by a twentieth century when the two parties were both loose coalitions, each of which contained liberals and conservatives. Over decades, the two parties sorted themselves into coherent blocs with tight-knit beliefs (which resemble political parties in most democracies). But the habits of the past shaped the response to Obama among reporters and business elites, who failed to detect the tectonic plates shifting underfoot. In a polarized age, Obama could not operate as presidents had in the days when Democrats controlled much of the white South, and Republicans still thrived in the Yankee North.

By temperament and ideology, Obama is a pragmatist. He gravitated toward the liberal Republican tradition, whose ideas, as we'll see, shaped most of his program—on health care, the environment, education, foreign policy, and other areas. But by 2009, the GOP was in the final stages of a decades-long purge that banished the last traces of liberal Republicanism from its ranks. Governing like a liberal Republican could not win Obama support from the now uniformly conservative Republican Party.

Judged by substance, Obama's agenda succeeded. Judged by style, it consistently rankled mainstream observers. Chuck Todd, the host of NBC's *Meet the Press* and an influential representative of mainstream political thought, summed up Washington's frustration with the forty-fourth president in a 2014 book titled *The Stranger*. The title reflected the trope of Obama as a foreign, ethereal figure, and its central premise cast him as a disappointment, concluding, "his legacy will be a generation of political division."

More telling than Todd's verdict is the criteria by which he arrived at it. *The Stranger* mostly dispenses with any judgment of Obama's policy outcomes, focusing instead on his political methodology. Todd's account of the stimulus, for instance, treats the episode primarily as an attempt to win the favor of Republicans in Congress. He concludes it failed, because "[f]ar from drawing up a truly bipartisan bill, Obama would claim the veneer of bipartisanship with only [moderate Republican Senators] Snowe, Collins and Specter for cover." Todd's own description showed that bringing on more Republicans would have required making the stimulus smaller (and less effective), but he frames bipartisan reconciliation and comity, rather than saving the economy, as the major stakes of the episode. Todd uses this lens to analyze the entire Obama presidency. He devotes several pages to the 2010 Deepwater Horizon oil spill, lacerating the administration for failing to satisfy public anxiety, while conceding its success in stopping the spill as an aside. ("Technically, what the government pulled off was quite the impressive feat," writes Todd. "But politically, this took a big toll on the Obama White House, and eventually they'd get no benefit for solving the problem.")

The point here is not to single out Todd, a shrewd and knowledgeable observer of national politics. His book is noteworthy because it provides an anthropologically accurate summary of how Washington and the news media viewed Obama in his own time. Millions of disappointed Americans saw Obama as Todd did. What they objected to was not the outcome but the methods.

The widespread feeling of disappointment in Obama can be understood if we contrast the aspiration of his 2004 speech, which elevated the idea of Obama to a plane above normal politics, with the day-to-day experience of his two terms, which was usually dismal, and frequently terrifying. The successful moments, when things were going well, usually amounted to drawn-out debates in Washington, with bills or regulatory proposals slogging through a tedious series of media leaks, complaints from dissatisfied Democratic allies, furious denunciation from Republicans, and perhaps a drawn-out last-ditch legal battle while its fate hung in limbo for months. It was a reality that could not match a romantic conception of politics as a noble triumph of good.

And that is just when things were going well. Often, they were not. Throughout Obama's tenure he frequently found himself facing apparent crises that threatened to rock his presidency to its very core. The source of the freak-out of the moment rotated in punctuated intervals. The episodes tended to be all-consuming for a period of time, after which they were almost completely forgotten. Mortal threats to Obama's presidency have included the Deepwater Horizon oil spill, the swine flu epidemic, the Christmas underwear bomber, the IRS scandal, healthcare.org, and the Central American refugee crisis, among many others. Depending on how you keep count, upwards of nineteen events have been described as "Obama's Katrina." In April 2014, at a time Obama had publicly beseeched his critics to consider the long run, the crisis of the moment was Russia's invasion of Ukraine. *New York Times* columnist Maureen Dowd scolded, "the American president should not perpetually use the word 'eventually.' And he should not set a tone of resignation with references to this being a relay race and say he's willing to take 'a quarter of a loaf or half a loaf,' and muse that things may not come 'to full fruition on your timetable.'" Obama likening his foreign policy approach to hitting singles and doubles further dissatisfied Dowd. "Especially now that we have this scary World War III vibe with the Russians," she wrote, "we expect the president, especially one who ran as Babe Ruth, to hit home runs." But once the World War III "vibe" disappeared, attention moved on.

A few months after, the crisis was the outbreak of Ebola, which held much of the nation in a state of terror. Panic enveloped not only the round-the-clock procession of cable television fearmongers but also sober observers like *New York Times* national reporter Michael Barbaro ("if Obama doesn't get [the] Ebola response right, it will define his presidency in a way that dwarfs ACA et al.") and veteran foreign correspondent Tom Ricks, who noted it was "starting to feel like President Obama's Katrina." As Obama failed to channel and soothe public anxiety, a Bloomberg News report diagnosed the Ebola episode as part of a pattern of botching the putatively crucial "performative" aspects of his job. "Six years in," the story concluded disapprovingly, "it's clear that Obama's presidency is largely about adhering to intellectual rigor—regardless of the public's emotional needs." Whatever the ultimate emotional trauma from the episode, the final Ebola death count in the United States was two.

Obama's restless, erstwhile supporters may think their dissatisfaction lies in his mastery of style over substance. The reality is just the opposite. Obama regarded the performative aspects of his job with a contempt he barely hid in public. (In off-the-record discussions with journalists, of which I have attended several, he did not hide it at all.) Obama faced constant complaints that he was not making Americans feel better about whatever had seized their attention at a given moment. The ever-shortening attention span of the public mind in the information age was an uneasy match for Obama's long-term horizons. Obama's friends and exasperated fans sometimes likened him to Mr. Spock, the Vulcan from *Star Trek* who lacks human emotion and struggles to comprehend it. While it was as frequently used to mock the president as it was to compliment him, Obama has embraced the model, even at one point taking time to eulogize Leonard Nimoy, the late actor who portrayed Spock, at a press conference. Careful, rational deliberation has been the hallmark of his governing style.

It would be a mistake, however, to conflate Obama's cool, calculating style with an aversion to risk. Obama thought carefully about the odds, but he proved himself willing to take big risks—often, more willing than many of his advisers and allies. Some of his greatest accomplishments, like pressing ahead with Obamacare in the face of apparent defeat, or approving the raid that killed Osama bin Laden, or even the decision to run for president in the first place as a freshman senator—overrode the objections of experienced allies who considered them far too perilous. To an unusual degree, the Obama presidency reflects not only the historical forces that gathered at a moment in time, nor even just the president's ideological beliefs, but also his character and mental makeup. The Obama presidency will be seen as the careful, patient application of the powers of office that paid off in ways that were often not evident on the surface—a long game with audacious goals, and a bold willingness to endure short-term costs in order to achieve them.

Throughout his presidency, Obama displayed a keen understanding of history. One of his most frequently cited quotes was a phrase, widely attributed to Martin Luther King, that "the moral arc of the universe is long, but it bends towards justice." Cynics often mocked the line as evidence of the president's complacency and naivete about the difficulty of the struggle to make the world a just place. But Obama never said that history moved in a constant, uninterrupted line toward progress. As he warned in a 2014 speech at the Lyndon Baines Johnson Library, "history travels not only forwards; history can travel backwards, history can travel sideways."

Good ideas advance in fits and stops. Demagogues and bigots will always have their day. Previous generations of Americans knew times when it seemed impossible to imagine slavery might be abolished, women given the right to vote, business subject to any government regulation. Redeemers, Red Scares and other reactionaries can wield their terrifying power. Progress tends to come in great dramatic bursts of action, and then recede.

Barack Obama's presidency represented one of those great bursts. It was a vision and incarnation of an American future. His enemies rage against and long to restore a past of rigid social hierarchy or a threadbare state that yields to the economically powerful. But he, not they, represents the values of the youngest Americans and the world they will one day inhabit.

Audacity

Chapter 1
America's Primal Sin

On March 7, 2015, Barack Obama stood at the foot of the Edmund Pettus Bridge in Selma, Alabama, to commemorate the fiftieth anniversary of the bloody, iconic civil rights march from that city to the capital, Montgomery. The historical juxtaposition was awe-inspiring. Five decades before, demonstrators had endured brutal attacks by police merely for attempting to exercise their right to vote. Now the site had been consecrated as a civic holy ground, and an African-American was presiding over the event as president. It had all happened within the lifetime of many participants—some of whom, like the demonstrator turned member of Congress John Lewis, were on hand. The mere sight of it attested to the triumph of the unimaginable.

The transformation embodied by the first black president, though, was not merely symbolic. Obama's presidency would be filled with reminders of the persistence of racism, but it was nonetheless true that his election could not have occurred fifty, or probably not even twenty, years earlier. For all the hatred and white racial paranoia that rose in opposition, the racial advancement that enabled his presidency continued as a result of it.

That Obama's presidency would ultimately reduce to his racial identity was inevitable from the moment of his election. In one sense, it is deeply ironic, since Obama's legislative record—unlike, say, Lyndon Johnson's, or Lincoln's, or the Reconstruction-era presidents—barely touched upon any explicit civil rights conflict. In another sense, however, it is perfectly appropriate. Obama's blackness is not merely a historical breakthrough but also the dominant fact of the political age over which he has presided.

Before the age of Obama, most Americans had an idea of what racial conflict looked like in the post–civil rights era. It looked like the O. J. Simpson trial of 1995, when white America and black America were both mesmerized by the same event, but came away from it with diametrical understandings, agape with mutual incomprehension. It looked like the urban riots of the late 1960s, or the Los Angeles riots in 1992, or Al Sharpton, or Bernhard Goetz, the New York subway vigilante who in 1984 shot four black teens who had (depending on one's perspective) either threatened him, or not. It was two races sharing a country but split into incompatible realities.

When Obama appeared on the scene, he seemed to hold within him the promise of something better. In a dazzling keynote speech at the 2004 Democratic National Convention, the not-yet-elected freshman senator described his white mother and African father, and seemed somehow to transcend race. "There's not a black America and white America and Latino America and Asian America," he said, "there's the United States of America." He attracted Republican admirers, like former president George W. Bush Secretary of State Colin Powell, Nebraska senator Chuck Hagel, and writer Christopher Buckley. The scene of his first, shocking political triumph three and a half years later, where he first convinced the skeptics he could snatch his party's nomination from Hillary Clinton, was the nearly all-white state of Iowa.

What transpired instead was neither the dream nor the nightmare, but something altogether different and unexpected. As Obama's primary battle with Clinton dragged on, her supporters failed to yield to the inevitability of his unsurmountable delegate lead. And their stubborn loyalty did not merely indicate a particular attachment to her. In Appalachia and the white South, especially, white Democrats continued voting for Clinton overwhelmingly, often expressing outright disgust for her opponent. In the spring of 2008, before Obama had clinched the nomination, the New Yorker's George Packer traveled to Kentucky, where he solicited a number of frank interviews to this effect. Some of these voters identified as Democrats, and had been happy to vote for Hillary Clinton or John Kerry but unwilling to do so for Obama. "Race," one voter told Packer, by way of explanation, "I really don't want an African-American as president. Race." That a black man became our commander in chief, that a black family inhabited the White House, that he was elected by a disproportionately high black vote, affected not just the few Americans willing to share their racism with reporters, but all Americans, across the political spectrum.

Social scientists have long used a basic survey to measure what they call "racial resentment." It doesn't measure hatred of minorities or support for segregation, but rather a person's level of broad sympathy for African-Americans (asking, for instance, if you believe that "blacks have gotten less than they deserve" or whether "it's really a matter of some people not trying hard enough"). Obviously, the racially conservative view—that blacks are owed no extra support from the government—has for decades corresponded more closely with conservatism writ large and thus with the Republican Party. The same is true with the racially liberal view and the Democratic Party: many of the Americans who support government programs that disproportionately offer blacks a leg up are Democrats. But when the political scientists Michael Tesler and David O. Sears peered into the data in 2009, they noticed that the election of Obama had made views on race matter far more than ever. By the outset of Obama's presidency, they found, the gap in approval of the president between those with strongly liberal views on the African-American condition and those with strongly conservative beliefs on race was at least twice as large as it had been under any of the previous four administrations. As Tesler delved further into the numbers, he saw that thinking on race was bleeding into everything, predicting, for example, opinions on health care reform far more closely in 2009 than they did in 1993, when the president trying to reform health care was Bill Clinton. In 2010, he found, "Whites who were racially resentful were less likely to support the health care reform law, even after controlling for age, gender, education level, income level, employment status, party identification, political ideology, the respondent's attitude towards President Obama and whether or not the individual had health insurance." Tesler called what he saw unfurling before him a "hyperracialized era."

In recent history, racial liberals have sometimes had conservative views on other matters, and racial conservatives have sometimes had liberal views on particular policies and initiatives. During Obama's time, race increasingly dominated everything. Consider another measuring tool, called "anti-black affect," a kind of thermometer that registers frostiness toward African-Americans. Prior to 2009, anti-black affect did not predict an individual's political identification (when factoring out that person's economic, moral, and foreign policy conservatism). Since Obama has taken office, the correlation between anti-black affect and Republican partisanship has shot up. Even people's beliefs about whether the unemployment rate was rising or falling in 2012—which, in previous years, had stood independent of racial baggage—were now closely linked with their racial beliefs. Other ways of measuring the question yielded similar results. A 2010 *New York Times* poll found that 52 percent of Tea Party sympathizers, as opposed to just 28 percent of Americans as a whole, believed "too much has been made of the problems facing black people."

Before the Obama era, racial conservatism and conservatism used to be similar things; during the Obama era, they became the same thing. This is also true with racial liberalism and liberalism. The mental chasm between red and blue America is, at bottom, an irreconcilable difference over the definition of racial justice.

The reason for this dramatic shift would come as a surprise. Most people who follow the news closely have understood for many decades that the Democratic Party has become the party of black Americans. Democrats generally favor expanding social programs that benefit African-Americans disproportionately, while Republicans oppose them. If you watch a Democratic nominating convention on television, you will see many black faces in the audience. If you watch a Republican convention, you will see almost exclusively white ones.

But this was not widely known to the people who don't watch conventions or follow political news closely. (There are a lot more of them than you might think.) During the several elections before 2008, only a minority of independent voters identified the Democratic Party as the one favoring higher levels of government aid for African-Americans. Close followers of politics

might have long associated Democrats with more liberal views on race and Republicans more conservative
ones. But, writes Tesler, "a substantial proportion of
the population had a difficult time making that connection before Obama ran for president."

America in the Obama era is not so much divided
by race as it is divided *about* race. When O. J. Simpson
was acquitted in 1995 of murder charges, whites across
parties reacted in nearly equal measure: 56 percent
of white Republicans objected to the verdict, as did
52 percent of white Democrats. Two decades later, the
trial of George Zimmerman produced a very different
reaction. This case also hinged on race—Zimmerman
shot and killed Trayvon Martin, an unarmed black teen
from his neighborhood in Florida, and was acquitted of
all charges. But in this instance the gap in disapproval
over the verdict between white Democrats and white
Republicans was not 4 points but 43.

Here is another indication of the transformed landscape. In 2007, radio shock jock Don Imus described
the Rutgers women's basketball team as "nappy-headed
hos." A poll found that 45 percent of Republicans and
61 percent of Democrats wanted Imus fired, a gap of 16
percentage points. Consider the contrast to a roughly
similar episode. In 2014—just seven years later, but
now in Obama's America—Los Angeles Clippers owner

Donald Sterling was recorded criticizing a girlfriend for "associating with black people." This time 68 percent of Democrats, but just 26 percent of Republicans, believed Sterling should have to sell his franchise—a partisan gap of 42 percent. Another poll that year found a similar-sized partisan gap on the question of whether *12 Years a Slave* deserved the Academy Award for Best Picture.

Ultimately Donald Trump represented this trend brought to its fruition. Unlike Mitt Romney, whose father campaigned for civil rights and refused to support Barry Goldwater on these grounds, Donald Trump wallowed in racism throughout his adult life. His father's housing empire, in which he worked, refused to lease apartments to black customers. In 1989, he took out a full page ad demanding the execution of five teenagers, four black and one Hispanic, for a crime they did not commit. He warned hysterically over a historic crime wave that existed only in his fevered imagination. He proposed unconstitutional bans on Muslim immigrants and called a judge unfit to preside over his fraud trial. The latter comment was so blatant in its racism—insisting an American could not do a job solely and explicitly because of his heritage—that even Republican House Speaker Paul Ryan had to admit was "sort of like the textbook definition of a racist comment." But less than a quarter of Republicans told pollsters they considered the comment racist, while more than four-fifths of Democrats disagreed. (Ryan supported Trump anyway.)

Americans had split once again into mutually uncomprehending racial camps, but this time along political lines, not by race itself. Race has occupied the minds of Republicans and Democrats alike throughout Obama's two terms, reordering the political landscape as profoundly as any event since the civil rights movement destroyed the Democratic Party's hold on the South. The aftershocks of this upheaval will last long after Obama's presidency.

On September 15, 2009, two boys on a school bus in Illinois got into a fistfight. A video of the melee emerged. Conservatives turned the story into national news. This was not just a fight between two schoolboys, the sort of thing that has gone on forever. One of them happened to be black and the other white, which transformed the event into a synecdoche for the changes conservatives perceived all around them. WHITE STUDENT BEATEN ON BUS; CROWD CHEERS, blared a headline on the *Drudge Report,* a massively popular conservative news site. "In Obama's America, the white kids now get beat up with the black kids cheering," concluded Rush Limbaugh, the preeminent conservative talk show host.

Obama's appearance on the national scene made conservatism obsessed with the subject of race. The most peculiar thing about the right's racial panic has been its fervent and apparently sincere belief that it is *not racist*. The social norm against racism has spread so widely that hardly anybody will openly confess to it. When University of Oklahoma fraternity members were recorded chanting, "There will never be a nigger SAE / You can hang them from a tree / But they'll never sign with me," a parent of one of the students professed, "we know his heart, and he is not a racist." In 2008, a Republican group in California distributed a fake Obama dollar bill, labeled "food stamps" and decorated with fried chicken and watermelon. The group's president denied being a racist. (She pointed out that she had once voted for African-American Alan Keyes.) In 2009, Georgia restaurant owner Patrick Lanzo displayed a roadside sign reading, OBAMAS [sic] PLAN FOR HEALTH CARE: NIGGER RIG IT. Lanzo insisted, according to a news report, that "he's not a racist." When Louisiana justice of the peace Keith Bardwell refused to marry an interracial couple, he argued in his own defense, "I'm not a racist. I just don't believe in mixing the races that way."

These episodes should not be taken as specimens of the authentic Republican base; very few Republicans would endorse sentiments even remotely as crude as this. (Close to 90 percent of Americans now approve of interracial marriage.) What they show, instead, are the odd ways in which white racial panic expresses itself in the context of a society that deems racism unacceptable. Conservatives find themselves trapped between their fear that racial norms have slipped out of control and indignation that they find themselves blamed for this state of affairs. In their mind, they find themselves victimized once by the hoodlums and welfare moochers closing in all around them, and again by a society accusing them of bigotry.

This mentality has a long historical pedigree. Racial conservatism is the belief that, at any given period, the balance of actual or threatened power is arrayed against whites. Fears of overweening government based in Washington had special purchase among slave owners, and then later among segregationists. After the Civil War, southern white supremacists attacked even formally race-neutral government programs like public education or other forms of social welfare. Striking down the 1875 Civil Rights Act, a conservative Supreme Court ruled, "[T]here must be some stage in the progress of his elevation when [a freed slave] takes the rank of a mere citizen, and ceases to be the special favorite of the laws." A mere decade after slavery had ended, and amid an epidemic of white terrorist violence and nationwide discrimination, conservatives perceived special favoritism toward African-Americans had gone on too long.

The conservative line often concedes that whites may have sinned against blacks in the past, and may even continue to do so here and there, but states that at the present moment the risk lies in taking things too far in the opposite direction. As prevailing standards of fairness have continued to advance, conservatives have retreated again and again to new lines of defense, always insisting that at any given moment, things have gone far enough (or, more often, too far). Indeed, conservative discussion of race pays vanishingly little attention to racism as an extant force in American life. On occasion, conservatives will blurt out what most of them believe, that racial discrimination has essentially disappeared. The conservative pundit David Gelernter, writing in the *Weekly Standard*, glibly referenced "the all-but-eradication of race prejudice."

In fact, the continued existence of racism in American life has been confirmed by a library of social science research. Experiments show that employers are less likely to call back job applicants whose resume (constructed by researchers) has a stereotypically black name, even if the resume touts equal credentials. Doctors feel less sensitivity to pain reported by black patients than white ones. The criminal justice system prosecutes defendants more severely for having killed a white person than a black person. People taking implicit association tests, which ask them to sort words that flash on a screen, are quicker to associate white faces with positive terms, and black faces with negative ones—even when they're aware of the experiment's design and trying their best to avoid prejudice.

And yet, despite the voluminous proof that racism continues to lurk deep in the American psyche, conservative thought treats it as dead and buried. Nearly every reference to racism you find in conservative media treats it either as a ploy by the left, or as a trait that liberals have but that conservatives do not. None of this is to say that all, or even most, conservatives hold racist beliefs. But denial or minimization of racism's persistence has become a defining conservative trait.

Just how deep does the connection run? A 2013 paper by University of Rochester political scientists Avidit Acharya, Matthew Blackwell, and Maya Sen found that counties in the South that had higher levels of slavery before the Civil War displayed continued right-wing tendencies. Even today, white residents of slavery-intense counties oppose affirmative action and vote Republican at higher rates than whites in low-slavery counties. The findings, they suggest, affirm that whites in high-slavery areas embraced racist social norms and institutions to control their freed black populations, and that the attitudes these produced have been passed down through generations. Such counties saw much higher rates of lynching in the decades after the Civil War than their lower-slavery counterparts. They also found that whites in southern counties that had very low levels of slavery voted for Obama in 2012 at about the same rate as whites in the north (46 percent). Not a single study of voting patterns has disputed that the extreme conservatism of southern whites sets them apart from whites in other regions, and that such conservatism grew out of a political culture driven by slavery.

Earlier research by the political scientists Donald Kinder and Cindy Kam found that whites who have higher levels of "ethnocentrism," or a preference for their own ethnic group, are more likely to oppose social programs that aid poor people because they perceive those programs as benefiting people unlike themselves. Interestingly, they found that ethnocentric whites approve of "universal" programs, like Social Security and Medicare, which they see as benefiting deserving constituencies.

These findings reveal a hidden racial basis for the passionate conflicts of the Obama era. Republicans relentlessly attacked Obamacare (the sort of means-tested program opposed by ethnocentric whites) for cutting funds from Medicare (the sort of program ethnocentric whites support). It was, after all, hard to construct a principled reason why the government should subsidize health insurance for people over sixty-five years old but not for working-age Americans too poor or sick to afford it. A famous Republican ad in 2012 showed an elderly white man, and the narrator said, in language that seemed to have been lifted directly from Kinder and Kam's research, "Now the money you paid for your guaranteed health care is going to a massive new government program that's not for you." In 2015, a YouTube star named Jamie Jones recorded a viral country music video, viewed more than two million times, called "Pissed Off Rednecks Like Me," which aired a number of right-wing cultural and political grievances, including, "Old folks they can't afford medication, this damn Obamacare's a joke." The song reflected the degree to which grassroots anger at Obama and his health care law had broken off from any semblance of conservative thought. It was simply an appendage of a cultural struggle.

After the civil rights movement had dismantled legal apartheid, conservative elites abandoned their fight against it. Nevertheless, Republican-led states imposed a wide array of measures designed to impose bureaucratic obstacles to registering voters and casting ballots—reducing early voting hours, requiring new forms of identification, and more. These laws disproportionately reduced turnout by minorities, and one paper found that states were far more likely to enact restrictive voting laws if minority turnout in their state had recently increased.

Through this process of constant revision—of forgetting old, losing battles and associating their side with a cause it opposed—conservatives have cleansed their own sense of honor. The American right thus feels little if any remorse for the legacy of racism. Indeed, conservatives consider themselves to the heirs to the civil rights movement. This belief, however strange, forms a crucial underpinning of modern conservative racial thought, and it has to be understood in order to grasp the pervasive sense of racial victimization that gripped the right during the age of Obama.

It is, of course, true that the Democratic Party was the party of the white South from the nineteenth century through most of the twentieth century, and the Republican Party was originally formed to resist the spread of slavery. This is another way of saying that American conservatism had a strong foothold in the Democratic Party until control of the party's leadership was wrested away from its white supremacist southern wing and into the hands of northern liberals. This process provoked fierce southern resistance, including breakaway third-party presidential campaigns by Strom Thurmond in 1948 and George Wallace in 1968, to protest the Democratic Party's embrace of civil rights. Eventually, white conservatives defected from the Democratic Party permanently and realigned with the GOP.

The most important single moment in this transformation came in 1964, when the conservative movement, up until that point an insurgent faction sidelined from power within the Republican Party, took control of its convention and won the nomination for Barry Goldwater. Though not personally a racist, Goldwater opposed the 1964 Civil Rights Act, which was supported by Republican Party moderates who fought bitterly against him. Goldwater drew support from conservative icons like William F. Buckley and Ronald Reagan, who expressed open disdain for the civil rights movement. "A new breed of Republicans had taken over the GOP," wrote a disgusted Jackie Robinson, who to that point, like a substantial minority of black Americans, had identified as a Republican, "As I watched this steamroller operation in San Francisco, I had a better understanding of how it must have felt to be a Jew in Hitler's Germany." The conservative movement's rise within the Republican Party drove out nearly all its remaining black support and opened the path for the party to gain the allegiance of (the far more numerous) white southerners. Indeed, conservative operatives like *National Review* publisher William Rusher explicitly argued that the Republican Party should court the white South as a strategy to build a conservative national majority.

The Republican Party's legacy as heir to the conservative tradition of the white South has become the subject of a furious campaign of denial and historical revisionism. During the Obama presidency, this strand of revisionism blossomed into a thriving subgenre of conservative polemic. A 2012 Ann Coulter book argued, "Liberals slander Republicans by endlessly repeating a bizarro-world history in which Democrats defended black America and Republicans appealed to segregationists. The truth has always been exactly the opposite." A 2014 conservative-authored booklet, *The Truth About Jim Crow,* dwells on the Democratic Party's historic role as defender of white supremacy, and the Republican Party's history of advocating abolition and

Reconstruction, and then elides the GOP's conservative takeover and embrace of the white South.

A 2012 *National Review* cover story by Kevin Williamson went slightly beyond repeating the rote historical fact that white southern conservatives used to be Democrats to spin a more convoluted, but equally warped, history that likewise fails to reckon with the undeniable links between conservatism and opposition to civil rights. Williamson, for instance, brushed aside Goldwater's opposition to the 1964 Civil Rights Act as overblown, placing more weight on the fact that the party platform called for its "full implementation and faithful execution." He did not mention that conservatives blocked convention plans for the party to endorse the law's "enforcement," and one calling the protection of the right to vote a constitutional responsibility—both obstructions that the moderate Republican George Romney bitterly denounced as "a surrender to the southern segregationists."

Versions of this backward history have recirculated endlessly in the conservative media in recent years. It forms the foundation of the right's belief in its own racial innocence. That innocence allows conservatives to believe, in all apparent sincerity, that they have become the primary victims of the racial dynamic.

It is certainly possible to find plenty of episodes of racism, or barely submerged racism, among Republicans during the Obama era. Republicans frequently made teleprompter jokes built on the bizarre assumption that Obama could not speak coherently without reading from a prepared text, or speculated that his memoir was secretly written for him by former sixties radical turned Obama Chicago neighbor William Ayers.

A related vein of racial paranoia imagined Obama as a kind of angry black nationalist, driven by concealed anger at its white minority. Such terror occupied Limbaugh's mind when he raved, in 2009, "The days of them not having any power are over, and they are angry. And they want to use their power as a means of retribution. That's what Obama's about, gang. He's angry, he's gonna cut this country down to size, he's gonna make it pay for all the multicultural mistakes that it has made, its mistreatment of minorities." Conservative author Dinesh D'Souza expressed a similar fear through his theory that Obama's worldview is best understood as a Kenyan backlash against European colonialism. His theory won the acclaim of figures like former House Speaker Newt Gingrich. "What if [Obama] is so outside our comprehension, that only if you understand Kenyan, anti-colonial behavior, can you begin to piece together [his actions]?" Gingrich asked. "That is the most accurate, predictive model for his behavior." Likewise former New York City mayor Rudy Giuliani's claim that the president, despite his incessant protestations to the contrary, does not love the United States. ("He wasn't brought up the way you were brought up and I was brought up, through love of this country.")

But the predominant characteristic of the Republican race obsession under Obama is not actual racism, or even racialized suspicions that Obama is seeking to undermine the country to punish it for its sins. It is, rather, a belief that race has become a weapon against Republicans. "This is a part of the war on whites that's being launched by the Democratic Party," declared Alabama congressman Mo Brooks, "and the way in which they're launching this war is by claiming that whites hate everybody else."

From a political standpoint, Republicans believe they face an unfair handicap: they must rely solely on appeals to reason, while Democrats enjoy the benefit of winning votes on the basis of race alone. "President Obama is asking for black votes as a matter of racial solidarity," editorialized the *Wall Street Journal* in 2014, "because he can't make the case based on results." (This was an astonishing way to think about race and voting, given that the entire pre-Obama history of African-American presidential voting, to the extent it was allowed, consisted of voting for candidates of a different race, while the pre-Obama history of white voting consisted almost entirely of voting for candidates of the same race.) The conservative columnist Byron York noted in 2009, as an aside, "the president and some of his policies are significantly less popular with white Americans than with black Americans, and his sky-high ratings among African-Americans make some of his positions appear a bit more popular overall than they actually are." York's claim makes no sense whatsoever if you think of every voter as having the same weight. It can be understood only as the expression of a belief that black voters belong to a different, racialized category.

Republicans likewise assessed that Obama, his party, and the national media have used false accusations of racism to intimidate them and insulate him from scrutiny. The party's own behavior reveals how seriously they took this belief. Since Obama's election, they sought out ways to neutralize his racial advantage by embracing black leaders of their own. To be sure, Republicans have always sought out ideologically acceptable black candidates in the interest of demographic outreach, just as Democrats do. But in the Obama years this desire took on a frantic quality to match the seriousness with which Republicans viewed the political power of Obama's identity. The GOP's first response following the election was to appoint Michael Steele, a failed Senate candidate from Maryland, as the director of the Republican National Committee. Steele's race gave him the freedom to say what most members of his party believed. Promising not to "soft-pedal" criticism "just because the President of the United States is a Black man"—a constraint Republicans believed had handicapped them fatally—Steele declared that Obama "was not vetted, because the press fell in love with the black man running for the office. . . . 'Oh gee, wouldn't it be neat to do that? Gee, wouldn't it make all of our liberal guilt just go away? We can continue to ride around in our limousines and feel so lucky to live in an America with a black president.'" Obama had won, Steele said at another point, because he "played the race card, and it worked beautifully."

Steele left his post in 2011, by which point his role in the political culture had been taken up by Herman Cain, a pizza chain magnate, radio host, and occasional conservative activist. Cain's central promise to Republicans was that nominating him would take "the race card," as he called it, "off the table." Cain also assured Republicans that, as they suspected, racial prejudice in modern America is mostly directed against them. "Most people have gotten past color," he said, "especially the Republican Party." The biggest racists turned out to be African-American Democrats: "A lot of these liberal, leftist folk in this country, that are black, they're more racist than the white people that they're claiming to be racist."

So eagerly did Republicans greet this message, and its messenger, that Cain shot to the top of national polling for the party nomination in the summer of 2011 despite having never held elected office, and having little experience in or knowledge of public policy. The fact that Cain attained front-runner status offered a secondary source of emotional satisfaction to conservatives, as it rebuked the calumny of Republican racism: Republicans were also willing to support a black man for president and, unlike the Democrats, they had arrived at this decision purely out of color-blind merit. When Cain won the Florida Republican straw poll in 2011, conservative columnist Mona Charen suggested "it wasn't that Republicans and conservatives were acting upon an affirmative action spirit—trying to prove that they too could pull the lever for a black guy.

It's that Herman Cain delivers a great speech, is willing to propose solutions commensurate with our problems, and is possessed of a remarkably sunny personality." Charen sardonically headlined her column, "'Racists' for Cain."

When Cain's campaign was soon derailed by a series of sexual harassment accusations, he ironically insinuated that he had only been targeted because of his skin color. "Do you think that race, being a strong black conservative, has anything to do with the fact you've been so charged?" asked a Fox News host. "I believe the answer is yes, but we do not have any evidence to support it," he answered. A pro-Cain organization pleaded, "Don't let the media 'lynch' another black conservative."

As Cain departed from the scene, his place was taken up by famed surgeon Ben Carson. A fellow black conservative, also lacking any political experience, Carson attracted presidential speculation merely by endorsing a few rote conservative ideas at a national prayer breakfast. Thrilled conservatives asked Carson to authenticate their theories on race, which he happily obliged. White liberals are "the most racist people there are," he told one conservative talk show host. Yes, he assured another, Obama plays the race card. Indeed, Carson garnered headlines for claiming that race relations have "gotten worse" under Obama and calling the president's health care law "the worst thing that has happened in this nation since slavery." And when he did become a candidate in 2015, he based his message almost entirely on absolving conservatives of racism, and enjoyed a brief period as front-runner before Trump supplanted him. Predictably, Carson defended his party's nominee. "No he's not a racist, but you know what the Left does," he announced on Fox News. "You know if you don't agree with them, you know, you're a racist, you're a homophobe, you're Islamophobic. You know they have a whole passel of terms they're going to throw at you and what people have to do is stop being afraid of these names." This was a perfect encapsulation of the Republican view that racism was not a real-world phenomenon, but only an accusation used by the left to silence the right. The Party experienced the Obama era as a period of racial trauma, and in the conservative mind, accusations of racism against Trump not only confirmed his righteousness, they identified him as a champion who would stand up against the bullying they believed they had endured.

It must be acknowledged that, while the conservative sense of racial persecution is rooted in faulty history and free-floating paranoia, it is not *entirely* groundless. The hyperracialized politics of the Obama era have victimized the right in a way that is completely real, and makes its resentment more explicable.

On September 9, 2009, Obama delivered a nationally televised speech before Congress on health care, intended to restore some measure of reason after an angry summer dominated by frantic and often unhinged Tea Party protesters at town hall meetings. In the middle of the speech, Obama pointed out that his plan would not provide coverage to illegal immigrants. Representative Joe Wilson, a Republican from South Carolina, screamed, "You lie!"

It was not a lie—Obama's claim was accurate. And even aside from its lack of merit, Wilson's outburst was wild and unusual. But several Obama supporters immediately concluded it was not only those things, but also the product of white racial hostility. "I think it's based on racism," explained Jimmy Carter at a public forum. "There is an inherent feeling among many in this country that an African-American should not be president." Maureen Dowd commented, "What I heard was an unspoken word in the air: You lie, boy! . . . Some people just can't believe a black man is president and will never accept it."

Of course, Wilson did not say "boy." Dowd had

merely extrapolated, and an imagined slur is not exactly a solid basis for impugning motive. It might have been the case that Wilson was driven to rage by the spectacle of the first black president. On the other hand, it may have instead been some combination of partisan exuberance or general ignorance or lack of self-control.

One way to answer the question would be to compare the treatment of Obama with that of the previous Democrat to occupy the Oval Office. Bill Clinton, too, endured unprecedented attacks that seemed to reflect the opposition's refusal to recognize his legitimacy as president. Many of these episodes, if they had happened to Obama, would have come across not just as influenced by race but obviously and overtly racist. The *Wall Street Journal* editorial page and other conservative organs speculated that Clinton may have had his aide Vince Foster murdered and had sanctioned a cocaine-smuggling operation out of an airport in Arkansas. North Carolina senator Jesse Helms said, "Mr. Clinton better watch out if he comes down here. He'd better have a bodyguard." Emmett Tyrrell, editor of the *American Spectator*, wrote a presidential biography entitled *Boy Clinton.*

If Obama had been called "boy" in the title of a biography, been subjected to threats of mob violence from a notorious former segregationist turned senator, or accused in a major newspaper of running coke, and also impeached, surely Obama's supporters would believe such things could only have happened to the first black president.

Yet many, many liberals believe that *only* race can explain the ferocity of Republican opposition to Obama. It thus followed that anything Republicans said about Obama that could be explained by racism was probably racism. And since racists wouldn't like anything Obama does, that rendered just about any criticism of Obama—which is to say, nearly everything Republicans say about Obama—presumptively racist.

Liberals aired their suspicions indiscriminately. Bill O'Reilly's 2014 Super Bowl interview with the president included the question, "Why do you feel it's necessary to fundamentally transform the nation that has afforded you so much opportunity?" *Salon*'s Joan Walsh asserted, "O'Reilly and [then-head of Fox News Roger] Ailes and their viewers see this president as unqualified and ungrateful, an affirmative-action baby who won't thank us for all we've done for him and his cohort. The question was, of course, deeply condescending and borderline racist." Yes, it's possible that O'Reilly implied that the United States afforded Obama special opportunity owing to the color of his skin. But it's at least as possible, and consistent with O'Reilly's beliefs, that he merely believes the United States offers every-body opportunity. *Esquire* columnist Charles Pierce has accused *Times* columnist David Brooks of criticiz-ing Obama because he wants Obama to be an "ano-dyne black man" who would "lose, nobly, and then the country could go back to its rightful owners." Timothy Noah, then at *Slate*, argued in 2008 that calling Obama "skinny" flirted with racism. ("When white people are invited to think about Obama's physical appearance, the principal attribute they're likely to dwell on is his dark skin. Consequently, any reference to Obama's other physical attributes can't help coming off as a coy walk around the barn.") Though the term *elitist* has been attached to candidates of both parties for decades (it stuck indelibly to John Kerry during his 2004 presi-dential campaign), the writer David Shipler has called it racist when deployed against Obama. ("'Elitist' is another word for 'arrogant,' which is another word for 'uppity,' that old calumny applied to blacks who stood up for themselves.")

MSNBC harped on the theme relentlessly. When Senate Minority Leader Mitch McConnell chided Obama for playing too much golf, Lawrence O'Donnell accused him of "trying to align . . . the lifestyle of Tiger Woods with Barack Obama." (McConnell had not men-tioned Tiger Woods; it was O'Donnell who made the leap.) After Arizona governor Jan Brewer angrily confronted Obama on an airport tarmac, Jonathan Capehart concluded, "A lot of people saw it as her wagging her finger at this president who's also black, who should not be there." Martin Bashir hung a monologue around his contention that Republicans were using the initials "IRS" as a code that meant "nigger."

Racial prejudice clearly influenced Republican hatred for Obama in the aggregate. But identifying racism in any individual episode was generally impossible, since most racists—especially those operating at high levels of national politics—take special care to avoid overtly racial comments. The result was a poisonous dynamic of mutually justified paranoia. Liberals believed racism lurked invisibly beneath the upsurge of right-wing rage that exploded at the outset of Obama's first term and never fully disappeared. Conservatives believed liberals used accusations of racism to delegitimize all opposition to Obama. Both sides had a point.

What's more, both sides frequently felt irritated about it. The wearing grind of a racialized politics of endless grievance is not quite what anybody had in mind when Obama first appeared on the national stage at the Democratic convention in Boston in 2004. The racialized partisan war, where liberals see racism everywhere, and conservatives see false accusations of racism everywhere, produced one odd point of agreement between the warring sides: the state of race relations was getting worse.

The left sensed that Obama's election had reawakened a white backlash that overwhelmed any progress he could achieve. ("The Truth About Race in America: It's Getting Worse, Not Better," announced a column in the left-wing *Nation*.) Obama has "made [racism] worse," complained actor Morgan Freeman in a CNN interview. (Despite Freeman's consistent support for Obama and his blaming the relapse in race relations on the right, conservatives widely circulated his comments as an admission that Obama had failed.) Polls showed most Americans thought race relations had deteriorated on Obama's watch. A depressing consensus settled in. "Obama's vision of a post-racial America," observed a *Washington Post* reporter, "looks even further away than it did that night a decade ago in Boston."

Obama always took the opposite view. He did not think his election banished racism, or that it was a sign racism has already been banished. He did, however, believe its power had waned, and would continue to wane.

Obama's optimism was the quality that most defined his star-making turn at the 2004 convention. It came through as well in his 2008 speech in which he addressed the vitriolic comments by his pastor, Jeremiah Wright. In that speech, he empathized with Wright's anger at America, which Obama explained as an understandable reaction to the brutal racism in which his older, former pastor was raised. It was Wright's failure to appreciate America's capacity to improve that he identified as his seminal error. "The profound mistake of Reverend Wright's sermons is not that he spoke about racism in our society," argued Obama. "It's that he spoke as if our society was static; as if no progress had been made; as if this country—a country that has made it possible for one of his own members to run for the highest office in the land and build a coalition of white and black, Latino and Asian, rich and poor, young and old—is still irrevocably bound to a tragic past."

This faith in American redemption placed Obama crossways with an important strain of thought on the left. The growing awareness of racism among liberals during his presidency gave new force and prestige to a belief that racism was endemic not only to its history but its very character. The left's profound affinity for the first black president has always been mixed with a caution. To celebrate the breakthrough represented by Obama, or to endorse Obama's cheerful assessment of American progress, would seem to downplay the persistence of racism and other evils. When liberals bring up the history of American race relations, they usually emphasize how little has changed, rather than how much.

Obama has always located himself between the despair of the left and the obliviousness of the right. There is both an element of conviction and political necessity behind this. Though the *intellectual* parallel between the two is clear, Obama's left-wing critics represent a small and relatively powerless faction, while his critics on the right control an entire party. Practically speaking, he had little to lose by raising the ire of the left. The danger of right-wing racial grievance, on the other hand, always posed a dire political risk. Obama's 2008 speech about race was forced upon him by media coverage of Wright's sermons; he made the address not as a way of opening up a new conversation about race, but as a way of ending it. "In the history of African-American politics in this country, there has always been some tension between speaking in universal terms and speaking in very race-specific terms about the plight of the African-American community," he told NPR at the outset of his campaign. "By virtue of my background, you know, I am more likely to speak in universal terms."

Defensiveness pervaded his treatment of the subject. Obama's ability to command a national majority always rested on presenting himself as a racial conciliator, rather than as a spokesman for black victimhood (as many whites viewed Jesse Jackson). Unlike the nearly all-white Republican Party, Obama represented a racially polyglot coalition. The imbalance was on display in December 2014, when Obama caused a minor stir with an interview to Black Entertainment Television. "When you're dealing with something as deeply rooted as racism or bias in any society," he said, "you've got to have vigilance but you have to recognize that it's going to take some time and you just have to be steady so that you don't give up when you don't get all the way there." Obama obviously intended his comment as another rebuke of the left and its tendency to despair rather than acknowledge steady improvement. Instead he offended the right. *Breitbart News,* a conservative site that frequently stokes white racial panic, put Obama's "deeply rooted" quote in its headline, and accused the president of "playing the race card." His mere acknowledgment of racism's existence—even while celebrating its rapid decline—was enough provocation for the right to present Obama as unduly angry.

When racial issues arose, it was never intentional. In 2009, a Cambridge, Massachusetts, police officer arrested the renowned Harvard professor Henry Louis Gates Jr., who had been reported as a burglar by a neighbor who spotted him attempting to pry open the door to his own house, having misplaced his key. A reporter at a press conference asked Obama about the incident, and he opined that the officer had "acted stupidly," and noted, "there's a long history in this country of African Americans and Latinos being stopped by law enforcement disproportionately." The comments thrust the administration onto the defensive. Obama invited Gates and his arresting officer to the White House for a widely publicized beer. The intended symbolism of the meeting was obvious: the president, not as civil rights advocate, but as a racial mediator between white and black.

The administration's fear of racial demagoguery sunk to its nadir in July 2010, at a moment when the Tea Party revolt was burning at its highest intensity. Breitbart's site revealed an explosive video showing Shirley Sherrod, an African-American employee at the U.S. Department of Agriculture, telling an audience that she had discriminated against a white farmer. It was a bomb planted in the center of Obama's coalition. Limbaugh had characterized Obama's economic pro-

gram as "reparations." Now a member of his administration, who was herself black, appeared not only to
be confirming it, but to be doing so with gleeful hostility. The administration, in a panic, forced her to resign
that day.

It emerged very quickly that Breitbart's story was a
smear. He had published a truncated video of Sherrod's
speech—the windup, essentially. She was recounting
a two-decade-old event, not a recent policy decision.
The point of the story was to reveal her temptation to
succumb to feelings of revenge—Sherrod's father had
been lynched—before deciding otherwise. Her speech
was a paean to universalism and the ethic of government as a vehicle for uplift of white and black alike, the
precise opposite of Breitbart's implication. After realiz-
ing its error, the administration tried to bring Sherrod
back, but she understandably declined, and the episode
went down as a disgraceful capitulation to a mob mentality whipped up by a disreputable, race-baiting pseu-
dojournalist.

Obama's 2012 election campaign turned out to be
a catalyzing event in both parties' racial calculus. The
2008 election had been conducted in the shadow of
Wright, and the president labored throughout his first
term under the vague apprehension that the transcen-
dent magic of his euphoric election would dissipate,

and white America would turn against Obama and his party. His reelection four years later, despite its smaller margin, nonetheless had more of a hardness about it. Precisely because his second campaign was no longer historic, and was conducted amid a sluggish recovery, it seemed to show the enduring power of Obama's base. After November 2012, Obama spent less time fretting about whether whites would abandon him, and some Republicans began to contemplate what they needed to do to attract minority support. Obama's approval rating in his second term soared into the middle and upper fifties, demonstrating his ability to capture the trust of Americans of all races.

The newfound freedom of reelection gave Obama more confidence to address racial issues explicitly. Also, in 2014, the Department of Justice began collecting data on police stops and arrests in order to study patterns of racial bias. That year, it issued twin reports on the shooting of Michael Brown in Ferguson, Missouri. The thoroughness and balance of both reports won widespread credibility not only on the left but also on the right.

The first report, vindicating officer Darren Wilson, persuaded even critics who had been initially outraged at his shooting of Michael Brown. The second report's devastating indictment of widespread racial bias in the city's municipal structure persuaded even many staunch right-wingers. The two, in combination, embodied Obama's approach to racial issues—factual and balanced without resorting to false equivalence, and acknowledging deep patterns of bias without assuming they explain every single event. The Ferguson reports managed the remarkable feat of bridging, at least momentarily, a racialized partisan divide. The next year, the administration created a "twenty-first-century policing" task force to encourage states and municipalities to reform their enforcement practices. The practices, which encourage awareness of racial bias and methods to reduce escalation, have spread to Los Angeles, New Orleans, Baltimore, Seattle, and many other smaller cities.

White racial backlash returned with a vengeance in the Republican primary. Even as Obama's popularity soared in his final year, Donald Trump catapulted himself from the fringes of reality television to win the nomination against a huge field of experienced and talented candidates. Trump managed this feat by shrewdly channeling the passions that had consumed the right-wing base. His embrace of conspiracy theories around Obama's origins, his crude bigotry toward Mexican-Americans and Muslims, and his appeals to nostalgic restoration of a bygone social order ("Make America Great Again") allowed him to outflank every opponent on the issue that mattered the most. Just as the Obama era made the most racially resentful white people Republican, within the party, the most racially resentful Republicans supported Trump.

Trump's election reflected a historically normal counterattack against racial egalitarianism, a more contained version of the white South fleeing the Democratic Party after the Civil Rights Movement, or the backlash against Reconstruction in the nineteenth century. But, as we will see in Chapter 7, the reactionary energy harnessed by Trump was unlikely to have the potency of those others. His ideas did not represent the future of the country envisioned by most Americans, and especially not the youngest ones who would have the most to say about that future. He was a deadly death rattle, a polarizing and even loathed figure ultimately destined to follow the likes of Charles Coughlin and George Wallace into ignominy, after exerting a painful price. At the end of the twenty-first century, the vision of American pluralism that is taught to American schoolchildren will not be Trump's any more than it will be Jefferson Davis's. It will be Obama's.

The Obama who spoke in Selma in March 2015 bore the confidence of a leader who believed he spoke for his country's future. His speech expounded on many of his original themes, and his aides later told a reporter that the president saw it as the culminating statement of his vision of America. He scolded despairing liberals who refused to acknowledge America's capacity to change. He mocked conservatives who had questioned his love of country for their "feeble attempts to define some of us as more American than others."

The most interesting idea running through Obama's speech was its tight embrace of the struggle for black freedom as not merely a part of the American story but as its epitome. Obama was commemorating the civil rights movement, but rather than treat it as a thing apart, he placed it at America's historical center, weaving black America's story and the larger American narrative into an inseparable fabric:

We are Lewis and Clark and Sacajawea—pioneers who braved the unfamiliar, followed by a stampede of farmers and miners, entrepreneurs and hucksters. That's our spirit.

We are Sojourner Truth and Fannie Lou Hamer, women who could do as much as any man and then some; and we're Susan B. Anthony, who shook the system until the law reflected that truth. That's our character.

We're the immigrants who stowed away on ships

to reach these shores, the huddled masses yearning to breathe free—Holocaust survivors, Soviet defectors, the Lost Boys of Sudan. We are the hopeful strivers who cross the Rio Grande because they want their kids to know a better life. That's how we came to be.

We're the slaves who built the White House and the economy of the South. We're the ranch hands and cowboys who opened the West, and countless laborers who laid rail, and raised skyscrapers, and organized for workers' rights.

We're the fresh-faced GIs who fought to liberate a continent, and we're the Tuskegee Airmen, Navajo code-talkers, and Japanese-Americans who fought for this country even as their own liberty had been denied. We're the firefighters who rushed into those buildings on 9/11, and the volunteers who signed up to fight in Afghanistan and Iraq.

Presenting the struggle for justice as the essence of American history, Obama implicitly consigned its reactionaries to their inevitable demise. Racism may be deeply rooted, but it is slowly withering. He was seizing back from the Tea Party, with its tricorner hats and partisan appropriation of the Constitution, the spirit of America's past. And he was likewise claiming its future—at one point, Obama spoke directly to the young, his strongest generational base: "And it is you, the young and fearless at heart, the most diverse and educated generation in our history, who the nation is waiting to follow."

In the same speech, Obama resolved the paradox that had bedeviled him when he first appeared in 2004, and throughout much of his presidency: To allow himself to be cast as a "civil rights leader" would forfeit his ability to be the leader of all of America. By fusing the civil rights story with the American story, he eliminated the contradiction. His role as the spokesman of one made him the spokesman of the other, since the struggle for black freedom was the apotheosis of the American story.

That race, America's primal wound, had been drawn into the foreground made public discourse during the Obama era frequently painful. New social media let Americans draw national attention to any racial confrontation, and the prevalence of cell phone videos made police violence against African-Americans into front-page news. It felt to many people as though the race problem was getting worse. And the incentive of the left to downplay progress for fear of encouraging complacency, and the right to deny Obama any credit, contributed to that feeling. But conditions were not really getting worse. They were actually getting better.

In 2012, Seth K. Goldman, a researcher at the University of Pennsylvania, discovered that white racial attitudes grew more liberal over the course of Obama's first election campaign and inauguration. Rather than the familiar images of blacks as athletes or entertainers, or associating them with crime and poverty, Obama provided an association of a leader. It was "a rare instance in which whites were massively exposed to a clear positive shift in the balance of black exemplars in mass media. Obama became the most salient black exemplar in the world, thus simultaneously reducing white racial prejudice." White racial prejudice declined over that period five times faster than it had over the entire previous twenty years.

A paper the next year found even more dramatic findings. Tatishe Nteta of the University of Massachusetts–Amherst and Jill Greenlee of Brandeis University discovered that whites who came of age during and after Obama's first campaign had more liberal views on race than older whites. Of course, racial views had liberalized over time, but they found an unusually pronounced effect. "The election of President Obama may have been a transformative historical event for today's youngest voters," they argued. The appearance of Obama on the national scene changed the way they thought about race, not only in the abstract but in their personal lives. The simplistic initial hope of Obama's giddy supporters that the symbolism of a black president could help heal, if not eliminate, racial prejudice turned out to have a real basis in fact.

And so the Obama phenomenon had made American politics more starkly racial, and it had also made racial sentiments more liberal. Michael Tesler noted that the transformation would continue to reshape American politics for decades. "The enhanced polarization of white partisanship by racial attitudes in response to Democrats becoming the *Party of Obama*," he wrote, "could therefore leave an imprint on the American political landscape that endures long after he leaves office." Obama was not only the effect of a new, more progressive generation. He was also its cause.

Chapter 2

Preventing the
Second Great Depression

S hortly after Barack Obama defeated John McCain, the incoming president received bracing advice from his economic adviser, and future Treasury secretary, Timothy Geithner. "Your legacy is going to be preventing the second Great Depression," Geithner told him. Obama rejected the prediction. "That's not enough for me."

The exchange took place in an atmosphere of slowly enveloping dread, as the world financial system was plunging into an abyss, the depths of which could only be barely discerned at the time. Obama, as it turned out, was correct—he would aim for, and accomplish, much more. But his dispute with Geithner illustrated two disturbing political facts that were beginning to shape the new administration's reality against its will. The first, Geithner's point, was that the economic crisis would impinge upon Obama's grand plans for fundamental transformation; it was not a momentary event but a defining one.

The second point, Obama's rejoinder, underscored a paradox about this. Preventing a second Great Depression would be a substantively gigantic achievement, but politically it would be minuscule. Presidents get credit for *responding* to disasters, not from keeping them from happening in the first place. Obama could not hope to recapitulate Franklin Roosevelt's towering place in the public mind as the man who had saved American capitalism, since Roosevelt had taken office at the depths of the Great Depression. If Obama succeeded, Americans would never experience the horrors from which his policies spared them. The prevention of a disaster would be a literal nonevent.

And so the onset of a financial cataclysm had a peculiar impact upon the new administration as it prepared to take office. Unlike George W. Bush after the 9/11 attacks, or Lyndon Johnson after the Kennedy assassination, the crisis did not invest the president with new agenda-setting powers. As the economy contracted, the political space around Obama compressed just as quickly.

The new administration's economic brain trust immediately agreed that Obama's first task should be to enact a massive economic stimulus program. The idea of a stimulus dated from theories developed during the Depression by the British economist John Maynard Keynes. According to Keynes, a recession created unusual circumstances during which the normal rules of government budgeting would not apply. In a deep recession, people tend to save their money rather than spend it. This sets off a vicious cycle: one person cuts back her trips to the restaurant, causing the restaurant to lay off waiters, who in turn have less money of their own to spend, creating additional losses of jobs and incomes. The first response was for the central bank to reduce interest rates, to encourage people and businesses to borrow more and save less.

If very low interest rates alone didn't do the trick, argued Keynes, the government should inject money directly into the economy, either by giving people money to spend, or by spending money itself—ideally on something worthwhile, but the point was simply to spend, period. The massive government spending during World War II was the stimulus that finally ended the Depression. Obviously, winning the war was of paramount value. But from a purely economic standpoint, there is hardly anything less efficient than building machines, then shipping them overseas, only for many of them to be quickly destroyed. What the war example shows is that, in a severely depressed economy, government borrowing to spend on anything at all can have a stimulating effect. Keynes even suggested that the government bury canisters of money, so that miners could be hired to dig them up. Obviously such a program would be absurd in normal times; only during the unusual circumstance of a severely depressed economy would it make sense to do anything at all to circulate more spending through the economy. It was also crucial that any new stimulus program be financed by temporarily increasing the deficit. If the government financed its new binge by cutting expenditures elsewhere or raising taxes, it would be canceling out its impact. In a depression, the government was the spender of last resort, and only Washington could borrow on the required scale.

And yet these notions—that more debt could actually be positive, and that the economic value of a stimulus program would stand unrelated to the enduring value of the project itself—run so contrary to instinct that they have always been difficult for laypeople to accept. Even many people who are paid to understand public policy for a living, like members of Congress and journalists, often had difficulty understanding it.

Keynes's theory was not notably controversial when it had been put into practice on a smaller scale. It had gained widespread acceptance among economists, both in academia and in the private sector. Even many conservative economists, like Harvard's Greg Mankiw, a frequent Republican adviser, endorsed the concept. In January 2008, a year before Obama took office, members of both parties responded to early signs of a slowdown by quickly passing a classic Keynesian stimulus that cut checks to taxpayers and retirees to encourage them to spend. One hundred sixty-nine of 194 House Republicans, and 32 of 48 Senate Republicans, voted for it.

Likewise, when a mild recession appeared in 2001, Kevin Hassett, a conservative economist who frequently advises Republicans, testified in Congress that "fiscal policy in recessions was reasonably effective," and would be even more effective if the scale of the response was larger and took effect more quickly. Paul Ryan jumped in to voice his agreement. "That is precisely my point," Ryan said. "That is why I like my porridge hot. I think we ought to have this income tax cut fast, deeper, retroactive to January 1st, to make sure we get a good punch into the economy, juice the economy to make sure that we can avoid a hard land-ing." Ryan wasn't arguing that lower tax rates would improve incentives, as the supply-side does, he was advocating a Keynesian stimulus. Richard Nixon had once famously declared, "We are all Keynesians now," and this held true, or true enough, through the Bush administration.

The Obama administration set out to apply this same formula to the crisis it found before it. The task, they discovered quickly, was far more daunting than any such previous effort. The first obstacle was that the size of the economic crisis dwarfed anything that had occurred in generations. In December 2008, economists forecast that the "output gap"—that is, the difference between the economy's potential size if it were healthy and the actual size to which it was projected to shrink—would be a staggering $2 trillion over the next two years.

Even the terrifyingly enormous size of the collapse that Obama's economists saw before them turned out, in retrospect, to be optimistic. Forecasters inside and outside government predicted the economy would shrink by 4.1 percent in the last quarter of 2008, and by another 2.4 percent in the first quarter of 2009. When Obama's advisers presented him with this forecast at a meeting in December, Christina Romer, a University of California, Berkeley economist who had studied the Great Depression, told him, "Mr. President, this is your holy shit moment." In reality, the economy shrank at a rate twice as fast as projected at the time—by 8.3 percent at the end of 2008, and by 5.4 percent at the start of 2009. "Holy shit" did not capture the true scale of the emergency.

As the Obama team drew up plans for its proposed stimulus, it ran up against certain limits of design. The point of a stimulus was to get money out the door as fast as possible; yet there were only so many projects that could be organized on short notice. Some of the more ambitious ideas Obama wanted to finance, like turning the electricity grid into a "smart grid" that could redirect energy to meet demand, required unsnarling years of red tape with hundreds of local communities. The usual dynamic, in which every corner of the bureaucracy demands more money for its pet project than it can get, was inverted. The president's advisers were asking every federal agency how much money they could spend on short notice, and the sum total still couldn't reach what they wanted to spend. Even with tax cuts accounting for 40 percent of the money they would spend, the stimulus still came to $800 billion—a huge amount by normal standards, but still far short of the amount needed to fill the projected output gap, and even farther short of the amount needed to fill the larger, actual output gap.

Obama's economic team could have come up with other ways to spend more money, but it ran into another obstacle. Even before Obama took office, a right-wing backlash was already under way, driving every element of the political, business, and media elite in precisely the opposite direction from where they needed to go to rescue the economy. It was a bizarre and horrible irony: just as the American economy faced a generational calamity, the political system's capacity to address it began to deteriorate.

As an intellectual matter, the case for fiscal stimulus was now far stronger than it had been in early 2008, or in 2001, the last two times Congress had enacted Keynesian measures. Both previous recessions were of a small enough scale that there was a case to be made for letting the Federal Reserve douse the fire by itself. But the economic collapse that followed the fall of Lehman Brothers was so vast that monetary policy alone couldn't possibly address it. To now argue against stimulus would be like someone who called 911 to put out a small kitchen grease fire later insisting that a five-story blaze could be handled without alerting the fire department. If there was ever a time in the last three-quarters of a century when fiscal stimulus was needed, it was 2009.

Yet at this moment, the Republican Party turned against Keynesianism. It is impossible to separate the strands of self-interest and genuine ideological fanaticism that drove this intellectual about-face. On the one hand, as we'll see later, Republican leaders consciously decided even before Obama's term began that their self-interest lay in denying him bipartisan support. To the extent that they still believed in Keynesian economics, they understood that the more effective the stimulus, the faster the recovery, and the harder time they would have regaining power. On the other hand, the party was also undergoing a radicalization, as many conservatives made the case that the Bush administration had failed because it abandoned true small-government conservatism, and that the party must return to stringent free-market absolutism. The two strands—self-interest and ideological fervor—fed into each other. As Upton Sinclair once said, it is difficult to make a man understand something when his salary depends on his not understanding it. Republicans came to believe what it was in their partisan interest to believe that temporary borrowing would not alleviate the crisis.

On January 28, 2009, Obama met with House Republicans to pitch them on stimulus. He got a frosty reception. Representative Roscoe Bartlett, then eighty-two years old, seized upon his authority as a Depression survivor to deliver the most memorable rebuke. "I was there" during the New Deal, he told the new president. "I don't remember any of the many government programs affecting the course of the Depression. Government programs didn't work then, I don't know why we think they would work now." It was not clear why Bartlett, who was five years old when Franklin Roosevelt took office, would necessarily remember the specific effects of government programs upon the economy, but fellow Republicans applauded his comments, which gained a temporary notoriety.

As Obama took office attempting to replicate Roosevelt's heroics, the Republican Party embraced the once obscure and dissident belief that Roosevelt had failed. "When Roosevelt did this, he put our country into a Great Depression," asserted Republican representative Steve Austria. "He tried to borrow and spend, he tried to use the Keynesian approach, and our country ended up in a Great Depression. That's just history." Or a view of history, anyway.

Some of this bizarre understanding was the product of a 2007 book by conservative columnist Amity Shlaes, *The Forgotten Man*. Republicans such as Newt Gingrich, Rudy Giuliani, Mark Sanford, Jon Kyl, and Mike Pence argued that it proved "it was the spending and taxing policies of 1932 and 1936 that exacerbated the situation." Senator John Barrasso found Shlaes's message so compelling that he brought it up in a confirmation hearing for energy secretary Steven Chu, where he evangelically gushed (to the probably dumbfounded Berkeley scientist), "in these economic times, a number of members of the Senate are reading a book called *The Forgotten Man,* about the history of the Great Depression, as we compare and look for solutions, as we look at a stimulus package."

The odd thing is that *The Forgotten Man* did not contain a new argument against the efficacy of stimulus, or an old argument, or even much of an argument at all. The book consists almost entirely of character portraits and meandering stories about obscure figures. It is much more like the transcription of an old person remembering the Depression than it is like reading an economic history of the period. To the extent that *The Forgotten Man* hints at an argument, it *contradicts* the revisionist case, asserting at one point, "The spending [in 1936] was so dramatic that, finally, it functioned as Keynes . . . had hoped it would. Within a year unemployment would drop from 22 percent to 14 percent." The book further notes that Roosevelt mistakenly pulled back on stimulus in 1937, which snuffed out the Keynesian recovery, which only returned to full health under the much larger stimulus of the World War II military buildup. That is to say, whatever wisps of an argument could be found in *The Forgotten Man* bolstered rather than refuted the case for stimulus.

Nevertheless, it was a handsome, weighty, 468-page tome that showed up around the time Republicans were ready to denounce stimulus as useless, and it became one of the sparks in a conservative opposition that flared out in all directions. One of the more common objections derided the bill as a "wish list" of long-standing Democratic policies. This had an element of truth—if you needed to spend a large amount of money as fast as possible, you'd logically begin by financing programs that already existed or had been planned, rather than dreaming up completely new ones from scratch. The attack missed the point of what a stimulus was supposed to do.

Indeed, as conservatives lashed out, many seemed to lack a clear understanding of the purpose of stimulus. Charles Krauthammer sneered, "a third of a billion for contraception, a billion to states to help them collect child support, nursing training—all this is worthy, but it ain't stimulus." The *Weekly Standard* denounced a provision to support state budgets, actually one of the most effective parts of the stimulus. State governments have to balance their budgets, and during a recession tax receipts crater and the need for spending on social services increases, forcing them to raise taxes and cut spending to stay balanced—both of which take spending out of circulation and make the crisis even deeper. For Washington to borrow money and give it to the states was a textbook way to stanch the impact of this anti-stimulus. Still, the *Weekly Standard* somehow insisted in an editorial that the provision couldn't stimulate the economy: "It's hard to argue that the $248 billion in transfers to the states will stimulate the economy. The money is being taken from one pot and put in another so that the states can balance their books and ensure the proper treatment of beneficiaries."

Karl Rove, the Bush administration adviser who retained enormous influence within the party as a pundit, fundraiser, and strategist, pointed out in a February 5, 2009, *Wall Street Journal* op-ed that the largest job losses had occurred in fields like manufacturing, professional business services, retail, hospitality, and the service industry. "It would be logical for policy makers to focus on job creation in these sectors," he argued. Instead, he complained, "Democrats want to spend $88 billion to increase the federal share of Medicaid. What American will be hired by a small business, factory, retail shop, hotel, restaurant or service company because of this spending?"

Of course, the theory of fiscal stimulus is not to pick out specific parts of the private sector to reinflate—which would involve much *more* heavy-handed government industrial planning—but to circulate spending throughout the economy and let consumers decide where to spend. Since Medicaid is a large portion of state budgets, increasing federal spending on it helped states limit the tax hikes and budget cuts they were carrying out to balance their budgets. In fact, a 2011 paper by economists Gabriel Chodorow-Reich and Zachary Liscow from the University of California, Berkeley, Laura Feiveson of the Massachusetts Institute of Technology, and William Gui Woolston of Stanford University measured the very thing Rove was scoffing at. Some states received more stimulus money for Medicaid per capita than others (based on variation in how much they spent beforehand). The economists found that every dollar of Medicaid spending in the stimulus recirculated enough to create about two dollars' worth of economic activity, a hugely efficient contribution to the recovery. "A state's receipt of a marginal $100,000 in Medicaid outlays," the paper calculated, "results in an additional 3.8 job-years, 3.2 of which are outside the government, health, and education sectors." Either Rove simply couldn't understand how a dollar spent on Medicaid could wind up in the hands of the service industry or construction or so on, or he didn't want to understand it, no matter basic economics and expert analysis.

This sort of seat-of-the-pants folk wisdom—which didn't even reflect a conservative theory of economics of any kind—seemed to blossom on the right. A major conservative talking point denounced a provision to re-sod the National Mall, which briefly became the go-to example of an outrageous boondoggle. Certainly, some forms of spending inject money into the economy faster than others, but hiring workers to plant new sod is not wasteful. In fact, unless you consider having grass on the National Mall an extravagance that a country like the United States can't afford, a period of mass unemployment is the best time to hire workers to plant new sod.

The only thing that united all conservatives was a conviction that the stimulus was a disaster. "It is an unholy marriage that manages to combine the worst of each approach—rushed short-term planning with expensive long-term fiscal impact," announced David Brooks. Krauthammer called it "one of the worst bills in galactic history."

It was not just the partisan opposition that was choking on (and in turn trying to strangle) Obama's request for stimulus. His program flew in the face of the fiscal conservatism that permeated the Washington establishment, the business and journalistic elite's belief that deficits were wicked and deficit reduction was thoroughly nonpartisan. Indeed, the rough definition of nonpartisanship that prevailed among right thinking types was a ritualistic demand that Democrats agree to cut social spending, and Republicans agree to increase taxes for the common good. The anti-deficit assumption ran so deep that hardly anybody who shared it even thought of it as a point of view. "Fiscal responsibility," as its advocates called it, was simply a form of virtue. That belief system turned out to be disastrously ill-suited for the moment of crisis.

Two weeks before Obama took the oath of office, the Congressional Budget Office, a nonpartisan government agency that tracks public finances, issued a new report that shocked Washington. The budget deficit for 2009, it projected, would exceed a trillion dollars, an unheard-of figure. This was, of course, the automatic outcome of the economic crisis, which had caused incomes (and thus tax receipts) to plummet, throwing millions of the previously secure into poverty, which automatically created a spike in benefits, such as unemployment insurance for workers who suddenly lacked a job, food assistance for people who no longer could feed their families, Medicaid for the now-uninsured, and so on. The trillion-dollar figure merely assumed current policies would remain in effect—that is, it did not account for any stimulus Congress would pass under Obama, which would push the sum higher still.

Plunked into a political culture that habitually considered deficits the most essential public problem in America, the report had the most damaging possible effect. It implicitly defined the crisis facing the country as excessive deficits, rather than a potential depression that could be averted in the short term only with *more* deficits. "If combined with the gigantic stimulus package of tax cuts and new spending that Mr. Obama is preparing, which could amount to nearly $800 billion over two years, the shortfall this year could hit $1.6 trillion," reported the *New York Times*. "But Mr. Obama and Democratic leaders in Congress said they were more determined than ever to pass a stimulus package by Feb. 16." That "but" contained an important, unstated assumption—that Obama's solution flew in the face of reality. Facing a record-high deficit, he somehow wanted the deficit to get even bigger. News reports, habituated to the premise that the deficit was always the top concern, covered Obama's warnings about the recession with deep skepticism. "In his first major speech since Election Day, Obama participated in an early version of a presidential ritual: preparing the country for an eventual economic recovery by painting an especially grim picture of the nation's fiscal standing at the start," reported the *Washington Post,* treating Obama's doomsaying as so much political hyperbole. "He acknowledged the staggering cost of his proposals and the enormous debt it would impose on future generations." All the media reports described Obama's plan with terms like *staggering* or *massive*—which it may have been when compared to previous stimulus plans, but not in comparison with the scale of the economic hole it was trying to fill. "The forecast Wednesday of a jaw-dropping $1.2 trillion one-year federal budget deficit will make it harder for President-elect Barack Obama to win broad support for a massive stimulus package that would add even more to the red ink," McClatchy newspapers reported. The *Hill,* a newspaper covering Congress, compared Obama's cries of economic alarm to the Bush administration's false warnings of weapons of mass destruction in Iraq: "Obama's tactics ring familiar to those President Bush and his administration used when they claimed that the evidence of weapons of mass destruction in Iraq could come in the form of 'a mushroom cloud.'"

The Republicans' fierce opposition, and the news media's myopic obsession with deficits, echoed and amplified the reality that ordinary Americans had never bought into the logic of Keynesianism. The popular tolerance of deficits often ran directly in contradiction to what economists of many stripes believed. When the economy was flush, as in the late 1990s, voters expressed more willingness to open the public purse strings. During tight times, they wanted the government to cut back. Keynesian logic would prescribe just the opposite: holding down deficits, or even running surpluses, when the economy was at full strength, and pumping deficit spending into the economy during a slowdown. Still, polls in 2009 found most Americans wanted the government to reduce deficits "even though it may mean it will take longer for the economy to recover."

What's more, the bank bailout, which had passed just a few months before, had generated a politically toxic backlash. The sheer injustice of bailing out institutions whose risky behavior had provoked the catastrophe outraged people on left and right alike. Republicans almost immediately began to use the term "bailout" to describe Obama's stimulus program, and many Americans had trouble distinguishing one from the other. By the following year, a plurality of Americans incorrectly believed that the bank bailout, which George W. Bush had signed a month before the 2008 election, had actually happened under Obama. Bailout, stimulus, debt—it all ran together in a singular crisis of Washington irresponsibility for which the new administration seemed responsible.

What people *could* understand was the old-fashioned concept of government waste. Republicans seized upon every program that sounded potentially frivolous and made it the centerpiece of their objection. When Obama obligingly removed the offending item—the administration cancelled funding to re-sod the Mall—they would pluck out a different one.

Most examples of "pork" came from the funding for state and local governments. Since states and municipalities could fund a wide variety of items, all the Republicans had to do was find a silly-sounding state or local initiative, anywhere in America, actual or proposed, and claim the stimulus paid for it. A plan by the city of Las Vegas to build a "mob museum" as a tourist attraction generated nationwide ridicule. There was no reason that paying construction companies to build a mob museum would do any less to stimulate the economy than paying them to build anything else; perhaps Las Vegas was right to believe that a mob museum would have durable appeal to tourists. But the Senate was forced to pass a restriction specifically prohibiting stimulus funds from going to the mob museum. Indeed,

Congress had to pass a measure barring stimulus funds from financing zoos, aquariums, golf courses, swimming pools, or casinos.

It was a farce, but there was no reasoning with it. Journalists eagerly scrambled for wasteful stimulus stories. Over the first sixteen days of Obama's presidency, Nate Silver found, the proportion of articles containing the word "stimulus" that also contained the word "pork" quadrupled. Republicans had won the public spin war in a rout.

This did not prevent the House—where Democrats held more than 250 seats, and which needed only 218 votes to approve anything—from passing a stimulus exceeding $800 billion on January 28. But Republicans held the line with such astonishing success that not a single GOP member crossed over to support the bill. Not even the deepest economic crisis, and a bill with hundreds of billions of dollars in tax cuts, and which bore the endorsement of the Republican-leaning (to put it mildly) U.S. Chamber of Commerce, could lure one stray Republican.

The drama passed over to the Senate, where the minority could block a bill from coming to the floor unless a 60-vote supermajority overruled them. Democrats began the session with just 58 senators. (The eventual 59th Democratic senator, Minnesota's Al Franken, was bogged down in a lengthy, ultimately successful re-count, and only took his seat on July 7.) Obama needed at least two Republican senators.

Three moderate Republican senators held the bal-ance of power: Maine's Olympia Snowe and Susan Col-lins, and Pennsylvania's Arlen Specter. The three were caught between a party leadership and an enraged conservative base demanding they oppose Obama, on the one side, and on the other, their states' blue lean-ings (and, perhaps, a substantive belief that stimulus was a good thing). Working together with conservative Democrat Ben Nelson, they positioned themselves as advocates of a somewhat smaller stimulus than the bill passed through the House.

The troika could never articulate a coherent eco-nomic rationale for their position, but instead seemed to start from the premise that a centrist should favor something smaller and more conservative than the Democrats, and work backward from that point. Their influence reflected horse sense of what kinds of pro-grams sounded stimulative to their senatorial ears. They cut funding for school construction and budget aid to states and, at Collins's insistence, funding for pandemic flu preparation, which Rove had singled out for ridicule. (After initially boasting of her role in elim-inating this item, it became a source of embarrassment for Collins after a major flu outbreak struck several months later.)

Surprisingly, the aftershocks of the moderates' high-profile intervention wound up playing to the Obama administration's favor, in a way that was not apparent at the time. Specter, in particular, faced a backlash so fierce that he soon realized he stood no chance of surviving a primary challenge by right-wing Republican Pat Toomey later that year. And so, at the intense prodding of the Obama administration, within a few months Specter seized his only chance to stay in office: he switched to the Democratic Party. Once Franken took office in July, this made Specter the 60th Democratic vote—and, rather than having to please the Republican base, Specter now had to compete for Democratic support in the upcoming primary, which made him the decisive, filibuster-breaking vote for some of the most important measures of Obama's presidency, including health care reform.

So while the moderates' pound of flesh ultimately paved the way for much of Obama's agenda, it substantially degraded the stimulus's impact. In response to the moderates' intervention, macroeconomic forecasting firms cut their forecast for jobs the stimulus would create. Obama was ultimately able to sign a stimulus projected to cost $787 billion, but his failure to secure an adequately sized response haunted his administration for years to come. More politically harmful than the smaller-than-ideal size of the stimulus was its timing. The administration's response to the crisis had occurred chronologically before the impact of the crisis hit home. Even if he had enacted a perfectly designed policy response, unemployment would have initially risen. But the stimulus granted was simply not large enough to accommodate the actual economic collapse, which turned out to be even larger than what Obama and his advisers had believed given the data available at the time. Thus the rise in unemployment after the stimulus passed (the rate briefly hit double digits) served to discredit the concept of stimulus altogether. Since it was impossible for Obama to convince the public that the crisis would have been worse if not for his policies, all they saw was that he had enacted his policies, and then things had gotten worse.

The moderate senators obviously bore heavier responsibility for the inadequacy of the stimulus than did supporters who wanted to maintain or increase its size. But the question has always loomed whether the Obama administration bears secondary responsibility. Could the administration have found a way to persuade the Senate moderates to authorize a larger or better stimulus?

It's obviously impossible to know whether a different legislative scenario would have yielded better results. It is certainly plausible. After all, the Obama administration only asked for an $800 billion stimulus. Moderate senators under intense political pressure to prove their independence from the administration were bound to cut down his request. By the well-established rules of Washington, positioning yourself somewhere between the two parties is how you establish your moderate credentials. Snowe, Collins, Specter, and Nelson obviously lacked any well-considered economic theory for their stance, beyond a general inclination that whatever the Democrats wanted was probably a bit too much. If the administration had requested, say, a $1.5 trillion stimulus, perhaps the moderates would have decided that $1.2 trillion, rather than $800 billion, represented the sensible middle ground. (On the other hand, it is conceivable they would have recoiled completely against any stimulus plan, and the effort might have collapsed, or taken much longer to pass.)

Still, the administration probably should have tried more to protect itself from the possibility, which turned out to be true, that economic forecasters had underestimated the size of the collapse. In January 2009, the administration published a report, written by two of its economic advisers, Jared Bernstein and Romer, predicting that the unemployment rate without a stimulus would top out at 8.8 percent and remain there through 2010. With the administration's stimulus, unemployment would peak out at 8 percent and decline starting midway through 2009. As it turned out, unemployment hit 10 percent and did not fall below 8 percent until 2012.

Republicans made this failed prediction the heart of their case against the stimulus. Obama's prediction became his promise, and the failure of the prediction became the failure of his agenda. In truth, the prediction failed because it underestimated the size of the problem, not the impact of the remedy. Unemployment before Obama took office was higher than Obama's economists (and most private sector economists) believed at the time. Outsiders like economics Nobel Prize winner and *New York Times* columnist Paul Krugman had been screaming from the rooftops about the danger of undershooting; the administration paid too little attention to the danger. The worst-case scenario envisioned from the outset by many of the administration's liberal critics had come true.

A cleverly designed stimulus could have contained built-in adjustments to increase its size if economic conditions deteriorated. Here is where the administration most clearly miscalculated. Obama and his advisers believed that, if their stimulus undershot, they could easily persuade Congress to spend more. A December 15, 2008, memo to the president-elect from Lawrence Summers, the incoming director of the National Economic Council, advised, "It is easier to add down the road to insufficient fiscal stimulus than to subtract from excessive fiscal stimulus."

In early February, an anonymous Obama adviser told the *New York Times* the same thing: "aides say this bill is not their only bite at the apple. Mr. Obama is willing to do more in the future. Congress, facing midterm elections, may also want to pass another small stimulus package next year." Likewise, Bernstein, looking back in 2011 on the administration's thinking at the time, conceded that they all overestimated how easy it would be to go back and ask for more stimulus. "If you're at the barber and they don't cut your hair short enough, you can always ask them to go a little further," Bernstein told Ezra Klein. "That's sort of how I thought about stimulus policy. I don't think we could have done more in February of 2009 based on political and implementation constraints. But I probably didn't recognize how hard it would be to go back to the barbershop."

All that said, the stimulus was still a gigantic success. Its failure to spend the optimal level can only be understood in a context in which it towered over everything that came before it. President Clinton, faced with a still-sluggish economy in 1993, had struggled to pass a stimulus of just $19 billion as his first major piece of legislation. The stimulus Congress passed at the beginning of 2008 cost $168 billion. Obama's stimulus cost nearly five times as much. As Michael Grunwald pointed out in *The New New Deal,* a history of the 2009 recovery act, even Franklin Roosevelt's New Deal had only consumed about 1.5 percent of the economy at its largest point. (That's why joblessness fell under Roosevelt, but only the more massive defense-led stimulus caused by the war brought full employment.) Obama's stimulus exceeded that. Obama had to overcome the sticker shock of a political system that regarded his program as staggeringly large—which, in comparison to any political response that had preceded it, it was. Obama may not have pushed the capacity of the political system to its maximum theoretical limit, but he pushed it extraordinarily far. No president in American history had ever proposed or enacted an anti-depression program remotely as aggressive.

Much of the stimulus's spending went to programs with an independent social value. Its spending on aid to the poor kept more than five million Americans out of poverty through cash grants. It invested in transportation infrastructure, scientific research, and a huge array of public goods. It also seeded long term reforms in health care, education, and green energy that, in the haste of the moment, barely registered but had far-reaching consequences that other chapters will explore. But its direct, primary purpose was to rescue the economy from calamity. In this it succeeded.

An enormous disconnect opened almost immediately between the way the political system viewed the recovery act and the way economists viewed it. Republicans flayed the bill relentlessly as the "failed stimulus," and vowed to repeal it. Most Americans sided with the critics; few Democrats could be found to defend it. A 2010 Pew Research Center survey found that only one-third of Americans believed the stimulus "helped the job situation"; nearly twice as many disagreed.

Experts held a diametrically opposing view. In July 2014, the University of Chicago Booth School of Business asked a panel of economists, chosen to represent a diverse array of perspectives, two questions about the stimulus. The first question asked if the U.S. unemployment rate was lower at the end of 2010 than it would have been without the stimulus bill. Weighted by confidence level, 97 percent of economists agreed, and only 3 percent disagreed. The panel also asked a second question. Considering the long-term consequences, such as the added debt it incurred, did the law's benefits exceed its costs? Seventy-five percent agreed that it did, another 19 percent were uncertain, and only 6 percent disagreed.

Among economists hired to model and forecast the economy for private businesses—that is, economists whose employers stand to lose money, not just prestige, if they're wrong—the pro-stimulus consensus was, if anything, even stronger. "In my view, without the stimulus, G.D.P. would still be negative and unemployment would be firmly over 11 percent," Mark Zandi, an economic forecaster who did work for the McCain campaign, told the *New York Times* in November 2009. "And there are a little over 1.1 million more jobs out there as of October than would have been out there without the stimulus." The macroeconomic forecasting industry has very little disagreement. Goldman Sachs, HIS Global Insight, JPMorgan Chase, Macroeconomic Advisers, and Zandi's own model all estimate that the stimulus increased gross domestic product in 2010 by somewhere between 2 and 3.4 percentage points, a huge difference, about equal to what the economy grows in a typical year. Among those who study the issue professionally and try to reach dispassionate judgments, the stimulus was a clear success.

Obama signed the recovery act into law on February 17, 2009, just four weeks after he had taken the oath of office. The stimulus mended the economic crisis's aftereffects—the waves of unemployment and financial distress rippling throughout the economy. Still untreated was its volatile core: a financial industry rife with speculation, risk, and opacity. The financial industry had created investment vehicles so complex even other banks and investors did not understand them; essentially, they packaged very risky investments as though they were safe.

The bank bailout, hastily enacted a month before the election, had shoveled hundreds of billions of dollars into the industry's maw and prevented a total meltdown. And yet, while no more banks collapsed, normal lending had not resumed. Nobody knew just how many bad assets they held. The banking system, while stable, remained paralyzed by fear, unable to supply businesses with the credit they needed to invest. Without restoring the banking system to life, the economy could not recover.

This was a new problem that Obama had not planned to handle during his campaign, and for which his economists could not draw much in the way of relevant experience, the last banking crisis of this scale having taken place during the Hoover administration. Obama and advisers debated possible responses, and eventually the president sided with now–Treasury secretary Timothy Geithner, who in February presented the administration's plan to save the banks. The basis for the plan was to have the federal government send examiners to scrutinize the assets of the nineteen largest banks, project how they would survive an extended economic downturn, and declare which banks were sound and which were not. Any firm deemed to be too short of capital to survive a downturn would have to raise more, or accept government control. Those that passed the exam would, presumably, reassure investors of their soundness.

Almost nobody liked the plan. As the *New York Times* reported on the day of Geithner's announcement, with complete accuracy, "the initial assessment of the plan from the markets, lawmakers and economists was brutally negative." House Republican whip Eric Cantor called it "fundamentally flawed" and a "shell game." In what was quickly becoming a political template for Obama's policies, the left and right denounced the plan with equal measure; furthermore, the left's opposition did not make conservatives soften toward it, nor did the reverse occur. Both sides treated the president's plan as though it sprang fully from the enemy camp. Liberals, believing the government needed to national- ize the banks, assailed the stress tests as woefully insuf- ficient. In February and March, Krugman wrote seven columns criticizing the bank rescue plan. The ridicule had penetrated deep enough into public consciousness that, when the administration announced the results of the stress tests, *Saturday Night Live* lampooned it.

But the program turned out to succeed. One way to measure its effectiveness was to look at the "spreads"— different ways of measuring the gap between the inter- est rate the federal government has to pay to borrow and the rate that banks pay to borrow from each other. Since everybody (or almost everybody) knows the fed- eral government pays back people who loan it money, lenders don't worry about default. When lenders are worried they might not get paid back by a bank, they charge them higher interest rates to reflect that risk. The spread between the latter (the bank borrowing rate) and the former (the federal government borrow- ing rate) had spiked catastrophically during the finan- cial crisis, reflecting pervasive fear that banks might fail. Before the stress tests, it was still around five times its normal level. After the stress tests came out, the spread deflated quickly, and within months reached a basic, healthy condition. The banks were not in as bad shape as investors feared, and could raise the capital they needed to protect themselves from failure. The crisis ended, and lending resumed. Alan Blinder, a former Federal Reserve vice chairman, called the plan "a modern equivalent of FDR's bank holiday," which restored public confidence in the banking system after a devastating series of bank runs during the Depression. Kevin Hassett, a conservative economist at the American Enterprise Institute, credited the stress tests as the "turning point in the Great Recession." Even Krugman conceded, five years later, that it had worked: "[Geithner] was right; I was wrong."

The crisis went far beyond collapsing banks. By November 2008 the economy had entered a surreal state, in which terrifying new developments arose so frequently they seemed numbing and incomprehensible. One of those events was the imminent collapse of General Motors and Chrysler. The American auto industry had fallen into a long decline in the 1970s and 1980s, recovered during the SUV craze that began in the 1990s, and then seemed to relapse. Now the recession had crushed automobile sales as frightened consumers postponed major purchases. Furthermore, the financial crisis had frozen up the credit markets. Suddenly GM and Chrysler could not pay back the suppliers who made their parts. Two iconic American firms were about to vanish forever. (Ford, which had happened to take out a large loan before the financial crisis, did not face imminent liquidation.) It was not just these titans and their massive labor forces that would disappear: the two sat atop huge chains of suppliers who would also perish—and, since those secondary firms also supplied Ford, would threaten its survival as well. In the Midwest, it would be a disaster on the economic scale of Hurricane Katrina, or an invading army. The rippling new waves of unemployment could destroy two million jobs, maybe three.

All three auto firms went to Congress asking for a bailout, but Congress, already scorched with anger against the recent Troubled Asset Relief Program, voted it down. (The tone-deaf executives admitted that they flew private jets to Washington, making them even more unsympathetic to the public.) In December, the lame-duck Bush administration made the principled (but also easy) decision that it could not make a final judgment on behalf of the incoming president. So Bush authorized the diversion of $20 billion of TARP money to keep the automakers afloat through February, at which point they would have to present plans to make them "viable."

When that moment came, Obama quickly rejected

the automakers' plan as unrealistic, and then had to make a horrible choice. Either he would let them die, or else essentially have his government take control of the auto industry. The prospect of turning General Motors into Government Motors was a new and potentially frightening extension of government's role, and Obama's own economists hesitated to recommend it. It was one thing to rescue the financial industry, which, as the provider of the credit that makes the entire economy function, has a uniquely indispensable function. Rescuing the manufacturer of an ordinary good, even a manufacturer that had formed a deep cultural imprint, seemed like a first step along a path whose conclusion could not be discerned.

What's more, they didn't know if it would work. There was no reason to believe the industry's interminable decline could be arrested, and certainly no reason to think that the people who could devise the strategy to pull this off would be a handful of economists with little or no experience in the industry. Obama's economic advisers deadlocked over what course to take, drawing up plans to revamp the industry without knowing if they'd succeed. In one decisive meeting, Obama asked Steven Rattner, head of the auto task force, the odds that his restructuring plan would succeed. "Fifty-one percent," he replied. In the wake of an unpopular financial bailout, an unpopular stimulus, and an unpopular bank rescue, yet another massive intervention seemed wildly profligate to most Americans—yet another handout of their money for irresponsible fat cats. Polls showed opposition by a staggering three-to-one margin. "Washington, the President, Congress, none . . . has any business running that car company—they'll run it into the ground," predicted Eric Cantor.

On March 30, Obama announced he would inject a final round of capital into the firms, but only if they undertook sweeping reforms. He arranged for Fiat to purchase Chrysler, replaced GM's chief executive officer, forced its employees (who earned more in wages, and much more in pensions, than their foreign-owned competitors) to accept cuts, and made their creditors accept pennies on the dollar.

This decision represented the moment when conservative opposition to Obama's agenda made the leap from anger to bug-eyed rage. Here was the final proof that Obama's true intention was not merely to rescue the economy but to seize vast new powers for the state. "There are many who question whether American capitalism will survive Obama," suggested the conservative journal *Human Events*. "The verdict is in. It will not. It *has* not. We are already living under the rule of economic fascism." Andrew Grossman, a senior legal policy analyst at the staunchly conservative Heritage Foundation, testified before Congress that Obama's plan constituted "a microcosm of the lawlessness that threatens our freedom and our prosperity." Limbaugh called the bailout "thugocracy" and the man who carried it out "Barack Peron," after the Argentinian strongman. The *Weekly Standard* called it "Gangster Government."

It was not merely the right wing of the Republican Party that was agog. Senator Bob Corker, a moderate Republican, called it a "power grab" that "should send a chill through those who believe in free enterprise." Mitt Romney, the archetypical New England mainstream Republican, and the Michigan-raised son of an automobile executive, explained that the government simply had no business taking such a step. "Of course, the financial system itself must not be allowed to collapse," he wrote the next year, "but individual institutions that do not show the capacity to right themselves should be allowed to fail. Non-financial businesses should also be allowed to fail; if they have future prospects, bankruptcy will allow them to re-emerge as stronger, viable employers."

The tropes devised by the right—gangsterism, bullying—bled into the center. A *Washington Post* editorial complained, "The Obama administration bullies

GM's bondholders." The *Economist* called Obama's plan "[a]n offer you can't refuse," fretting it would set a "terrible precedent."

By committing more taxpayer funds, and injecting his administration into the inner workings of General Motors, Obama took an enormous gamble. If it failed, he would have confirmed the most devastating criticisms lobbed against him—he was a socialist, a crony capitalist, a bungling free-spender. Instead the administration's plan succeeded. By 2014, automobile sales climbed to their highest level since 2006. The industry and its suppliers added 400,000 jobs. In less than five years, the government sold off its holdings, recovering $70 billion of the $80 billion it had spent beginning with the Bush administration. Over the first two years alone, the bailout and restructuring had saved more than two million jobs and generated $284 billion in income that otherwise would have been lost, according to the Center for Automotive Research. And it had eliminated the possibility of setting off a second, deeper economic spiral emanating from the Midwest. By 2015, the unemployment rate in Michigan had fallen to its lowest level since 2001.

What's more, it had almost certainly saved taxpayers a great deal of money. The auto companies are not merely employers. They also run small welfare states, supplying their workers with pensions and health care benefits. Had they gone under, the federal government would have had to take over the cost of their pensions, through its Pension Benefit Guaranty Corporation, which backstops corporate pensions that fail. Likewise, workers who lost health insurance would have become eligible for federal tax credits. All told the federal government saved more than $100 billion that it would have lost had it allowed GM and Chrysler to go bankrupt—ten times over what it spent.

By 2010, the *Economist* had conceded "an apology is due Barack Obama." The president had not used his control of General Motors to advance a political agenda; his policy had worked as well as it could have. To be sure, a hardened libertarian could still oppose the intervention on the principled ground that the government should not bail out a failing firm under any circumstances, regardless of the cost to the economy or the taxpayers. But it turns out there aren't many libertarians in foxholes. By 2012 the auto bailout had recovered enough popularity that even Romney was attempting to position himself as having supported a similar plan all along. "Under no circumstances would I do anything other than to help this industry get on its feet," he insisted during the first presidential debate.

"And the idea that has been suggested that I would liquidate the industry, of course not." That was a preposterous revision of his own history. Romney's actual stance at the time of the bailout, and through 2011, when he competed for the Republican nomination, was that only the private sector, not the government, should spend money to save the auto companies. But the whole reason the bailout posed such an agonizing choice for the administration was that private financing could not be found. It was an amazing turnabout. Nobody could have imagined in the spring of 2009, when nearly three-quarters of the country opposed the auto bailout and Obama's critics were invoking fascism, that three and a half years later the Republican nominee would fervently deny that he had ever disagreed with it.

So it would go, too, for the deficit obsessives, despite signs to the contrary. By the beginning of 2010, anti-deficit fervor had completely overtaken Washington. A fashionable new doctrine of "expansionary austerity" took hold. The moderate version of this theory accepted Keynesian economics, but held that the national debt had grown to dangerously high levels that threatened economic growth. In January, two esteemed economists, Kenneth Rogoff and Carmen Reinhart, published a paper whose conclusion seemed to vindicate the fears that Obama's centrist critics had been raising from the outset. They found that when a country's national debt exceeds 90 percent of the size of its economy, its growth slows sharply. Their conclusion appeared to confirm the worst nightmares of the deficit hawks: the United States was heading into a trap. Once its debt hit the dreaded threshold, its economy would slow, which would in turn reduce income, and thus taxes, driving debt even higher, a cycle that would feed on itself and make escape increasingly impossible. To imagine what this kind of fiscal black hole might look like, an example was readily apparent in Europe. Greece had become a fiscal basket case, too indebted to pay back its creditors, and on the brink of social disintegration. Centrist opinion leaders like the *Washington Post* editorial page, *New York Times* columnist Thomas Friedman, and members of Congress from both parties all cited the dreaded 90 percent point of no return.

The moderates among the deficit hawks did not abandon Keynesianism altogether. Rather, they insisted that, unless it was paired with measures to reduce the debt over the long run, additional short-term stimulus might do no good. "While the additional spending could help fill the output gap, there is no guarantee that there will be sufficient demand for the mammoth amount of borrowing that would require," warned Maya MacGuineas of the Committee for a Responsible Federal Budget. Foreign governments would stop snapping up Treasury bonds needed to finance Washington's debts, which would force the government to give them a higher rate of return, causing interest rates to rise, which would slow down the economy.

It goes without saying that, with the ideological center running toward panic, the Republican Party had entered into full-fledged delirium. Geithner later recalled traveling to China, where officials told him that GOP representative Mark Kirk—known as a relative moderate—had warned Chinese officials not to buy Treasury bills, because the U.S. government was sowing hyperinflation and risking a default on its debt. House Republican Paul Ryan of Wisconsin, already emerging as a party thought leader, told a television reporter in the spring of 2010, "we are on the same path as Greece"—where rioting was breaking out in the streets. This was no partisan ploy—conservatives genuinely believed inflation was poised to return, and that interest rates would spike, or were already doing so. Advertisements for gold flooded conservative media, pitching frantic Republicans on a safe investment that would protect them from Obama's coming debasement of the currency. It was not merely the fever swamps of the right, or hucksters exploiting it for profit, that believed this. The most financially sophisticated corners of the Republican Party whipped itself into a terror. As early as May 2009, the *Wall Street Journal* editorial page instructed its readers that higher interest rates were already appearing. (They never came.) In 2010, Eric Cantor invested $15,000 in a fund betting on higher inflation. That, too, never came.

But it took years for the hysteria to fade away quietly (with no apology ever given by the hysterics) and Republican terror reached its most berserk stage in Obama's first term. And so, when Republicans won a rout in the 2010 midterm elections and took control of the House, the new majority did not treat its victory like an ordinary transfer of power. It swept into Washington bearing the hellfire determination of a party summoned by the people to spare the republic from imminent collapse.

In their belief that the midterm election had granted them a mandate that overrode Obama's, the Republicans were not alone. Their pose as champions of fiscal rectitude placed the new House majority firmly in tune with both popular and elite sentiment. Even elites in the business and media world who knew better believed that the problem of excessive deficits overrode the problem of elevated unemployment. (It did not hurt that, after the bailout and the bank reorganization had stabilized the financial sector, the economy was no longer terribly scary for college-educated workers.)

Obama's advisers wanted additional stimulus, but they did not dismiss concerns about long-term debt, either. They believed that they could strike a compromise with Republicans to bring down the long-term debt, which would ease the fiscal panic gripping the country, thus opening room for more short-term stimulus. That strategy proved naïve.

In 2010, Obama appointed two long-time Washington fixtures, former Clinton administration budget director Erskine Bowles and former Wyoming senator Alan Simpson, a Republican, to head a commission to devise a bipartisan plan to reduce the long-term deficit. The commission had no chance of success, because the two parties could simply not even agree on the basic parameters of a deal. Most Democrats would accept cuts to retirement programs like Medicare and Social Security only if they were balanced by increased taxes on the rich; Republicans would only accept a plan without any tax increases at all. The commission attempted to thread the needle with a vague scheme to eliminate some tax deductions, but the gimmicky plan was too specific in its intention to raise tax revenue to be acceptable to Republicans, while also too vague to credibly identify the savings it claimed was needed.

And yet the Simpson-Bowles plan (or, more accurately, the Simpson-Bowles plan to come up with a plan later on) became a kind of political holy writ. It satisfied the unfulfilled aspiration that originally attracted many of Obama's supporters when he appeared on the scene at the 2004 Democratic National Convention: that Obama's presidency would represent the idea of a better, more elevated, less partisan style of politics. That Simpson-Bowles was in fact a nonsolution for the wrong problem did not detract from its symbolic appeal.

The plan's lack of specificity, along with the no-new-taxes-ever stance of congressional Republicans, guaranteed its downfall. Predictably, this collapse became central to the indictment of Obama. Even figures like Paul Ryan held up Simpson-Bowles as evidence of the president's failure. "I thought it advanced an adult conversation that we needed to have," he told sympathetic reporter Mike Allen in 2011. "But the president just took us a few steps backwards by ignoring the commission's findings, by ignoring its conclusions." Ryan had actually served on the Simpson-Bowles commission and voted against the plan, making his proclaimed disappointment bizarre. Yet this sort of comment could pass by unchallenged because "Simpson-Bowles" did not mean an actual set of policy commitments but a symbol of the administration's failure to end political conflict.

This set the stage for possibly the greatest domestic blunder of Obama's presidency. When Republicans seized control of the House, they cast around for a vehicle to exert their newfound power, and settled on the federal debt limit, which is sometimes called the debt ceiling. The debt limit is a requirement that Congress approve any increase in borrowing by the federal government, without which the Treasury Department would literally default on any spending commitments that exceed available revenue, triggering a potential worldwide economic meltdown. It is an archaic ritual, dating from World War I, and used by virtually no other advanced economies. The debt ceiling vote had been used by the opposition party to posture against the administration's fiscal policies (as Obama himself had done as a senator), and also to attach mutually agreeable policy changes. Neither party's leadership had ever entertained refusing to raise it, nor had it ever before been used as a weapon to force the president to sign otherwise unacceptable policies. Republicans briefly considered using the debt ceiling as leverage to extract concessions after they won the 1994 midterm elections, but the Clinton administration squashed the ploy by making clear it would not give in to what it called "blackmail."

When House Republicans announced that they would refuse to lift the debt ceiling at all, or perhaps do so only in return for trillions of dollars in spending cuts, the Obama administration took it as an opportunity to strike a deal. If Obama had refused to bargain in the face of threats, like Clinton had, he'd have been isolated from mainstream opinion. Influential deficits hawks, like the Committee for a Responsible Federal Budget and the *Washington Post* editorial page, urged Obama and Congress to use the threat of a default to agree to some Simpson-Bowles–like plan. Numerous Senate Democrats insisted they, too, would refuse to lift the debt ceiling without reforms. Still, Obama appears to have genuinely believed he could persuade Republicans to abandon their theological opposition to higher taxes. Administration officials insisted, both publicly and privately, that the potential crisis of a default would force both parties to compromise.

The plan backfired. Obama, remarkably, succeeded in persuading House Speaker John Boehner to trade higher tax revenue in return for cuts to retirement programs. But Boehner could not bring along his members, who opposed on principle any increase in tax revenue or any compromise with the administration, and the deal collapsed. As the debt limit approached and economic catastrophe loomed, the administration frantically drafted a fallback plan. It created a bipartisan "supercommittee" that would try to make the agreement Boehner could not sell to Republicans, and if it failed (which, of course, it did), automatic cuts to domestic spending would take effect. The president assumed those cuts, called "sequestration," would prove so painful that Republicans would agree to replace them with some kind of compromise, in part because they cut tens of billions of dollars from the defense budget.

Instead Republicans let them take effect and Obama was forced to negotiate a ransom instead of a solution. The cuts in sequestration, along with additional budget reductions the administration agreed to, amounted to a sizable anti-stimulus, sucking nearly $400 billion out of net spending over the first four years. It reduced employment by more than half a million jobs a year by 2014, according to the Congressional Budget Office. Even more damaging, the possibility that Congress would deliberately trigger the calamity that would ensue from a debt default caused consumer confidence (as measured by Gallup) to plunge. The agreement did lift the debt ceiling through the 2012 election, prevent-

ing a second showdown. But essentially, the administration had succumbed to the political establishment's
misguided fixation with deficits and its own naïveté to
allow the passage of a small anti-stimulus bill. Obama
had not grasped the willingness of the Republican Congress to use catastrophe as leverage in a game of chicken
to win policy concessions. He learned the lesson, but at
a price.

Obama's reelection came as a devastating blow to
Republicans, many of whom, including those in Mitt
Romney's campaign, expected victory right up until
the returns were announced. They had believed the
American public would punish Obama for his radical policies. Romney's defeat robbed them not only of
a chance to repudiate a president they feared and despised, but of their broader hope that normal political methods might suffice to restore the America they
believed had been taken from them. The Republican Congress returned in 2013 in a grim, despairing
mood. Rather than deflating their messianism, however, the defeat actually stoked it. In 2011 Republicans
had anticipated that the next year they might be voted
into power. In 2013 their only path to power was to
seize it, leading to yet another debt ceiling tantrum. It
was an extraordinarily brazen strategy. "The reason

this debt limit fight is different is, we don't have an election around the corner where we feel we are going to win and fix it ourselves," explained Paul Ryan, in a burst of candor. "We are stuck with this government another three years."

Repeatedly and consistently, the Republicans would use the threat of economic calamity to impose their agenda—not in spite of the fact that the public had rejected it, but precisely for that reason. Indeed, the 2013 House Republican list of demands in order to lift the debt ceiling reprised almost the entire GOP domestic policy platform from the last election. The demands included delaying Obamacare for as long as the debt ceiling would be raised, deep cuts to tax rates, deep deregulation of the environment and Wall Street, and cuts in a wide array of social spending. If successful, normalizing debt ceiling extortion would have recast the entire balance of power between the legislative and executive branch. Had they succeeded in extracting any ransom from Obama, American government would have changed. Instead, this time the administration held firm, simply refusing to give Republicans even a token concession.

The climate of elite opinion was changing in a way that bolstered Obama's firmness. In 2013, researchers at the University of Massachusetts–Amherst discovered that the Reinhart-Rogoff paper, and its famed 90 percent debt threshold of doom, was wrong. Its findings depended on the omission of important data, simple spreadsheet errors, and other mistakes. When corrected, the widely touted conclusion evaporated. By this point budget projections were already undercutting the debt hysterics. In 2010 the national debt was projected to rise to more than 200 percent of gross domestic product by 2040. In 2014 it was forecast to rise to less than half that level. The widespread, influential belief that a debt crisis of civilizational scale beckoned had seen both its factual and its theoretical basis collapse beneath it. By Obama's second term, the doctrine of expansionary austerity was in full intellectual and political retreat, even among hardened conservative ideologues. Nevertheless, even in the darkest moments of deficit panic, the Obama administration continued pumping stimulus into the economy. Even though the general concept had lost favor, many individual components of the stimulus retained public support, and piece by piece, the administration had managed to stretch out its efforts after 2009. A bill extending emergency unemployment benefits, low-income tax cuts, incentives for business to hire—it all added up. Indeed, such additional stimulative measures combined amounted to nearly $700 billion over the next several years, not much below the cost of the original recovery act. It had all simply happened in too small, incremental, and undramatic a form to capture much public attention.

Thus, in largely unnoticed ways, the administration chipped away at the budget sequestration that had held back the recovery. After the failed 2011 negotiations, Obama recognized that Republicans would never strike a "grand bargain" where they would trade higher tax revenue for cuts to retirement programs. Instead Obama struck modest deals, and he found the person to strike them with in Paul Ryan. After the 2012 election defeat, the fierce and even crazed tone of his attacks on the administration gave way to a pragmatic recognition that Republicans lacked the means to roll back his reforms without the presidency, and that shutdowns and confrontations merely made it harder for Ryan's party to regain the public trust they would need to win back the White House. His earlier "we are stuck with this government another three years" defiance had become a sour realism. Ryan agreed in 2013 to ease the sequestration cuts for two years, and then did so again in 2015 for two more years—essentially conceding that most members of his party could not live with them any more than Democrats could. By 2016, 90 percent of the sequestration cuts had disappeared, and with them the shackles Washington had placed on the recovery. The era of crisis and showdowns had ended. Normal, functional governing had quietly returned.

Almost as quiet were changes to the tax code Obama had left behind. The stimulus had included a tax credit for workers at the bottom of the income scale. Its primary purpose was to get more cash into the hands of people who could spend it, and it succeeded. But the tax credit also served a long-term social objective of making the tax code more progressive, and in 2015, Obama struck a deal with the Republican Congress to make those tax cuts permanent, in return for making permanent a series of supposedly temporary business tax cuts that had been routinely extended for years.

Here, again, was an Obama initiative that in isolation may have seemed relatively unimpressive (and barely made a ripple.) But in 2013, the administration had also allowed expiring Bush-era tax cuts on incomes over $450,000 to lapse, bringing higher Clinton-era tax rates into effect. The combined effect of lower taxes on the middle-class and poor, and higher taxes on the wealthy reduced incomes for the highest-earning 1% by an average of 5% per household, and increased incomes for the lowest earning tenth of households by an average of 9.7%. With vanishingly little attention, Obama had moved the needle against income inequality. The burden of the tax code had been a central point of contention between the two parties since Ronald Reagan. Republicans have poured every ounce of political capital into shifting the tax burden off the rich and onto everybody else, and Democrats have pushed in the opposite direction. Obama's victory on this front, while not a permanent one, reset the balance.

For most of his presidency, Obama labored under the comparison between the recovery over which he presided and those of previous presidents, like Bill Clinton and Ronald Reagan, who enjoyed swifter returns to prosperity and full employment. But it is not a fair comparison. Historically, a financial crisis inflicts deeper and longer-lasting harm on an economy than does a normal recession. A fairer comparison would juxtapose the United States against other economies that suffered through the same systemic crisis it endured in 2008.

By the beginning of his final year in office, the signal fact of Obama's economic performance was that his administration had avoided the errors to which many European economic policy makers had fallen prey. A powerful impulse to do exactly the wrong thing had swept over much of the developed world, completely overtaking many European leaders (who imposed brutal austerity budgets that retarded their own recoveries) and bringing along large segments of the American public and elites. Obama had faced down this movement and, for the most part, gotten the better of it. Of the twelve countries that had a systemic financial meltdown in 2008, only two, the United States and Germany, had returned to their pre-crisis GDP by the end of 2014. (Germany by that point was teetering on the brink of a second recession.) "Unhappy with the economic recovery in the United States? Could be worse," pointed out *Washington Post* economic columnist Catherine Rampell in December 2014. "Specifically, we could be *literally any other country in the world* that also just went through a major financial crisis." Unemployment in the European Union by 2015 was running at levels nearly twice as high as in the United States. In 2014, the United States created more new jobs than it had in any year since 1999.

In 2012, economic journalist Noam Scheiber published *Escape Artists: How Obama's Team Fumbled the Recovery.* It was a deeply reported account that delivered a mixed but ultimately negative verdict, ultimately concluding that the administration's strenuous efforts to save the economy would fail. Two years later, in light of the economy's strength, Scheiber revised his conclusion, conceding, "my verdict on the administration was overly harsh."

In May 2012, Republican candidate Mitt Romney, who had lacerated Obama's policies for allegedly killing jobs, promised that, if elected, he would bring the unemployment rate, then just over 8 percent, down to 6 percent by the end of his term. It is fair to say that, if he had won, and unemployment had dropped to this level by the end of 2016, Romney would be touting his success. But in fact, after Romney lost, the unemployment rate fell below 6 percent by the fall of 2014. By 2016, it had fallen to 5 percent. By the standard set out by his Republican opponent, Obama's economic record was a rousing success.

In many parts of the country, it did not feel like prosperity had returned. The residents of those towns were hardly mistaken. The world of blue-collar prosperity of the postwar years, when boys could walk out of high school and into a job at the local plant, earning middle-class wages and a secure pension, began to disappear in the 1970s and 1980s. That's why Bruce Springsteen wrote songs about hollowed-out towns—"They're closing down the textile mill across the railroad tracks / Foreman says these jobs are going, boys, and they ain't coming back"—a quarter-century before Obama took office. The hollowing out of these towns persisted for decades, and in some ways grew worse. Even Trump's promise to "Make America Great Again" was a slogan he had first started using during the Reagan era.

Decades worth of economic stagnation in much of the country was a problem on a scale no president could hope to reverse at once. It did not help that the Republican Congress clung to its contractionary policies solely out of partisan calculation. The Republican Congress refused Obama's repeated entreaties to upgrade public transportation infrastructure as supposedly unaffordable, but swallowed its objections when Trump proposed an even larger and costlier version of the same idea. The pattern of Republicans embracing Keynesian policy during their own administration, and opposing it during Democratic ones, allowed them to weaponize economic discontent.

The recovery took years to replace the jobs lost during the recession, and the elevated levels of joblessness allowed employers to refrain from giving their workers higher wages. For most of Obama's term, wage gains were largely confined to the rich. But as unemployment finally returned to normal levels, workers finally gained the bargaining leverage they needed, and wages began to creep back up. In 2015, income for workers in the middle rose more than 5 percent—the highest gain ever measured since the Census began recording this figure in 1967. Income actually grew the most for workers at the bottom, and the least for those at the top, with the poorest earning tenth of the income spectrum seeing a 7.9 percent hike in its income, the next-highest decile enjoying a 6.3 percent increase, the middle tenth a 5.2 percent increase, and the richest tenth an increase of 3.9 percent. The endlessly recirculated charge that Obama's taxes and regulation had buried entrepreneurship, dooming Americans to stagnant wages, was ultimately itself buried by economic reality. Against the backdrop of decades of stagnation, the upsurge in wages felt inadequate to many blue-collar workers in depressed regions. But broad-based prosperity, and an economy that delivered a better life for average Americans, had finally returned.

Chapter 3
Obama Cares

A certain measure of Obama's success was the inevitable product of a Democratic president enjoying huge majorities in both chambers of Congress for his first two years, successes any Democrat would have enjoyed. But some of Obama's most important achievements came about because of decisions he made that cut against the instincts of many of his fellow partisans.

Unlike the economic crisis, the American health care crisis was not a discrete episode, but a humanitarian and economic disaster that built up slowly over the decades. The United States stood alone among its peers as the only industrialized democracy that did not offer access to medical care to all its citizens. As a result, Americans had come to live with cruelties that would be unimaginable in most of the world—people unable to treat fatal cancers; children unable to receive antibiotics when ill; broken bones left uncast; surgeries forever postponed . . . The examples went on and on.

At the same time, the United States spends considerably more on health care than any of its peers without obtaining detectably superior results. Before Obama took office, the United States spent about twice as much per person on health care as countries like Canada, France, and the United Kingdom. For decades, the cost of health care had grown much faster than the cost of other goods and services. Even though the government covered a far smaller proportion of its citizens than governments in countries with universal health insurance systems, per capita spending by the government alone—exempting the enormous private sector spending in the United States—exceeded all but a handful of its peers, simply because the cost was so high. The system was the worst of all worlds: ghastly, bloated, cruel, combining the worst elements of big-government inefficiency and dog-eat-dog private sector callousness.

For people who could get insurance through their job, the cost problem was a huge, albeit mostly hidden, bite out of their paycheck. For those who worked on their own, or whose employer did not provide insurance, the system was a true nightmare. The individual market was rife with "adverse selection"—that is, the people most interested in buying insurance were the sickest ones who needed insurance the most, driving up the cost, and further pricing out all but the most desperate customers. The individual insurance market was geared almost entirely around making sure an insurer didn't get stuck footing the bill for a sick person. Any customer with a preexisting condition could be charged exorbitant rates, or denied coverage altogether. Older customers (who are at higher risk of illness) could likewise pay unaffordable rates. And insurance companies protected themselves from becoming stuck with an expensive customer by tacking on all sorts of fine-print conditions that would let them cut off reimbursements, or kick the customer off their plan altogether, if his or her costs reached a certain point. Three-quarters of Americans who went bankrupt due to medical costs actually had insurance; it's just that the insurance they had didn't actually protect them from catastrophe.

No wonder even customers who *could* afford to buy health insurance on the individual market didn't like it. Forty-five percent of customers with nongroup insurance plans rated their coverage "fair" or "poor." Just over a third as many Americans with group insurance gave their plan such a poor rating—18 percent of people with employer coverage, 17 percent with Medicare, and

16 percent with Medicaid rated their coverage "fair" or "poor." A market where insurers had to scrutinize each patient for signs of weakness, and ruthlessly weed out the most vulnerable, was a comprehensive failure. Merely toting up the tens of millions of Americans without any health insurance failed to capture the dysfunction in the system. All but the lavishly rich were one misfortune away from medical ruin.

The normal structure of any public problem is that, the worse the situation, the greater the pressure to solve it. If your country is enmeshed in a disastrous war, then the more soldiers die, the more people demand peace. If your city's atmosphere is choked with pollution, the smoggier it gets, the more citizens will demand cleaner air.

The American health care system is the rare disaster that defied this dynamic. The worse it got, the harder it became to solve. The system's increasing bloat simply meant that more and more doctors, hospital administrators, insurers, drug companies, and medical equipment suppliers had a stake in perpetuating the status quo; every dollar of waste was a dollar of somebody's income. And the more Americans lost their insurance, the more the remaining majority who had it came to fear change—they, too, saw themselves as the lucky or deserved beneficiaries of the status quo, and clung more tightly to the insurance they had.

Harry Truman, Lyndon Johnson, Richard Nixon, and Bill Clinton all attempted and failed major overhauls of the system, which seemed over time to grow increasingly impervious to change. But among Democratic activists, health care reform remained a cherished cause, the centerpiece of their idea of what a presidency ought to accomplish. Obama, like his rivals for the 2008 nomination, pledged to attempt health care reform, and his contacts during the campaign with ordinary people victimized by the system deepened his conviction. The plan his administration devised broke open the political vise that had thwarted reform for decades.

Obama proposed to cover the uninsured by blending two ideas that had worked elsewhere: Medicaid, a Johnson-era program to cover the most destitute, would be expanded to cover uninsured people with incomes up to around $15,000 a year (or more for a family). People with incomes above that level who needed insurance, and couldn't obtain it through their job or Medicare, would be able to purchase a private plan through new exchanges, modeled after an innovative program that then-governor Mitt Romney had successfully implemented in Massachusetts in 2006.

The exchanges would solve the adverse selection problem by creating a balanced pool of healthy and sick customers alike. Insurers, who before could mainly charge whatever they wanted, could now only charge older customers up to three times as much as they charged the young; they could not charge higher rates to customers with preexisting conditions, nor could they cut off payments to a customer who came down with an expensive condition. In the past, some states had tried to make insurance available to sick patients by preventing price discrimination against the old and sick, without doing anything to ensure younger or healthier customers bought plans, too. Those reforms always failed, since sicker customers would rush in, driving up the cost of premiums, driving out healthier customers, causing prices to rise even higher, and making the product unaffordable. Since insurers wouldn't be able to turn away people who were sick, there had to be an incentive for healthy people to buy a plan—otherwise, they would save money by skipping out on insurance until they got sick (driving up premium costs for everybody who *did* buy insurance). Romney's solution was an "individual mandate"—a requirement that everybody buy health insurance, so they couldn't free-ride off the system and the companies could have a more balanced risk pool. Such a mandate has always been unpopular—a fact Obama exploited against Hillary Clinton by opposing it during his primary campaign—but as president he acknowledged it was necessary to make the plan work.

Of course, you couldn't require people to purchase insurance unless they could afford it, so the government would make insurance available by providing tax credits to people buying insurance in the exchanges. (It already subsidized the cost of health care for people who get it through their job by making employer-provided health insurance tax deductible.) But where would the money come from? Romney had gotten a big lump payment from the federal government, which at the time had a Republican administration eager to pay the cost for an experiment in market-friendly health reform that might become a model for the party. Obama would have to come up with the money to pay for the tax credits, along with the expansion of Medicaid.

Obama had promised during the campaign not to raise taxes on families earning below a quarter-million dollars a year. He could raise some money by increasing investment income taxes on the rich, but not enough. Obama convinced the medical industry that reform was likely to happen, and that they could ensure the outcome was something they could live with by cutting a deal. This was, in fact, what happened: hospitals, doctors, and drugmakers agreed to hundreds of billions of dollars in new taxes or in cuts to Medicare reimbursements, in return for the government agreeing to subsidize tens of millions of new paying customers.

Understandably, Obama's critics on the left and right alike both complained about the seediness of giving stakeholders such influence over the shape of the bill. But the industry had played a major role in killing previous efforts at reform in the past, and neutralizing its opposition gave Democrats their best chance to succeed. For better or worse, this kind of horse-trading was how even the best kinds of major legislation often got written, and it went both ways: the threat of a health care bill that might be written without the industry's input was enough to persuade it to pony up its share of the hundreds of billions of dollars needed to cover the uninsured.

Financing the health care bill was a massive political achievement, the solution to a puzzle that had confounded generations of liberals. (The last time Washington had created a new entitlement—the Bush administration's expansion of Medicare to cover prescription drugs—it simply added the entire cost to the deficit.) But the Obama administration hoped to do more than cover the cost of its new spending. It aspired to gradually overhaul the economics of American medicine.

Doctors and hospitals have traditionally been paid by Medicare or by insurers to conduct more treatment, and these incentives have shaped the practice of health care. A 2008 Dartmouth study had examined Medicare spending across the country and found vast disparities between regions that could not be explained by either the differing needs of their communities or by differing outcomes. The only explanation was that economic incentives, including traditional billing practices, had driven the doctors and hospitals in some communities to prescribe more tests, procedures, and drugs, to no benefit. (Indeed, in many cases, the risks of extraneous procedures *outweighed* the benefit.) The study concluded that some 30 percent of American medical costs could be eliminated without any harm to patients whatsoever. The trick was cutting out useless or harmful care without eliminating the necessary kind. In 2009, Atul Gawande, a surgeon and health care journalist, described in the *New Yorker* how McAllen, Texas, spent twice as much per Medicare beneficiary as El Paso, Texas—a city with a similar demographic profile—without yielding any detectable improvement in its residents' health. Obama and his aides read the story, which hardened their belief that health care reform needed to (in the administration's shorthand) "bend the curve." That is, they recognized that health care waste could not be eliminated quickly or easily; instead, they hoped that the graphs depicting health care costs rising well beyond the inflation rate into perpetuity could be gradually altered, bent down to a more sustainable trajectory.

Obama's health care efforts included a wide array of experiments designed to introduce some rationality into the process of paying for medical care. The stimulus contained $20 billion to encourage doctors and hospitals to convert their record-keeping from the old pen-and-paper files stashed in manila folders to electronic form, in the hope that this would allow better sharing and use of medical data. His health care plan authorized a half-billion dollars a year for a new institute to compare the effectiveness of different kinds of medical treatments, which could help distinguish practices that make people healthy from those that don't. It created new "Accountable Care Organizations"—doctors who would band together and be paid for keeping their patients healthy, rather than for performing more care. It imposed new financial penalties for hospitals with high rates of patient readmissions. (Under the old system, if a patient acquired an infection in the hospital, they would just go back for more treatment, netting the hospital a second payday.) It capped the tax deduction for the most expensive health insurance plans, giving employers an incentive to shop for more affordable plans for their employees. And it created an Independent Payment Advisory Board, composed of health care experts, whose recommendations for cost savings would automatically take effect if medical inflation rose too quickly, unless overridden by Congress.

Obama did not believe his reforms could solve America's cost predicament immediately. The plan was to attack the problem from all directions with aggressive and continuous experimentation. Doctors, hospitals, insurers, patients, and the federal government would all be armed with new information and new incentives to seek out the best kinds of medical practice, not just the most expensive.

Obama's plan to overhaul health care was certainly radical in its ambitions—not only its attempt to at long last offer all citizens access to basic medical care but to also revolutionize the economics of a gargantuan industry that had sprawled out of control for decades. It was not, however, radical in its methods. The cost reforms had been modeled after the recommendations of bipartisan health care experts, including those of Mark McClellan, a Medicare adviser under the Bush administration. The most important new mechanism for covering the uninsured also had Republican roots: a new, regulated individual market, which prevented insurers from excluding customers with health risks, required those who were uninsured to obtain coverage, and offered tax credits to make doing so affordable.

When Romney ran for president in 2008, he repeatedly held up his plan in Massachusetts as the basis for a national reform proposal. "We have to have our citizens insured," he declared in a 2007 Republican presidential debate. "What you have to do is what we did in Massachusetts. Is it perfect? No. But we say, let's rely on personal responsibility, help people buy their own private insurance, get our citizens insured, not with a government takeover, not with new taxes needed, but instead with a free-market based system that gets all of our citizens in the system. No more free rides. It works." Even the most conservative elements within the Republican Party deemed Romney's health care a sound basis for a national plan. The influential right-wing talk show host Hugh Hewitt called Romneycare a "brilliant bit of legislating," touting its individual mandate in particular. *National Review*, which normally demands ideological purity of Republican candidates, was just slightly less gushing. Its editorial endorsing Romney for president allowed that "not every feature of the health-care plan he enacted in Massachusetts should be replicated nationally," but insisted he had "more authority than any of the other Republican candidates about this pressing issue."

And before Obama pursued it, the individual mandate—which Republicans eventually decided was the most extreme and oppressive element of Obamacare—was seen as a decidedly conservative idea. The Heritage Foundation had endorsed it in the 1990s as part of an alternative to the Clinton administration's ideas. Even *Reason*, a libertarian magazine, endorsed it in a 2004 article headlined "Mandatory Health Insurance Now!"

"Romneycare" was particularly exceptional given that conservatives have embraced health care policy reforms only insofar as they could be used as alternatives to Democratic plans; their interest in the topic would spike only when Democrats brought the issue to the fore, and most of their energy would go into opposition. Their advocacy of alternative ideas mainly served to discredit any Democratic proposals, rather than serve as the basis for negotiation or a program they would put into effect if given the votes to do so—indeed, once Democrats adopted their ideas, Republicans would promptly abandon them. The Heritage plan in the

1990s formed the basis for a proposal endorsed by Republican Senate leader Bob Dole and most of his party during the Clinton-era health care fight. When Clinton's plan no longer had a chance of passing, and moderates looked to take up Dole's idea, he repudiated it.

The pattern continued as Obama took up reform in 2009. Obama advocated that his plan include a "public option"—that is, every exchange would include a government-run plan to compete against those offered by private insurers. The public option had taken on an oversize role in the hopes of liberal activists, who had organized for decades around the goal of a "single-payer" plan, in which the government would replace private insurers, as it does with Medicare. Initially, Republicans likewise made the public option the focal point of their opposition to Obamacare.

Two of the most conservative Republicans in Congress, Oklahoma's Tom Coburn and Wisconsin's Paul Ryan, proposed their own alternative health care plan in May, near the outset of the debate. It, too, closely resembled a national version of Romneycare, promising "universal access to affordable health care for all Americans." Coburn and Ryan proposed to heavily regulate the new insurance exchanges, preventing insurers from "cherry-picking" the healthiest patients and requiring them to cover the same treatments offered by Congress's own health insurance plan. Even liberal policy analysts applauded their proposal.

Ryan and Coburn framed the public option as the central point of disagreement. "Nothing will rally ordinary Americans against the president's plan," they wrote, "more than his allies arguing too forcefully for a system run by politicians and bureaucrats in Washington—what we call the 'public option' in the Obama plan." As the debate bogged down in Congress, Romney wrote an op-ed holding up his Massachusetts-based reform as a national model. "Our citizens purchase private, free-market medical insurance," he wrote. "There is no 'public option.'" Eventually, the most moderate Democrats insisted upon discarding the public option from Obama's bill. One might think its removal would have opened the way for Republicans to embrace Obama's plan, or negotiate a compromise. Nothing of the sort happened because the Republican health care alternatives served merely to justify Republican opposition to Democratic plans.

By February 2010, Obama's plan was on the ropes, and he held a summit to find common agreement. There Ryan and Coburn denounced ideas they had endorsed the year before. "You're defining exactly what kind of health insurance people can have; you're mandating them to buy this kind of health insurance," complained Ryan, whose plan had done the very same thing. Coburn urged Obama to forget about expanding coverage altogether and focus instead on promoting healthy eating habits.

In early 2009, Ryan had also promoted a plan to create a government board of fifteen experts charged with "promoting transparency in price, quality, appropriateness, and effectiveness of health care" and given authority to "enforce compliance of health care providers with the guidelines, standards, [and] performance measures." Ryan's proposal turned out to be nearly identical to the Independent Payment Advisory Board in Obama's plan. Indeed, it won praise from health care experts supporting the same idea in Obama's proposal. Now Ryan predictably decided not only to oppose IPAB but to fixate on it as the most sinister, socialistic device in Obama's plan—"a panel of fifteen unelected, unaccountable bureaucrats."

Conservative activists, often incoherent with rage, flooded town hall meetings with members of Congress in their home districts. It was at this point that the Republican Party settled on a belief that Obamacare was not merely misguided but evil, a threat to freedom the magnitude of which could not be found in decades of history. Pennsylvania Republican Rick Santorum even compared those opposing the administration's proposals to be on par with no less a figure than Nelson Mandela (once demonized by the pro-apartheid conservative right). "He was fighting against some great injustice," he effused, "and I would make the argument that we have a great injustice going on right now in this country with an ever-increasing size of government that is taking over and controlling people's lives—and Obamacare is front and center in that."

In Congress, debate dragged on for months on end, projecting dysfunction and uncertainty. Most of the individual elements of the plan fared well in opinion polls, but hardly anybody knew how the plans would work. A Democratic pollster reported hearing repeatedly from independent voters during the health care debate, "Republicans all hate it, and the Democrats cannot agree what to do, so how good can this proposal be?" The political scientists John Hibbing and Elizabeth Theiss-Morse published a book in 2002 that explained an important dynamic about public opinion during this period. Americans, they found through a deep study of focus groups and survey data, don't have well-informed or even terribly firm beliefs about policy. They have little conception of ideological divisions between parties, and believe that people in politics should be able to cooperate to accomplish shared goals. Thus, Hibbing and Theiss-Morse wrote, "they are consequently turned off by political debate and deal making that presuppose an absence of consensus. People believe these activities would be unnecessary if decision makers were in tune with the (consensual) public interest rather than cacophonous special interests." Unsurprisingly, public opinion turned staunchly against Obama's plan.

At one point in June, David Axelrod, Obama's chief political adviser, confronted the president with grim polling data. Axelrod later told Jonathan Cohn, who subsequently reconstructed the law's passage in *The New Republic*, that Obama replied by bringing up a thirty-six-year-old woman with cancer he'd just met during a trip to Wisconsin. "She's married, has insurance, and she's still going broke. She's absolutely beside herself because she feels like she may not make it and that she'll leave her family with this huge debt." Obama urged Axelrod to press on despite the political cost.

During the endless health care summer, many glum Democrats came to doubt that a bill would ever pass (or that, if it did, it would do much good). That original concern for the victims of the cruelties of the American health care system that had animated Obama and his allies was falling out of fashion. Deficit hawks increasingly came to see the goal of covering the uninsured as an unaffordable luxury, even though health care reform was also aiming to reduce the cost of health care to the federal budget. One *Washington Post* editorial complained that Obama's coverage proposal would "heap more dessert on an already calorie-laden plate." Another lectured, "We think that it is not asking too much, given the dire fiscal straits, for Washington to show that it can swallow distasteful medicine while, and not after, it passes out the candy." (It was telling that a bastion of centrist, and often center-left, thought was analogizing the provision of basic medical care to poor, sick, and desperate Americans as "dessert" and "candy.") Elite opinion curdled along with popular opinion. Fred Barnes, a conservative reporter, declared shortly after Labor Day, "unless Obama has suddenly transformed public opinion, [then–speaker of the House Nancy] Pelosi and Senate Majority Leader Harry Reid won't be able to find enough Democrats, even among the usually malleable Blue Dogs, willing to vote for ObamaCare." Numerous Democrats in Congress and the administration wanted to pull the plug, perhaps stripping down their grand reform ambitions to a small expansion of health care for children.

Still, key Democrats like Max Baucus, who chaired the Senate committee that would sit at the center of the legislative action, believed, reasonably enough, that they could win back public approval if they could persuade at least a few Republicans to join with them. Not all of them understood that, by summertime, the white-hot intensity of conservative fervor made such a defection impossible. A dwindling handful of Republicans was even willing to negotiate, though they could not be pinned down on specific policies that would win their vote. Even when Democrats asked the most open-minded Republican senator, Olympia Snowe, for particular legislative demands that would enable her to support a bill, Snowe simply requested more time. And even her sense of how much more time would be needed remained completely open-ended.

On September 24, 2009, Democrats finally got their 60th supporter, when Massachusetts appointed interim senator Paul Kirk to replace the deceased Ted Kennedy (whose illness rendered him unavailable for all but a handful of votes). In November, the House passed a reform bill. The next month, the 60 Senate Democrats followed suit, breaking the filibuster without a single vote to spare.

Soon that margin was gone: on January 19, Massachusetts held a special election to replace Kennedy, and Republican Scott Brown pulled off a victory in the heavily Democratic state. Brown had based his opposition to Obamacare on the most parochial grounds—since Massachusetts had a good health care plan in its own state, he argued, its residents had no reason to pay more taxes to subsidize coverage for residents of other states. But the political world treated his victory as a kind of referendum on Obamacare to which Democrats across the country were morally bound.

For weeks, nearly the entire political world assumed health care reform was dead. They took as a given that, since the House and Senate bills were not identical, both chambers would apparently have to reengage the issue. "Barack Obama's two signature initiatives— cap-and-trade and health-care reform—lie in ruins," gloated Charles Krauthammer. It was not merely the partisan opposition that reached this conclusion. Even hard-core liberals like Massachusetts representative Barney Frank and New York representative Anthony Weiner, both of whom regularly lambasted Obama for his lack of partisan resolve, panicked in the wake of Brown's victory and urged their party to give up. "If there isn't any recognition that we got the message and we are trying to recalibrate and do things differently, we are not only going to risk looking ignorant but arrogant," said Weiner. Frank declared, "our respect for democratic procedures must rule out any effort to pass a health care bill as if the Massachusetts election had not happened."

Many members of Obama's administration agreed. One adviser emailed Cohn, sadly, to admit reform was "Dead, DEAD DEAD." Rahm Emanuel, Obama's chief of staff, resumed his efforts to negotiate a children's health care expansion, or any other mini-reform that could be seen as progress, however meager. Mark Penn, the chief political strategist for Hillary Clinton's 2008 campaign, publicly implored the administration to give up on comprehensive health care reform. Dana Milbank, a moderately liberal *Washington Post* columnist, argued that Emanuel, a longtime skeptic of the feasibility of passing health care reform, had been proven correct. "Obama's greatest mistake was failing to listen to Emanuel on health care," Milbank wrote. "The president disregarded that strategy and sided with Capitol Hill liberals who hoped to ram a larger, less popular bill through Congress with Democratic votes only. The result was, as the world now knows, disastrous." Milbank's premise—that health care reform stood no chance of passage—was, by that point, so widely shared that it barely required defending.

But health care reform was not dead. The House and Senate had each passed a bill already. The most common procedure was for the two chambers to negotiate an agreement that would iron out differences between the two bills, and then the House and Senate would vote again on the identical measures. With Brown now in place to provide the 41st vote to block passage, the Senate could no longer pass an amended version. (By this point, Olympia Snowe, who had originally supported the legislation in a committee vote and could have broken a filibuster, had turned irrevocably against it.)

There was another way, though. If the Democratic House simply passed the bill the Senate had passed, it would become law—the only point of a House-Senate conference was to force the two chambers to vote on the same piece of legislation. If the two chambers wanted to negotiate changes, they could do it in a separate budget reconciliation bill. The strange rules of Congress allow that such legislation cannot be filibustered; the only limit is that the bill can only address budgetary issues. Since the points of difference between the House and Senate mostly concerned budgetary aspects of the health care law, reconciliation was the perfect vehicle.

In retrospect, the decision to advance a bill that had already passed both chambers was obvious. At the time, the Washington establishment regarded it as foolhardy. "If we took a vote now, we would not have 51 votes for that approach," a Senate Democratic aide told the *New York Times*, when the decision to proceed or quit hung in the balance. "The president would have to do a major sales job." Former Bush administration aide Yuval Levin gasped, "The apparent decision to push Obamacare through reconciliation gives new meaning to the term political suicide," adding that it would almost certainly fail. Unlike a great many conservative opinion makers, who confined themselves to generalities, Levin had the ability to immerse himself deep into legislative debates, using the terms that marked true experts in the field. Megan McArdle, a libertarian blogger, called him "an ultrawonk who appears to have had the entire text of the PPACA [The Patient Protection and Affordable Care Act—the official name of the Obamacare legislation] tattooed on the inside of his eyelids for quick reference." Levin's deeply argued analyses always landed on the forceful conclusion that the law was a "disaster," or a "monstrosity," or a "calamity," or that "catastrophe is a function of the law's very design."

It was this decision to push forward, which Obama took against the advice of many members of his party and even his own administration, that most clearly displayed the role played by his personal qualities in his presidency's historic success. He showed guts, moral resolve, and the capacity to keep his head while all about him were losing theirs (and blaming it on him). When the House of Representatives passed the Patient Protection and Affordable Care Act on March 22, 2010, and Obama signed it into law the following day, it was the triumph of the vision of generations of activists and intellectuals consummated by the vision of Barack Obama.

The long and harrowing passage into law of Obamacare, as it came to be known universally, did not end its travails. After conservatives had grown so confident of its demise in the fall of 2009 and again after Scott Brown's election, its ultimate triumph felt to them not just like a setback but indeed a travesty, even a crime. Mitch McConnell called it the "single worst piece of legislation passed in the last 50 years in the country." Representative John Fleming of Louisiana has described Obamacare as "the most dangerous piece of legislation ever passed by a Congress" and "the most existential threat to our economy . . . since the Great Depression." Ken Cuccinelli, the former Virginia attorney general and Republican gubernatorial candidate, compared it to the Fugitive Slave Acts. And having failed in Congress, the crusade to destroy instead mutated into a rearguard guerrilla campaign spilling across the legal, electoral, and even cultural realms.

On July 1, 2012, Paul Ryan made an unusually revealing public comment. He was appearing on *This
Week*, a Sunday morning talk show, opposite Vicki
Kennedy, widow of the late Democratic senator. Kennedy extolled the security the new health care law would
provide to vulnerable Americans. "These are rights
and benefits that the American people embrace and are
excited about," she said. "Families can go to sleep re-
laxed and happy knowing that their children who have
asthma or diabetes or allergies are covered by insurance and aren't barred because they have a preexisting
condition." Ryan gave a completely honest response. "I
think this, at the end of the day, is a big philosophy
difference," he explained. "What Mrs. Kennedy and
others were saying is this is a new government-granted
right. We disagree with the notion that our rights come
from government, that the government can now grant
us and define our rights. Those are ours. Those come
from nature and God, according to the Declaration of
Independence, a huge difference in philosophy."

Conservative activists and intellectuals express
views like this regularly. They believe individuals
should be responsible for their own medical needs—or,
if they cannot afford it, that they should appeal to private charity. This conviction may be the most striking
aspect of the distinct economic libertarianism that sets

the Republican Party apart from the major conservative parties in every other developed economy, all of
which have broad-consensus acceptance of universal
coverage. Yet conservatives grasped from the outset of
the debate, as during previous health care reform debates, that opposing the goal of universal insurance put
Republicans in an untenable spot. Instead of a frontal
attack on Obamacare's goals, the right instead concentrated its energies on making the case that it would fail
to achieve them. It was not enough for conservatives to
deny that the costs and benefits of Obamacare amounted
to a worthwhile trade-off. Instead they denied that the
costs and benefits would look anything like what its
supporters, or even neutral authorities such as the Congressional Budget Office, predicted. The law would be
a complete fiasco, a train wreck.

"Just as economic shortages were endemic to Soviet
central planning," wrote *Weekly Standard* editor William Kristol, "the coming Obamacare train wreck is
endemic to big-government liberalism." On the right,
the inevitability of Obamacare's failure was repeated so
often it became an axiomatic truth. To deny it was to
deny conservatism itself. In 2010, David Frum, a former
Bush administration speechwriter turned fellow at the
American Enterprise Institute, wrote a column arguing
that Republicans in Congress could have enticed Dem-

ocrats to settle for a smaller, less offensive bill had they been willing to compromise. Frum was not even endorsing Obamacare—but the mere fact that he called into question the party's totalistic opposition made his view anathema on the right; AEI fired him shortly thereafter. Two years later, a paper published by AEI spelled out the correct line: "The Affordable Care Act (ACA) is too misguided to succeed, too dangerous to maintain, and far too flawed to fix piecemeal." Its title, "When Obamacare Fails"—"when," not "if"—deliberately captured the most important premise. The notion that subsequent events might force anyone in the party or its intellectual apparatus to reconsider their opposition to the hated law was unthinkable.

Shortly after its passage, a wide array of conservatives filed suit to block the law's enactment. The rationale behind the lawsuit held that the individual mandate violated the Constitution, because if the government could require people to purchase health insurance, it could require nearly anything—it could require people to buy broccoli! (Numerous conservative legal scholars invoked the imagined case of a broccoli mandate, and three conservative Supreme Court justices cited it.) As observers like Yale law professor Akhil Amar pointed out, this was a silly basis to oppose a law, since many powers could be stretched to absurd limits. If the government can levy income taxes, it can raise the tax rate to 100 percent; if the government can institute a draft, it can require universal service and lifelong terms. The lawsuit made sense only in the context of the panic about "rampant socialism" that had enveloped the right.

The Supreme Court ultimately rejected the constitutional challenge, but the workings of its decision remain shrouded in mystery. The Court ultimately decided the individual mandate could be upheld as a tax on the uninsured. Most Court observers believe that Chief Justice John Roberts, a conservative appointed by George W. Bush, stood poised to overturn the law, then suddenly changed his mind, fearing a 5–4 vote to strike down such a high-profile law would imperil the Court's public legitimacy.

While the Court narrowly left Obamacare mostly intact, it tore a chunk out of its structure. The law, as written, threatens states that if they turn down its Medicaid funds to cover the poorest of the uninsured they will lose *all* their Medicaid funding—related to Obamacare and otherwise. The Court deemed this threat excessive, and instead made it voluntary for states to accept Medicaid expansion. (Two liberal justices agreed to this aspect of the ruling. Most Court observers also believe that they did so in return for Roberts's vote to leave the rest of the law in place.)

The result left a significant hole in Obamacare's coverage. Even without the threat of withholding all Medicaid funds from states that didn't accept the Obamacare expansion, it made no financial sense for any state to turn down the money—the federal government still financed 90 percent of the Medicaid expansion, so states that turned down the funds only saved a mere 10 percent of the cost, in return for which they would have to spend, by most calculations, much more when their uninsured citizens showed up at emergency rooms with serious conditions, or were unable to work due to a physical or mental illness that could have been treated. Turning down the federal government funding ninety cents on the dollar would cost those states billions of dollars.

Still, given the option to turn down funds to cover their poorest uninsured citizens and in the process thumb their nose at Obama, twenty Republican-run states leapt at the opportunity. The decision left those states with an ungainly hybrid the law's authors never envisioned: the poorest of the poor could still obtain Medicaid, and uninsured citizens in or around the middle class could buy insurance through the exchanges, but struggling adults in between those levels were locked out.

Slowly, some of the initially recalcitrant states, like Iowa, New Hampshire, Pennsylvania, Louisiana, and Arkansas, joined, but the fight to complete the project of universal health insurance for all citizens settled into an extended, state-by-state slog that may take years or even decades to complete.

When Massachusetts opened its Romneycare health care exchange, the state undertook a massive public outreach campaign to inform citizens of the new insurance options that were available, along with the requirement that they purchase coverage. Even the Boston Red Sox helped get out the word that everybody had to get covered, and affordable plans were available.

Just as it had followed the Massachusetts model in designing its exchanges, the Obama administration hoped to replicate its public outreach. In this case, it hoped to enlist the National Football League in a public service campaign to raise awareness. When Republican leaders sent letters warning the NFL not to collaborate with the hated Obamacare, the league acquiesced. Republicans also targeted "navigators"—consultants who often work for churches, state governments, or charitable organizations, helping poor people fill out often confusing paperwork. House Republicans sent the navigators letters making sweeping demands for documentation that seemed to have the intent of burying them with paperwork. (Sample line: "This request also includes, but is not limited to, any documents provided by [or communications with] representatives from HHS, CMS, CCIIO, Enroll America, or any other entity including federal or state governments discussing individuals to target or solicit for enrollment under the PPACA including discussions or documents related to geographic area.") Several Republican-controlled states imposed unnecessary licensing requirements on navigators, forcing at least a couple of hospitals to drop out in response. Their sudden love of bureaucracy and Washington red tape had no explanation except a burning desire to gum up the works by any possible means.

Meanwhile, conservative activists financed a guerrilla campaign to persuade the young to boycott the exchanges, in an attempt to skew the age composition of the exchanges and set off the death spiral they hoped for. One group, "Generation Opportunity," sponsored parties with free pizza and games to lure students to hear pitches about why they'd be better off going uninsured. (Its campaign trademark was a frightening Uncle Sam–esque clown, who appeared in creepy online videos peering into the private parts of terrified patients.) YG Network, a conservative advocacy group founded by former staffers for Eric Cantor, started an anti-Obamacare advertising campaign targeting the young, including a satirical ad on *Saturday Night Live.* FreedomWorks, an antitax organization that helped finance Tea Party activity, held rallies where supporters could burn their "Obamacare card." (Such cards did not actually exist, so FreedomWorks had to supply them.) Dean Clancy, the group's public-policy director, explained, "We're trying to make it socially acceptable to skip the exchange."

The war to destroy Obamacare burst through on another front: conservative activists came to believe that they had one final chance to stop the hated law, by shutting down the government. Over the summer, they grew frenzied with the conviction that this strategy represented a chance at salvation for the America they knew and loved, and set out to persuade Republicans in Congress to embrace it. Many powerful figures in the party's congressional leadership, eager to prove that they shared their supporters' hellfire passion, agreed. "You want to delay implementation? Don't fund it," declared Florida senator Marco Rubio at a Republican Senate breakfast in July. "If Republicans in both houses simply refuse to vote for any continuing resolution that contains further funding for further enforcement of ObamaCare, we can stop it," insisted Utah senator Mike Lee. A spokesman for Lee announced that the shutdown would constitute "the litmus test of whether you do or do not support ObamaCare."

This premise was, in fact, completely erroneous. The Affordable Care Act had funded its own implementation already. Shutting down the government halted only government functions that needed continuous authorization to keep their doors open. Eventually Republicans in Congress realized this, but by that point, they had already committed to the strategy. And so, just as the exchanges opened, the Republican-led Congress had staged a futile shutdown of the federal government, the kind of self-destructive gesture usually employed by radical protesters rather than parties that have control of a national legislature. By the time the hullaballoo died down, when Republicans gave up and reopened the government two weeks later, national attention focused on a problem almost nobody had anticipated: the website where people could shop for insurance policies in the new exchanges did not work.

Perfectly playing into Republican arguments about the dangers of turning health insurance over to the federal government, the site, healthcare.gov, turned out to have been shoddily constructed, and launched without what software writers would call a full "beta testing" stage. Confusion spread through the Obama administration for days, and the full horror of what had transpired settled in slowly: the most important domestic reform in decades of American government rested on a single point of failure that lay in the hands of a few overwhelmed techies.

More than two weeks into the debacle, Obama and his key advisers had yet to decide whether the faltering website could be repaired, or whether they needed to build a new one from scratch. In a frantic scramble, Obama appointed Jeffrey Zients, a highly regarded executive turned adviser to his budget office, to recruit software engineers to revive the failed website. As miserable as the effort to build the website was, the campaign to rebuild it was equally impressive. By the beginning of December, after just a month and a half of work—an impressively rapid schedule for such a herculean assignment—the site was functional.

The two-month delay in the website's operation did little direct damage—customers still had a full month to shop for insurance plans that could not begin coverage until January 1. The indirect damage, on the other hand, proved massive. Just as the administration itself had initially missed the story of the website failure, so, too, had the news media. It corrected its mistake, and then overcorrected. From mid-October through November, the question at hand was not whether the website failure amounted to a gigantic debacle—all sides agreed it did—but whether the Obama administration as a whole had become one as a result. Former Bush adviser Matthew Dowd, asked if Obama had replicated a disaster on the scale of the Bush administration's botched response to Hurricane Katrina, agreed, "from a political standpoint, it's eerily similar to President Bush in the fall of 2005." A portentous front-page *New York Times* story reported that the controversy "raises questions about his competence in the same way that the Bush administration's botched response to Hurricane Katrina undermined any semblance of Republican efficiency." *National Journal*'s Ron Fournier, a columnist with an uncanny knack for locating himself in the midpoint of national opinion at any given moment, compared the health care rollout to Katrina and Iraq, rolled into one.

The website's failure gave credence to every Republican attack against Obamacare, of which there were many. A surge of coverage of the new law gave sympathetic coverage to overblown or even false claims that the new law was raising premiums, creating deprivation, and unlikely to ever function as intended. An NPR-sponsored debate, held on January 2014, put forward the question, "Is the Affordable Care Act Beyond Repair?" But as the administration repaired the website and the law itself confounded its skeptics and worked more or less as intended, public attention collapsed. *Washington Post* reporter Sarah Kliff tracked mentions of Obamacare in major national publications during this period. From October, when healthcare. gov had failed, to December, when it began to work, mentions of the law fell by half. Coverage in January, by which point the law's collapse was barely plausible, was about a quarter as intense as in December. Lacking media follow-up, the widespread impression of disarray formed during this period of national obsession with the website's crash and the potential failure of the law proved difficult to dislodge.

Hard as it may be to believe, many leading conservatives had at one point dismissed the possibility that Obamacare would even fulfill its most important objective of expanding access to health insurance. When some fragmentary evidence during the law's rollout suggested that a high proportion of new customers on the exchanges already had insurance, conservatives transformed this highly preliminary bit of data—which even then was contradicted by other data—into the conclusion that the new law would yield no reduction in the uninsured rate. House Speaker John Boehner announced in March 2014 that the law had caused "a net loss of people with health insurance." Boehner was echoing what had become a conservative truism. "What you have basically done is a churn where you've knocked people off their old insurance and then gotten them on the exchanges," insisted *National Review* editor Rich Lowry, appearing on *Meet the Press*. Obamacare "created more uninsured people than it gave insurance to. And it promises to create even more," argued Lowry's colleague Jonah Goldberg. Krauthammer proclaimed the law would result in "essentially the same number of uninsured."

A wide array of measures have disproven this. The National Health Interview Survey found that, among Americans aged 18–64—which excludes older people already eligible for Medicare—the uninsured rate dropped from 22.3 percent to 12.8 percent. The Department of Health and Human Services found that some 20 million additional Americans gained access to insurance due to the law. For those inclined to distrust figures coming from the government, Gallup's survey had found that the percentage of American adults lacking health insurance, which had ranged from 17 to 18 percent of the population in the years before Obamacare's coverage expansions began, dropped to 11 percent by 2016.

Health insurance is not a product from which customers tend to draw active enjoyment, like a beach vacation or a nice bottle of wine. It's a product you tend to use only when something has gone wrong. It also carries a certain inherent level of nuisance, like shelling out for premiums and deductibles, or discovering that some doctors and hospitals aren't covered in your plan. The newly insured now have some of the same hassles that people with insurance have had to cope with.

But, as insurance goes, the exchange plans have turned out to be reliable and affordable, if not a source of joy. A PricewaterhouseCoopers report found, "Across the board, at every level, average exchange premiums are lower than this year's average premiums for employer-sponsored coverage." Surprisingly, customers actually liked their exchange plans more than people with employer-sponsored coverage. A 2015 J. D. Power consumer survey found customers on the exchanges reported an average satisfaction rate of 696 out of 1,000, compared with 679 for people with employer coverage.

The first several years of the exchanges proved to be a period of flux. Working Americans who didn't have coverage through their job were not used to having the chance to purchase affordable health insurance on their own, and insurers were not used to selling it to a mass market. When the exchanges opened, premiums came in 18 percent under the level that the Congressional Budget Office had predicted. That shockingly positive news turned out to reveal a mixed blessing. Insurers had set their rates in many markets too low, and many found they could not compete in the new markets, and had to drop out. Customers on the exchanges needed to shop around every year in order to find affordable plans. Big insurers like Aetna pulled out of the exchanges, reducing options, and insurers in most markets raised their premiums.

The state of the exchanges varies from state to state. While 19 percent of consumers would have just one insurer in their market, according to the Kaiser Family Foundation, more than three-fifths of consumers would still have three or more from which to choose. Even at their higher levels, premiums will be almost exactly what the Congressional Budget Office had forecast when Obamacare passed. For all its birth pangs, the new individual marketplace, unlike the one that had existed before 2014, was functional and giving people the chance to get access to medical care.

Behind these numbers lay a humanitarian revolution, millions of lives transformed, in mostly quiet ways, from fear, pain, and impoverishment to normality. Lisa Gray, a consultant in suburban Washington, D.C., had expensive insurance that did not cover the cost of chemotherapy when she discovered she had leukemia in 2013. Starting in 2014, she could buy an exchange plan with a monthly premium that covered her treatment and had a premium thirty percent less. "A couple years earlier, I think I would have been done," she told the *Los Angeles Times*.

Obamacare did not conjure the subsidy that allowed people like Gray to be covered by magic. It transferred resources from the rich (through higher taxes) and the healthy (through higher premiums) to the poor and the sick. The alternatives they faced before, and would have continued to face without Obamacare, would have been to suffer, to go broke, or to die. Dean Angstadt, an uninsured logger in Pennsylvania, decided after regular Fox News watching that he should boycott Obamacare, until his friend prevailed upon him finally to enroll when he needed heart valve surgery to save his life. He may not have liked Barack Obama, but he owed him.

When cold actuarial logic was applied to the *cost* of health care, once again Obamacare's conservative critics were shown to have fundamentally misunderstood how the law could simultaneously expand access to the uninsured and also tamp down long-term medical inflation. It seemed to them like a simple paradox. "You don't need a PhD to see that the promise to expand coverage and reduce costs is a crude deception," wrote Krauthammer in 2009, in what was a common talking point on the right. But the designers of Obamacare never planned to reduce the amount the government spent on health care, at least not in the short term. They planned to bring about an immediate increase in spending, by bringing tens of millions of Americans into the system, while slowly holding down the expected increases in the average price everybody pays. The official forecasts projected that the law's new spending to cover the uninsured would exceed its cuts to Medicare, but that its revenue increases would bring about a net reduction in the deficit. Republicans relentlessly assailed these projections as a scam, numbers on a page manipulated to appear to reduce the deficit. "This legislation was supposed to end that asphyxiating growth [in health care costs]. It will not," concluded David Brooks. "This bill is full of gimmicks designed to get a good score from the Congressional Budget Office."

What actually transpired since then surprised everybody. The cost of health care has risen at a much slower pace than anticipated not only by Obamacare's critics, but also its supporters. In just the first five years since the law's enactment, the Congressional Budget Office has had to revise down its estimate of its cost five times. From 2014 through 2019, the first five years of Obamacare's enactment, the American health care system, public and private combined, will have spent some $2.5 trillion less than projected *before the law's enactment.* The cost of medical care has come down so fast that the federal government itself is now spending less than it was projected to spend on health care even had Obamacare never existed.

Additionally, in the years since Obamacare's enactment, the cost of medical care has risen at the slowest rate since before the enactment of Medicare. In the first half decade after the law's enactment, health care costs rose at a slower pace than general prices for the first time since 1959, when such records started being kept. Not even the wildest Obamacare optimist expected medical inflation to fall so low, so quickly. Nobody can say with any certainty just how much of this economic miracle can be attributed to Obamacare—both the direct impact of its reforms, or its broader signal about the need to make medical care more cost-effective—as opposed to other changes in medicine that may have occurred anyway. But, as we'll see below, a wide array of evidence shows that the law's reforms have worked.

Obamacare's cost reforms started taking effect almost immediately after the law's passage in 2010, and well before its new coverage took effect at the beginning of 2014. Yuval Levin—he of "catastrophe is a very function of the law's design" conclusion—believed that Obamacare would begin pushing up health care costs well before the exchanges opened. As early as the spring of 2010, he maintained that "in the interim it is likely to begin wreaking havoc with the health care sector—raising insurance premiums, health care costs, and public anxieties." It is fair to say that, had health care inflation started to rise after 2010, or even if it had remained at its projected level, Levin would have started making the case that he had been proven right.

Instead, the opposite happened. As the law's cost reforms took effect, health care inflation began falling. By the beginning of 2013, health experts had begun to debate how much this surprising success had to do with Obamacare. Some, cautious of declaring premature victory, attributed the drop to lingering effects of the recession. Levin embraced that view with gusto. In early 2013, he predicted that health care inflation would soon spike as the economy recovered, mocking supporters of the law who believed health care costs "just magically remain very low" for their "rosy" and "very implausible" faith in the law.

But health care inflation didn't resume the upward trajectory he predicted. Instead it confounded him by continuing to stay at a historically low level. By the end of 2013, he was formulating a completely new argument: without acknowledging his previous insistence that Obamacare would absolutely cause a spike in health care inflation, or his subsequent belief that the fall in health care inflation would be temporary, he now maintained that the fall in health care costs was inevitable. The "major slowdown in cost inflation began in 2003 . . . began in dramatic fashion five years before the recession." (And yet, despite this "dramatic" event, he spent years insisting the very opposite would happen.)

Levin, again, was anything but alone. The *Wall Street Journal* editorial page insisted over and over that Obamacare would increase rather than decrease health care inflation. In March, the editors noted rising costs in Massachusetts—which had expanded coverage but had not undertaken any cost reforms—and called it "merely a preview of what the entire country will face if Democrats succeed with their plan to pound Obama-Care into law in anything like its current form." Later that year, it proclaimed, "Once the health-care markets are put through Mr. Obama's de facto nationalization, costs will further explode." (Not may, *will*.) In October, an editorial warned "no one should entertain the illusion that it will reduce costs," and predicted "the result is going to be higher costs."

This is worth calling attention to because the author of those quotes was awarded the 2011 Pulitzer Prize for his series of hysterical denunciations of Obamacare that year. The Pulitzer committee does not award prizes on the basis of ideological agreement, but the *Journal*'s selection reflected a sense in which the opposition to Obamacare had appeared to carry the day. Activists and intellectuals supporting the law never matched the passion or the certainty mustered by its opponents.

The shocking drop in health care spending transformed the long-term state of the federal budget. But, from a political standpoint, it might as well never have happened, because as far as most Americans knew, it hadn't. A 2015 national poll asked respondents if they thought Obamacare was spending more than expected, less than expected, or about as much. A mere 5 percent offered the correct response, which is that it has spent less than projected. Just 10 percent more said spending had come in around expectations. Forty-two percent stated the law was spending *more* than expected, and another 40 percent did not know. Obama has repeatedly touted the law's twin successes at expanding coverage and holding down costs, but this side of the story never broke through reflexive skepticism about government's ability to get anything right. (Extremely few Americans watch presidential speeches all the way through, or even the news stories that, at most cover one or two lines from them.) The fashionable, cynical dismissal of the law's ambitions to bend the curve never dissipated, even in the face of powerful evidence.

There is a good reason for the pro-Obamacare side's caution about declaring victory in the quest to bend the curve: they cannot be certain they are right. Economics is a complicated field. Predictions are difficult. Even a policy change that seems to make logical sense is not assured of working. Obamacare's advocates tended to follow the professional norms of the social sciences, one of which is an appropriate hesitation to reach a strong conclusion without overwhelming evidence. The conservative opponents come from a right-wing tradition that has usually distrusted academia as a bastion of liberal bias. Conservatives have been strangers to doubt, immune to self correction, and able to maintain unwavering opposition to Obamacare. Hardly any equivalent has been found on the left.

And yet the evidence that Obamacare's reforms have succeeded in bending the curve is strong. There is no proof, because, as with the stimulus, it's unprovable: we cannot know for certain what would have happened to medical costs absent Obamacare. The evidence can be found not only in the larger trend of surprisingly depressed medical costs, but also in the clear success of many of the law's experimental initiatives.

The penalties for hospitals with high levels of patient readmissions paid immediate dividends. As soon as Obamacare started docking reimbursements for hospitals whose patients acquired illnesses in them, the rate of hospital-acquired illnesses dropped, by a staggering 17 percent over the first three years alone. The law also put into place financial incentives to penalize hospitals whose patients frequently had to be readmitted for additional care. (Under the old system, if a patient had to come back, it just meant more revenue.) The patient readmission rate dropped from 19 percent to 17.5 percent, which meant some 150,000 patients a year avoided having to go back to the hospital.

Not all the law's reforms fully took hold. Capping the tax deduction for employer health insurance proved controversial. Conceptually, the idea makes perfect sense. Money your boss spends paying for your health insurance is not taxed, while the money he or she spends on wages is (when you pay income tax). This imbalance creates a bias that encourages employers to compensate their workers with more expensive health insurance rather than higher wages. Health economists on both the right and the left have proposed to even out this imbalance by reducing, or even eliminating, the tax deduction for employer-sponsored insurance. In fact, most conservative proposals to replace Obamacare took the same approach even further. Obamacare's version became known as the "Cadillac tax"—a tax (or, more accurately, the scaling back of a special tax break) only impacting the most expensive, "Cadillac" plans.

Substantively, the Cadillac tax started working just as designed, prompting a growing number of businesses to shop for more affordable insurance plans to cover their workers. "Companies hoping to avoid the tax," reported the *New York Times* in 2013, "are beginning to scale back the more generous health benefits they have traditionally offered and to look harder for ways to bring down the overall cost of care." But the disruption angered workers who had expensive plans, and some of those workers—especially ones who had negotiated for their benefits through a union—demanded change. The Cadillac tax had enemies in both parties, and despite its sterling support among economists, few members of Congress wanted to defend it. In 2015, as part of a budget deal, Congress delayed implementation of the tax. Democratic presidential candidates Bernie Sanders and Hillary Clinton both denounced it, leaving its future viability in serious doubt.

But on the whole, Obamacare has instigated a revolution in the economics of health care that has reverberated. The first few years of the new Accountable Care Organizations—those groups in which doctors banded together to form their own medical group that provides coordinated care, and were paid for keeping their patients healthy rather than by how many services they performed—also showed promise. The experimental ACOs saved $300 per patient per year. And their patients reported levels of satisfaction with their medical care similar to those of patients in traditional insurance plans, and actually had an easier time getting in to see their doctor. And the new exchanges gave consumers an easy way to compare prices.

Obamacare's reforms have poked and prodded the system from every direction—hospitals, doctors, insurers, and patients—and those pokes and prods all seemed to be having their intended effects. The direct, measurable impact of each individual reform was small. But they sent a cumulative signal to the entire industry that it had to change. And the reforms were proof of concept of the whole theory behind the administration's plan to bend the curve: massive amounts of waste sloshed through the health care system driven by perverse economic incentives, and correcting those incentives could yield measurable improvement.

In 2015, Atul Gawande returned to McAllen, Texas, ground zero for runaway waste in the health care system when he described it six years earlier. Gawande described how the entire industry was eliminating wasteful and fraudulent treatments—"savings on an unprecedented scale," as he put it. McAllen was now undergoing a revolution. In the next three years alone, the city's hospitals were spending $3,000 less annually for every Medicare patient.

The Affordable Care Act will not end the problem of inefficient medical care, just as it will not end the problem of people who can't afford insurance. Few things in history simply end. But it created an inflection point on a historic scale—the entire American health care system will now be delineated as having a period before Obamacare and a period after. It was a revolution that succeeded after so many attempts before it had failed. Obamacare will be seen as one of the most ambitious and successful social reforms in the history of the United States.

Donald Trump, in keeping with his party's animating impulses, ran for president calling Obamacare a "disaster." He promised to replace the law first with "something terrific," which he frequently assured audiences would take care of every American's medical needs at much less cost. At one point, forced to describe his plan, he rattled off a handful of off-the-shelf Republican proposals, which would have allowed insurers to cherry-pick the healthiest customers and left people with serious medical needs or low incomes no way to afford decent coverage. It seemed obvious that the candidate lacked even a cursory understanding of how the law worked, what changes he would bring about, or how he could possibly fulfill his promise of fabulous medical care for all.

Once elected, Trump told reporters he wanted to maintain the law's protections for patients with preexisting conditions. Possibly the incoming president failed to grasp that these safeguards required the other elements in the law in order to function, and was in his mind clumsily walking through the steps Obama (and Romney before him) had taken. Perhaps he was misleading the public about his support, or perhaps he still had no real idea how the law worked and what trade-offs he would need to accept. It was impossible to tell. Either way, he did understand a simple political logic: thanks to Obamacare, millions of Americans now had access to health insurance. Throwing them off their insurance would cause immense political blowback.

Many Republican staffers working on their plans to fulfill the promise to repeal Obamacare quickly arrived at the same conclusion. Republicans had already passed dozens of bills to repeal the law, satisfying their base's anger. But they did so in the comfortable knowledge that Obama would veto their bills, sparing them any responsibility for the pain, suffering, and death their plan would create. "We're not going to use that package. We're not dumb," one Republican staffer told reporter Caitlin Owens. They hoped instead to tinker with the insurance requirements and age discrimination laws, so that insurers could charge a bit more to older customers and less to young ones, and sell skimpier plans. It would make the law more generous to the healthier, and more costly to the sick, but it would not destroy its central achievements. Republican senator Lamar Alexander, an unrelenting critic of the law, conceded repeal would not eliminate the law's central achievements. Alexander warned against the fantasy that the law could be quickly repealed. "[T]his will take several years to completely make that sort of transition to make sure we do no harm, create a good health care system that everyone has access to and that we repeal the parts of Obamacare that need to be repealed," he said. And whatever came next, Republicans must "be the rescue party instead of the party that pushes millions of Americans who are hanging by the edge of their fingernails over the cliff." "The cliff" was the cruel system in place before Obama, and even his enemies were reluctant to return to it.

To be sure, the most rabid of the conservatives would never give up their desire to repeal the law altogether. But the hesitation of the Republican leadership to follow through on its own rhetoric showed just how thoroughly Obama had transformed the politics of the issue. Before his reform, the uninsured could be easily discounted by Congress. Since responsibility for their suffering could not be traced to any specific political figures—the whole system was simply ignoring them—it was not a political problem. Obamacare turned 20 million previously uninsured Americans into beneficiaries of defined programs who could be easily identified if Congress stripped away their coverage. Republicans may not like paying for social programs, but neither do they like angry victims descending on their district offices, or stories in the local news about a mother who died of a treatable illness because her representative in Congress voted to end her health care subsidies.

In 1947, Harry Truman, in consultation with leading architects, proposed that the White House add a new balcony to its south-facing side. Truman's idea made aesthetic, functional, and fiscal sense (as it would replace unsightly awnings that required frequent replacement). But Truman's public standing had sunk at the time, and the idea unleashed "a huge stir of disapproval and ridicule," as historian David McCullough recounted. The "Truman Balcony," as his Republican opponents dubbed it, seemed to symbolize his haplessness and arrogance. Over time, the controversial porch would become a cherished part of the building's grandeur, and its name, originally intended as an epithet, transformed into a tribute to the president who dreamed it up.

Truman's dream of a federal program to provide universal access to health insurance took longer to come to fruition. When Clinton attempted to fulfill it, Republican critics labeled his plan "Clintoncare" (or "Hillarycare," after the first lady, who had a strong hand in the project). When Obama took up the goal, Republicans called it "Obamacare." The fusing of the president's name and health care created a belittling juxtaposition, conveying the gulf between the grandiosity of the ambition and the president's smallness—or perceived smallness.

Clinton's administration resisted the term, and so did Obama's, but by 2012 the president gave in and conceded that the Patient Protection and Affordable Care Act could bear his name, if its opponents wanted. The term has already lost much of its hostile connotation, and as it embedded itself into the medical economy, it slowly created a constituency on its behalf. Possibly Republicans will come to regret affixing the name of their partisan adversary to a measure that provides every American a guarantee against misfortune. Thus have materialized the fondest hopes that Obama harbored on the evening of March 23, 2010, when he celebrated signing into law his party's eternal, elusive dream—gathered with his staff on the Truman Balcony.

Chapter 4

To Halt the Rise
of the Oceans

On June 3, 2008, on the brink of securing his party's presidential nomination, Barack Obama delivered a grandiose address to his overjoyed supporters containing what was destined to become his most widely ridiculed promise. "If we are willing to work for it, and fight for it, and believe in it, then I am absolutely certain that, generations from now, we will be able to look back and tell our children that this was the moment when we began to provide care for the sick and good jobs to the jobless . . . this was the moment when the rise of the oceans began to slow and our planet began to heal." To Obama's critics, the notion of slowing the rise of the oceans seemed to capture the delusional arrogance they saw in the freshman senator. To his supporters, the line captured the existential scale of the challenge that lay before them. As early as the nineteenth century, scientists had observed that the release of carbon dioxide into the atmosphere trapped heat that would otherwise have escaped into outer space.

By the outset of the twenty-first century, their warnings had taken on increasingly frantic tones, as global temperatures soared, glaciers melted, and sea levels rose alarmingly higher. And as the scientific basis for their fears grew steadily stronger, the political basis for any response seemed to erode. Climate change is a problem the American political system is practically designed *not* to solve. The costs of inaction all lie far in the future, while politicians survive from election to election. (Indeed, Mitt Romney, accepting the Republican nomination four years later, ridiculed Obama's idealism, telling his supporters, "President Obama promised to slow the rise of the oceans and to heal the planet. My promise is to help you and your family.") Limiting emissions does not offer any tangible benefits—merely the absence of disaster, or more likely, just its mitigation. The fossil fuel industry has powerful allies in politics, including a handful of Democrats in states that heavily produce coal and oil.

What's more, even successfully jolting the American government into overhauling its entrenched patterns of energy use would merely serve as the precondition for the far more daunting task of coordinating agreement across the globe. The carbon any one country dumps into the atmosphere does not merely warm the air over that country—it spreads its effects across the world. Carbon pollution presents a classic collective action problem: any one country has every incentive to use cheap, dirty energy, letting others bear the costs of reform. Even worse, there is no obvious or intuitively fair basis for allocating the costs between rich and poor countries. The poorest countries can correctly point out that the old, industrialized giants grew rich by filling the atmosphere with the carbon from oil and coal, and have a larger burden for mitigating the damage they inflicted on the rest of humanity. On the other hand, those rich countries can reply that we know far more about the damage of carbon emissions now than we did during the heyday of Western industrialization—and, in any case, allowing the developing world to follow the West's dirty energy path would court disaster.

The first major attempt to forge an international agreement—in Kyoto, Japan, in 1997—left developing countries out completely. The next major world conference—in Copenhagen, Denmark, in 2009—foundered upon the inability of rich and poor countries to agree on their level of obligation. In the two decades preceding Obama's presidency, effective action to halt climate change had come to seem unimaginable. Meanwhile, the horrors of an ever-warming planet, with its rising seas, mass extinctions, droughts, famines, waves of refugees, and abandoned coastal cities, has grown terrifyingly real.

The Obama administration had taken shape in the midst of a worldwide economic meltdown that pushed the threat of a slowly warming planet far from Americans' minds. Yet, in Obama's mind, the economic emergency he suddenly faced did not blot out the long, slow planetary emergency of unchecked climate change. The two crises served to complement each other, in a way. The president's first task upon taking office was to find a way to get hundreds of billions of dollars out the door, and green energy provided something upon which to spend it.

The stimulus poured $90 billion worth of subsidies into technologies to reduce greenhouse gas emissions. It also extended tax credits for wind and solar power, the scheduled expiration of which threatened to smother those infant industries. The results of the infusion were nearly immediate: Before the stimulus, the Department of Energy predicted that it would take until 2030 for American wind power to produce 40,000 gigawatts of electricity per year. After the stimulus extended tax credits for wind energy, the 40,000 megawatt target was reached by 2010—two decades sooner. The wind boom continued, nearly tripling total wind energy capacity over the eight years Obama held office, as a new generation of taller, more efficient turbines came on line. At the same time, the price of manufacturing solar panels plummeted, setting off an explosive rise in their use. During Obama's tenure total solar energy capacity in the United States increased more than thirty times over. In Obama's second term, it even became economical to build entire power plants employing solar power; fueled largely by the tax credits, utility-scale solar power increased some thirty times over during the Obama presidency.

Following a classic pattern of American capitalism, in which the government supplied financing for new technologies—as it had with the railroad, the telegraph, and canals—the stimulus provided more than $30 billion in loans for green energy companies. A handful of the firms that received financing went bust, of course, just as happens in the private sector, but Republicans turned a couple of the high-profile failures into the symbol of what they claimed to be the insolvency of the administration's agenda. During his presidential campaign, Mitt Romney brought reporters to the shuttered headquarters of Solyndra, a solar company that had received federal loans and gone under. As he'd hoped, the resulting news coverage echoed Romney's contention that Solyndra had been a boondoggle emblematic of failed big government, or even corrupt "crony capitalism." (The success of the attack also bore out the administration's fear during the crafting of the stimulus that any spending seen as wasteful would serve to undermine the whole measure.)

In reality, failures like Solyndra were the exception rather than the rule. Of the Department of Energy's $34 billion in loans, a mere $780 million, or just 2 percent, had defaulted. When interest payments were included, the loans broke even for the government, while financing transformative new green technologies. The loans "seed[ed] the ground for an energy revolution," concluded *Scientific American.*

The stimulus also created a new agency, the Advanced Research Projects Agency–Energy, to fund cutting edge energy technologies. Modeled after a similar agency in the Department of Defense—which established, among other things, the Internet—ARPA-E funded research into green energy technologies whose commercial applicability lay far off in the future: advanced batteries, turbines, and ultraefficient solar cells. Because its work, by design, will not come to fruition in the short term, it is too soon to assess ARPA-E's success in producing breakthrough technologies. But the agency has won a cult following among green energy techno-enthusiasts, and even grudging respect among a small handful of attentive conservatives. Fred Smith, the Republican founder and CEO of FedEx, has said, "Pound for pound, dollar for dollar, it's hard to find a more effective thing government has done than ARPA–E."

At the international climate conference in Copenhagen in 2009, the United Nations tried, and failed, to create a binding worldwide agreement to bring down greenhouse gas emissions. Nevertheless, in the wake of that failure, some concrete goals emerged, including a pledge by the United States to reduce its emissions by 17 percent below its 2005 levels. That 17 percent figure became Obama's ante at the international negotiation card table. If the United States wanted China, India, and other developing countries to veer off the dirty energy path, the 17 percent promised cut was the concession it needed to make. That pledge would not guarantee a successful international deal, but without it, a deal would be impossible.

Obama had a plan to fulfill America's obligations: the United States would pass a cap-and-trade law. Cap and trade is a market-based policy for reducing emissions, under which the government sets a limit (the "cap") on total emissions, and then allows businesses to buy and sell permits for those emissions (that's the "trade"). Cap and trade has impeccable moderate Republican credentials. It was designed as an alternative to blunt government regulations that specify exactly what technologies every industry must use to reduce its emissions, without regard for their cost. Cap and trade assumes that firms can identify the cost of reducing their own emissions more cheaply than the government can, and that a market-based system can allow the companies with the cheapest opportunities to reduce their emissions to make the cuts. As with health care, Mitt Romney pioneered an early version of the idea as governor of Massachusetts, and he promoted a crafty administrator named Gina McCarthy to undersecretary for policy at the state's Executive Office for Environmental Affairs to implement his vision. Romney backed off the idea shortly thereafter when he decided to seek the 2008 Republican nomination. Still, Republicans like Newt Gingrich and John McCain publicly supported the idea through 2008, and it seemed plausible to imagine that Obama might attract bipartisan support. Even Marco Rubio, as recently as 2008, had positive things to say about cap and trade.

And the administration would certainly need Republicans to pass cap and trade. Democrats still sat two senators short of a filibuster-proof majority at the beginning of Obama's term, and they couldn't even win all of them since those representing coal and oil states viewed cap and trade as a surefire career-ender. (Democratic senator Joe Manchin, from coal-rich West Virginia, went on to survive the 2010 midterm elections by dramatizing his opposition to cap and trade in a television ad depicting himself shooting a copy of the bill with a rifle.) What's more, unlike health care reform, a Democratic Party goal for decades, global warming had only recently matured into a first-rank priority.

Just as turned out to be the case with health care, it might have been possible for Democrats to pass a climate bill with just fifty votes in the Senate through budget reconciliation, but moderate Democrats broke ranks to prevent such a measure. Cap and trade's survival thus depended on attracting Republican support.

This was not going to be easy, no matter the urgency. As scientists have grown more convinced of the theory of anthropogenic global warming (the scientific name for the phenomenon that the release of carbon and other heat-trapping gasses increases global temperatures), the GOP has rejected it. Senator James Inhofe, the chairman of the Senate Committee on Environment and Public Works after the 2014 election, even wrote a book titled *The Greatest Hoax: How the*

Global Warming Conspiracy Threatens Your Future.
Its thesis is both self-evident and shared by a good
number of his fellow Republican legislators. Representative Lamar Smith, chairman of the House Science
Committee after the 2010 elections, has mocked climate
scientists as "alarmists" who follow "malfunctioning
climate models."

Numerous polls have shown Republican voters growing more skeptical that human activity is contributing
to climate change—a shift that reflects the hardening
of climate science denial into a pillar of Republican
doctrine. The ascendance of this reactionary stance
drove Republicans who had once straightforwardly
accepted the theory of anthropogenic global warming
to nervously edge away from their heresy, or to flee in
disarray. Romney, who had once declared, "I believe
that climate change is occurring—the reduction in the
size of global ice caps is hard to ignore," recast himself
in 2011 as uncertain. ("Do I think the world's getting
hotter? Yeah, I don't know that but I think that it is.")
Tim Pawlenty, who also sought the 2012 nomination,
was called out by a moderator during a presidential
debate for having once declared "cap greenhouse gas
pollution now!" (The mortified Pawlenty confessed his
position had been "a mistake.")

This retreat from any semblance of reason was

well under way in 2009, as Democrats in Congress attempted to cobble together Republican support for cap and trade. The House, where Democrats enjoyed a majority swollen by two straight landslide elections of voters reacting against a failed Republican administration, could absorb the defection of forty-four Democrats and still find a majority to pass a cap-and-trade bill. Cap and trade's fate would lie in the Senate. Yet the anti-Obama tide of reaction that swept away the remnants of Republican moderation on fiscal stimulus and health care in the wake of the 2008 election likewise wiped out any GOP willingness to limit climate change. John McCain had endorsed cap and trade as a presidential candidate, and his senatorial friends Lindsey Graham of South Carolina and Joe Lieberman of Connecticut hoped to build a cross-party coalition. (In 2005, Graham had joined a cohort of fellow senators to visit the Arctic Circle, where they witnessed firsthand the impact of climate change upon Inuit who had seen their environment transformed. He pronounced himself "moved.") But McCain's defeat seemed to embitter his disposition against the upstart president. McCain and Lieberman had worked out a bill in January 2009, but a primary threat back home by fellow Arizonan J. D. Hayworth, a bombastic conservative, made McCain increasingly skittish. By February, McCain had retreated from plans to announce support for a specific bill to plans to announce support for "principles." Soon after, McCain abandoned plans to declare support for those principles, too.

By 2010, the list of potential Republican supporters had dwindled—perhaps Susan Collins, perhaps Graham (even without his mentor McCain). But by June, Graham, also facing a threatened primary challenge, had abandoned any climate legislation, and was recanting his belief in climate science as well. ("I think they've been alarmist and the science is in question.") As happened with health care, the nervous Republican sympathizers couldn't name specifics that would nail down their support; they seemed to want other Republicans to join them, and no such support was forthcoming.

In fact, Republican senators all knew support for cap and trade would run the risk of producing a primary challenger that might end their career. New Hampshire senator Judd Gregg, who had once supported limits on carbon emissions from power plants, admitted, "Nothing is going to go anywhere in this climate, as we go toward an election, that involves cap and trade." Cap and trade perished quietly in the summer of 2010.

The death of cap and trade plunged environmental-ists into a profound gloom. A postmortem story in the *New Yorker* on the bill's failure lamented, "perhaps the last best chance to deal with global warming in the Obama era, was officially dead." Paul Krugman called 2010 "the year in which all hope of action to limit cli-mate change died."

The failure of that bill in 2010 set off bitter recrimi-nations, many of which laid the blame on the presi-dent's alleged lack of commitment. "Obama never fully committed to the fight," complained the *New York Times* editorial page; he displayed "no urgency on the issue, and little willingness to lead," concluded *Roll-ing Stone.* The administration's critics did have a point that the Obama administration concluded relatively early that cap and trade stood no chance of passage. In that sense, it did display a lack of urgency for passing a bill for which it could detect no path to obtaining sixty Senate votes, instead focusing its legislative energies on bills that did. Where the critics went wrong was their assumption that Obama's fatalism about cap and trade *caused* its failure. There was never a plausible chance for Democrats to corral the combination of Republi-cans and oil and coal Democrats they needed to break a filibuster.

The critics were also wrong about something else: their dejected assumption that cap and trade represented the last chance to take major action against climate change under Obama. As it turned out, there was another.

In December 31, 1970, Richard Nixon signed the Clean Air Act. The dispatches from that era feel unfathomably remote. The law passed Congress with Pearl Harbor war-resolution levels of support: In the House, 374 members favored it, with just one Nebraska Republican opposed. The Senate passed it 73–0. "Anti-pollution laws," explained the *New York Times,* "did not excite political rivalry." The law embodied a brand of environmental absolutism that would make Al Gore blush. It mandated that power plants use the best available technology, with no apparent thought given to the cost. No law as remotely grand or sweeping could pass Congress in the modern era. But the law turned out to have an enduring power and relevance that few anticipated when Obama took office.

The Clean Air Act requires the Environmental Protection Agency to regulate "air pollution which may reasonably be anticipated to endanger public health or welfare." Scientists in 1970 did not recognize that carbon dioxide contributed to global warming; they were more concerned with the human health effects of carbon monoxide and other chemicals. But as the scientific case for climate change hardened, environmentalists filed suit to force the EPA to regulate carbon emissions like other pollutants. In 2007, the Supreme Court ruled in the environmentalists' favor. In 2008, the agency officially deemed carbon dioxide a pollutant, and sent its finding to the White House. The Bush administration refused to open the email, thus, incredibly, running out the clock on any legal obligation on its own part.

The Obama administration opened all its emails from the EPA, thus resolving the question of whether Washington had an obligation to regulate carbon emissions. But just how vigorously the administration would exercise its regulatory authority, few people knew at the time. The green energy subsidies in the stimulus, just a few weeks into the administration, would turn out to represent the extent of Obama's legislative achievements on climate change. The administration's legacy would instead rest upon regulation.

The administration issued a sweeping array of rules. In 2012, the administration tightened fuel efficiency standards for cars, from 29.7 miles per gallon to 54.5 miles per gallon by 2025. The next year, it required cleaner-burning gasoline, the impact of which would remove the equivalent of 33 million cars from the road every year. ("There is not another air-pollution-control strategy that we know of that will produce as substantial, cost-effective, and expeditious emissions reductions," noted the executive director of the National Association of Clean Air Agencies, an organization representing state and local air pollution regulators.) In 2010, it tightened emission standards for trucks and buses, and tightened them again in 2015. It raised energy efficiency standards for federal buildings, for a wide array of home appliances, and began the process of writing emissions standards for airplanes.

The administration's climate record also benefited from simple blind luck. The recession that began in 2008 temporarily drove down energy usage. (When people cut back on their spending, they do less driving, don't run the air conditioner as high, and so on.) Unlike the temporary dips in emissions that accompanied previous recessions, though, this time emissions did not resume their upward trajectory as the economy recovered, a break with decades of history. As a result, greenhouse gas emissions in the United States peaked in 2007. Furthermore, revolutionary improvements in drilling technology produced a boom in inexpensive natural gas. Natural gas is not clean compared to emissions-free technologies like nuclear, solar, and wind energy, but it is much cleaner than coal, producing about half as much carbon dioxide, and the gas boom helped drive down carbon emissions. (The most common process of drilling for gas, fracking, does release methane, a particularly threatening greenhouse gas, but in 2015 the administration created regulations to limit methane leaks, too.)

All these things—the administration's green energy stimulus and array of regulations, the temporary emissions dip from the recession, and the gas boom—combined to revive an opportunity that had appeared to slip away. Now the United States had a chance to fulfill the ambitious commitments it had made in Copenhagen.

To redeem its promise, the administration had to fill one remaining hole, a huge one: power plants, which account for 40 percent of all emissions in the United States. Power plants presented a massive regulatory challenge. Unlike cars, or appliances, or fuel, which are used and replaced frequently, power plants are built and stay in operation for decades on end. What's more, there is no technology that can meaningfully reduce carbon emissions from coal, America's most common source of electrical power. The only cost-effective way to make a coal plant clean is to shut it down. Thus the only meaningful standard one could impose for a coal plant would result in all of America's coal plants shutting down—which, even if phased in slowly, would carry large costs and likely provoke a revolt from people suddenly staring at huge electric bills. Modest regulations could slightly reduce the carbon emissions from coal plants, but not nearly enough to put a dent in their emissions. The EPA's choice, as David Roberts, a writer who focuses on environmental issues, put it, seemed to be "either a firecracker or a nuke."

During Obama's first term, the nuke was useful, as nukes tend to be, only as a threat. The idea of the EPA regulating carbon dioxide as a pollutant was so abhorrent to power companies and some Republicans that it brought them to the bargaining table during the cap-and-trade negotiations. When negotiations collapsed, however, the prevailing assumption was that the entire ability to regulate existing plants had become a useless tool, paradoxically too powerful to actually deploy. As recently as 2011, fossil fuel industry lobbyists and their Republican allies believed they could find enough Democratic support to pass a restriction on the EPA's ability to regulate carbon emissions. (One giddy lobbyist told *Politico*, "the chances are better than ever.") Democrats eventually held enough support to prevail, but the fact that opponents believed they were in range of a bipartisan vote to eliminate the agency's regulatory authority over carbon shows just how thoroughly the cause of climate regulation had fallen on the defensive.

Toward the end of 2012, the administration began to seriously consider a different plan, based on a concept developed by the Natural Resources Defense Council. The idea was to create state-by-state targets for power plant reductions, and give each state the flexibility to meet those targets as it saw fit—usually by closing some, but not all, of its coal plants, and having their utilities install more clean energy sources. Creating standards for states, rather than for plants, allowed the EPA to escape its all-or-nothing "ban or leave" dilemma.

Few observers outside the administration took seriously the possibility that Obama would throw himself into such an ambitious plan. "I think this has the proverbial snowball's chance in hell of actually happening," wrote liberal *Slate* columnist Matthew Yglesias in December 2012. In his second inaugural address, Obama promised aggressive action on climate change, but commentators saw it as just so much empty rhetoric. "Many took note of Mr. Obama's promise to tackle global warming in his inaugural address," Edward

Luce wrote sadly in the *Financial Times* a few months later. "That was the last anyone heard of it." The *Washington Post*'s Chris Cillizza concluded, "[G]iven the fraught politics around doing anything major on the issue . . . it seems likely that Obama will go small-bore rather than major overhaul if he wants to get something through Congress." In June, "First Read," the NBC News daily political crib sheet, reiterated Washington insider opinion: "Yes, the president will announce some executive actions, but to do what he really wants he needs some legislative action, and this Congress is just not going to prioritize anything having to do with climate. . . . Opponents have successfully stopped previous climate-change policy efforts by simply turning the issue into a pocketbook issue by labeling it as an energy tax or a rate hike on average Americans' power bills. And there's no reason to think this same tactic won't work again."

In August 2015, Obama finally announced the final version of the Clean Power Plan. The new standards required power plants to reduce their emissions 32 percent below their 2005 levels by 2030. Since it merely updated an old law, the Clean Air Act, rather than creating a new one, there was no vote in Congress. That meant the Clean Power Plan had no legislative theatrics—no dramatic votes, no coy interviews with wavering lawmakers, no fevered town hall rallies. There was not much of anything for the media to cover, since all the work went on inside the administration. The drama-free process failed to convey the historic scope of the policy change Obama had brought to bear.

The GOP of the Obama era was now dominated by climate science skeptics and other determined opponents of any government action to limit climate change. But the party's tattered and besieged moderate wing, now powerless to influence its own leaders, was not entirely extinct. Obama's reforms incorporated the market-friendly structure that had once attracted such moderate Republicans, and some of them responded favorably. Christie Todd Whitman, the EPA administrator under George W. Bush (and a dissident from that administration's indifference to climate change), praised the Clean Power Plan as "the most flexible thing" the EPA had ever done. Whitman, along with three other former Republican EPA administrators from the Nixon, Reagan, and George H. W. Bush eras, coauthored a *New York Times* op-ed urging their party to support Obama's "achievable actions that would deliver real progress." Ted Gayer, an economist and former adviser in George W. Bush's Treasury Department, conceded the Clean Power Plan "does a good job of providing compliance flexibility, which is the key to containing costs." Obama had, again, adapted the best elements of moderate Republicanism and applied them to a world in which all traces of moderation had been driven from the Republican Party.

Obama's regulatory offensive is, of course, vulnerable to reversal by Donald Trump or the Supreme Court, since it rested upon executive action rather than a law that would need to be overturned by Congress. But its design gave it enduring influence. Its flexibility and gradually tightening standards allowed states long-term planning, the effects of such decisions to play out over years. Since the only cost savings offered by coal was that the infrastructure that uses it was already built, once states had begun transitioning to new sources of green energy, it would not save any money to tear down windmills or solar panels and resume digging up coal. Indeed, one beauty of solar and wind energy is that, unlike fossil fuels, which must be extracted from the ground continuously, they run on their own. Trump promised to bring back coal mining jobs by eliminating regulations. But the revival of coal was a fantasy. Natural gas power plants had replaced coal at a rapid clip in part because they were now dramatically less expensive. Stopping coal's decline would come at prohibitive cost.

Republicans filed a legal challenge to halt the Clean

Power Plan. In January 2016, the Supreme Court issued a stay halting its implementation pending the resolution of the lawsuit. But the death of Justice Antonin Scalia in February 2016 deprived conservatives of the fifth Republican-appointed justice they would almost certainly require to overturn the plan. Even without a Democratic-appointed justice to replace Scalia, the Court would have just four justices potentially willing to overturn the regulations. A 4–4 tie would leave the final word in the hands of the U.S. Court of Appeals for the D.C. Circuit, controlled by a majority of Democratic appointees.

During the debate over cap and trade, when they weren't questioning the legitimacy of global warming— an argument that had the harmful side effect of reinforcing the party's deserved reputation for hostility to science—Republicans began to emphasize a second, and newer claim: reducing greenhouse gases in the United States would make no difference, since the rest of the world wouldn't follow. "We can't do it alone as one nation," John Boehner said. "If we've got India, China, and other industrialized countries not working with us, all we're gonna do is ship millions of American jobs overseas." They continued to make this case after cap and trade failed. "If we could have a pact with other countries in which everybody would reduce their emissions, I would sign on," is how Charles Krauthammer put it in 2014. "In the absence of it, all that we're doing is committing economic suicide in the name of do-goodism that will not do an iota of good."

The skeptics were correct that, without securing cooperative reductions from other countries, American emissions controls would do little good. And they had good reason for their fear. As China industrialized, it followed the same path of cheap, dirty energy that the United States and Europe had blazed a century before. Over the past quarter century, its emissions had quadrupled. Lifting the oppressive burdens of Chinese poverty required massive industrial development—which meant huge quantities of carbon, and the process had no end in sight. As recently as 2009, analysts believed China's carbon emissions level would continue to rise, not reaching its peak until 2050.

This vast new source of global warming in the East, just as the West was making a dent in its emissions, provided the single largest reason for the sense of helplessness among the environmentalist movement. Worse, most of the developing world longed to replicate China's astonishing new prosperity.

It is hardly selfish for developing countries to refuse

to force their impoverished people to shoulder the burden of averting climate change. (Even now, China burns less than half as much carbon per person than does the United States.) But there were also reasons to believe China would not simply burn its way to affluence. Its cities are already choked in smog from coal, and Communist Party elites must breathe the same air as ordinary workers. What's more, China has aspired to global leadership, and the rise of climate change created a new avenue for that country to exert its influence. And the prospect of a global transition to green energy created a void for a new industry it hoped to anchor. For markets domestic and beyond, China has invested vast sums in green energy, erecting wind turbines everywhere, and pumping out inexpensive solar panels for global export. In the first half of 2016, China increased its solar capacity by 20 gigawatts—which is nearly three-quarters as much solar power as already existed in the U.S. Its wind energy production has increased tenfold in a half-dozen years, and the country is in the midst of what one analyst called "the largest build-out of hydroelectricity the world has ever seen."

In 2013, when the Obama administration first signaled its intention to implement the Clean Power Plan, and thus to live up to its emissions targets, it began to negotiate with China. Later that year, the two countries jointly pledged to phase out hydrofluorocarbons, a potent greenhouse gas used in air conditioners and refrigerators, and which would have grown to a fifth of greenhouse gas emissions by midcentury if unchecked. The next year, the two countries agreed to deepen their cuts in overall greenhouse gas emissions. Obama, already pledged to the 17 percent 2020 target, promised to push emissions levels down 26–28 percent by 2025. China pledged its emissions would peak by 2030—two decades before what had not long before been the expected date—and to draw a fifth of its power from renewable sources by that time.

When the Chinese government announced its participation in the bilateral agreement, American conservatives rolled their eyes. Their skepticism that China would curtail its emissions rested upon the premise that maintaining its prosperity required it to burn ever-increasing amounts of dirty energy, forever. "China almost certainly won't take significant steps to reduce carbon emission," explained *National Review.* "That's because the legitimacy of the Chinese Communist party's government rests squarely on economic development. Energy—often produced by dirty coal—allows that economic development to occur, lifting millions out of hand-to-mouth poverty." This analysis relied upon a fatally flawed assumption: that producing more energy required producing more carbon emissions. The ratio of carbon emissions to energy produced is called "carbon intensity," and China's carbon-intensity ratio has dropped precipitously. In 2009, China promised to reduce carbon intensity 45 percent from its 2005 level by 2020. It is well on track to achieve this (as of 2015, it was already down 34 percent) and is now promising to deepen the cut to 60 or 65 percent—evidence that China not only had begun the process of producing more energy without producing more carbon, but more important, has begun thinking seriously and practically about what it will mean to steward the majority of the world's future population.

The energy revolution in China has laid the groundwork for a future scarcely anybody could have imagined just a few years ago. For most of the 1.3 billion people globally without access to electricity, building new solar power is already cheaper than fossil fuel generation. And so, the possibility has come into view that, just as the developing world is skipping landlines and moving straight into cellular communication, it will forgo the dirty-energy path and follow a clean one. The global poor can create a future of economic growth for themselves without burning the world.

The revolutionary developments in China primarily

reflect decisions the Chinese government made for its own reasons. But the administration's diplomacy and domestic reforms surely played an important role. A *Wall Street Journal* editorial published in June 2014 provided one of the rare times that American conservatives acknowledged that Obama's strategy was not merely to unilaterally reduce American emissions, but to entice China into cooperative reductions. "Mr. Obama's logic seems to be that the U.S. should first set a moral example by imposing costs that reduce our prosperity," scoffed the *Journal.* "This will then inspire China (8.7 billion tons), which produces and consumes nearly as much coal as the rest of the world combined, to do the same to its 300 million people who still live on pennies a day. Good luck persuading [Chinese president] Xi Jinping." Given that events exactly followed the sequence that Obama's critics mocked, it seems fair to credit the strategy for helping to produce this very outcome. Obama's Clean Power Plan attracted close attention abroad, and especially in China, where reporters found that Chinese limits on carbon emissions came as a direct response to Obama's own targets.

By the end of Obama's second term, green energy had expanded at a pace even its most optimistic devotees could not have imagined a few years before. Political willpower and technological innovation fed into each other, and as one of the dynamics accelerated, the other would accelerate in turn. The United States and China, the two largest greenhouse gas emitters in the world and, respectively, the leaders of the industrialized and the industrializing economies, had unique power to set the terms of the global climate bargain. A commitment to reduce emissions in the United States, Europe, China, and elsewhere created incentives for green energy entrepreneurs to develop new technologies to reduce energy use and harness emissions-free sources. Those innovations drove down the price of clean energy. And the availability of affordable clean energy made it easier for political leaders to commit to reducing emissions, knowing they can do so without imposing punishing price increases on their constituents.

Because these developments have reinforced each other, innovation has advanced more quickly than straight-line projections could forecast. In a March 2011 post for *Scientific American*'s website, technologist Ramez Naam compared the rapid progress of solar power to Moore's Law, the famous dictum that described the process by which microchips grew steadily more useful over time, doubling in efficiency every two years. The price of solar power had fallen in two decades from nearly $10 a watt to about $3. By 2030, he predicted, the price could drop to just 50 cents a watt.

Four years later, in the spring of 2015, Naam re-visited his post and admitted his prediction had been wrong—it had been far too conservative. The price of solar power had *already* hit the 50-cent threshold. In the sunniest locations in the world, building a new solar power plant now costs less than coal or natural gas, even without subsidies, and within six years, this will be true of places with average sunlight, too. Taller turbines, with longer and more powerful blades, have made wind power competitive in a growing swath of the country and by 2023, new wind power is expected to cost less than new power plants burning natural gas. Experts predicted in 2000 that wind-generated power worldwide would reach 30 gigawatts by 2010; when 2010 arrived, it was 200 gigawatts, and by 2014 it reached nearly 370, or more than 12 times higher. Predictions in 2002 stated that installations of solar power would add one new gigawatt per year by 2010. It turned out to be 17 times that by 2010 and 48 times that amount last year.

Meanwhile, the coal industry has gone into free fall. In 2009, 523 coal plants operated in the United States. More than 200 of them have since shut down, displaced mostly by natural gas plants. Only one coal-fired plant has been green-lit since 2008, and new regulations make it virtually certain that no coal plant will break ground in the United States ever again.

The energy revolution has rippled widely through the economy. In the first half of 2016, renewable-energy installations accounted for 70 percent of new electrical power. As the energy mix has grown cleaner, people have found ways to use less of it, too. Incandescent bulbs have been replaced with efficient LEDs in what Prajit Ghosh, director of power and renewables research at energy company Wood Mackenzie, refers to as a "total bulb revolution." Tesla has introduced a new home battery, the "Powerwall," and broken ground on a plant in Nevada, called the Gigafactory, with the capacity to churn out 500,000 lithium-ion battery packs per year, which will allow it to cut battery costs by a third and sell less expensive electric cars. And these are only a few of today's greener technologies. Laboratories from Cambridge to Silicon Valley are racing to develop next-generation batteries, as well as ultraefficient solar cells, vehicles, and kitchen appliances. For more than a century, everything that consumed energy was designed without a thought to the carbon dioxide that would be released into the air. Now everything from buildings to refrigerators is being designed anew to account for scientific reality.

This is a story of ingenuity, but the energy market has been disrupted because governments disrupted it; progress came not in spite of our government but because of it. The private sector developed LED bulbs because Washington required higher-efficiency lighting. The post-crash stimulus package pumped $90 billion into green energy subsidies, as China and Germany made similar public investments. Obama's regulations may have ramped up the pressure on old, fossil fuel industries. But, far from being "job-killing regulations," they helped set off a period of intense innovation and discovery.

On December 12, 2015, the Obama administration's work reached its culmination when negotiators for 196 countries gathered in Paris approved the first agreement in world history to reduce greenhouse gas emissions. The Paris talks succeeded where those in Copenhagen failed for two reasons. One was that the clean energy revolution—which had been nurtured in places like the United States, China, and Germany—had come to fruition. In 2009, placing the future of your country's energy sector in the hands of technologies like solar and wind power was a leap of faith. Half a dozen years later, the price of new clean energy sources had fallen to the point where politicians could embrace them with confidence.

The second distinction lay in the different agreement structure. Copenhagen, and other previous climate negotiations, all tried (and failed) to establish overall caps on greenhouse gas emissions, doling out enforceable caps to each country. Paris turned that structure upside down. Instead, each country would submit its own targets for reductions. The more forgiving bottom-up structure worked. The pledges collected in Paris closed about half the gap between continuing the world's old energy policies unabated and the reductions that would be needed to stay within the temperature limits recommended by climate scientists.

The Paris agreement represented a staggering triumph of cooperative diplomacy, credit for which must be spread across the globe. But Obama's role in nurturing the accords is singular. Only in the United States does one of the two major parties question the validity of climate science. So, while presidents from Australia to Norway had to hammer out difficult negotiations with industries and fellow politicians to propose emissions targets they could live with, only Obama had to face down an opposition party that denied that dumping unlimited carbon into the atmosphere amounted to a problem.

An agreement to carry out half the necessary greenhouse gas emissions could be seen as a glass half-full—or, alternatively, half-empty. The environmental community is filled with people who tend toward the latter interpretation, as you might expect of people who spend their days contemplating mass extinctions, the flooding of major coastal cities, deadly heat waves, and other unspeakable horrors to be endured by future generations. Accordingly, headlines from Paris conveyed tightly restrained optimism, emphasizing that the real work lay ahead. It is certainly true that the world has not been saved. But the Paris agreement did not only ratify vast change on a planetary scale—it also implemented steps to ratchet up its goals over time. The negotiators agreed to reconvene every five years and attempt to tighten their collective targets. If green energy innovation proceeds in the half decade after Paris at anything like the pace of the half-dozen years after Copenhagen, securing deeper emissions reductions will be simple.

Political willpower and technological progress operate in tandem. As many governments set out to reduce their emissions, scientists and entrepreneurs, some of them subsidized by those governments, produced cheaper and more effective technologies. And as the price of green energy came down, more governments found it easier to embrace low-emission policies. More willpower produces more innovation, and on and on.

The Paris agreement represents a clinical sample of the extended time horizons on which Obama's mind operated. The problem of climate change itself is the ultimate long-game objective, the polar opposite of the sort of issue where a president can expect immediate gratification, but one of absolute, paramount, long-term significance. Obama set out to tackle a challenge at a time all his critics and many of his allies urged him to turn his attention elsewhere. And when the first attempt at a solution failed, he devised a second one, and pursued it even in the face of widespread skepticism from opponents and well-wishers alike. All the elements of the plan—the regulatory reforms, the patient diplomatic work—came together slowly. His plan's prospects evolved, almost invisibly, from fanciful to inevitable.

Some of Obama's critics on the left have complained that, unlike Franklin Roosevelt's New Deal, his administration has left no imprint upon the landscape to rival the Hoover Dam or the Tennessee Valley Authority. But the imprint of Obama's climate legacy is everywhere—rows of houses covered in panels, wind turbines stretching across the plains, glistening new solar power plants arising in the desert.

But if there was a single aspect of Obama's legacy most vulnerable to reversal, it was his achievements on climate change. Trump openly derided climate science, surrounded himself with advisers who did the same. (He even derided wind turbines as ugly and bad for tourism.) He pledged to pull out of the Paris Climate Agreement, to end the Clean Power Plan and eliminate all federal regulation of greenhouse gas pollution.

Unlike other extreme positions Trump had taken, most of which would inflict an immediate harm to many Americans, his rigid opposition to any policy response against climate change stood a good chance of remaining in place because its effects would only sink in long after he departed. Trump had little incentive to conform to reality or the needs of his constituents. Containing climate change ultimately requires not just continuing Obama's policies but expanding and deepening them, ultimately weaning the economy off carbon altogether. The most hopeful scenario, which had finally come into view at the end of Obama's term, was rendered hopelessly optimistic by Trump's election. And the damage wrought would likely be irreversible: a glacier cannot easily be un-melted.

This did not mean the task of sparing the planet from the worst effects of runaway global warming was hopeless, though. Obama had thrown the federal government's regulatory and diplomatic resources into organizing an international response to the crisis. With that government now in the hands of climate science deniers, leadership would have to arise in other places. States and cities, especially massive California, had already begun efforts to reduce their emissions beyond what Washington required. Other countries, having committed to an energy future, expressed reluctance to turn back in the wake of Trump's election. Obama will remain the president who launched the green energy revolution in the United States and forged the first international agreement on climate change.

In some ways, the work of the green energy revolution has already changed the economic calculus irreversibly. By the end of 2016, American power plants had already met their 2024 emissions reduction targets, thus fulfilling Obama's promises under the Paris climate agreement. Even if Trump managed to halt all further progress, a case could be made to the world that America had upheld its end of the bargain, and the agreement could remain in place. Many developing countries (which tend to be located in the sunniest parts of the world) can now build a new solar plant at lower cost than one using fossil fuels. A strong enough international consensus might resolve to outlast Trump and wait for him to be replaced by a more rational successor. Obama's efforts will be honored by future generations, while they will regard Trump's with horrified incomprehension. The cause will not disappear, nor will all the progress that Obama drove. Obama will go down in history as the first American president to take up the fight against the planetary catastrophe of global warming, and he will not be the last.

Chapter 5
To Stanch a Bleeding World

On October 9, 2009, the Nobel Committee announced it had awarded its Nobel Peace Prize to Barack Obama, who had not yet completed his ninth month as president. The committee's choice astonished and even embarrassed the Obama administration, which had barely settled into office. The committee's unusual reasoning credited Obama anyway, for what might be more accurately described as goals rather than accomplishments: he had "created a new climate in international politics," taking care to mention such feats as, "Multilateral diplomacy has regained a central position," and, "Democracy and human rights are to be strengthened" (which is far from boasting that they actually had been strengthened). This was a peculiar basis for bestowing such a prestigious award. Multilateral diplomacy had been a hallmark of American diplomacy for decades, until the administration immediately preceding Obama's. And "creating a new climate in international politics" meant, mostly, restoring the climate that had existed until 2001. In other words, Obama had been awarded the Nobel Prize for the achievement of not being George W. Bush.

The contrast between Obama's approach to handling world affairs and that of his predecessor did not merely dominate his foreign policy at the outset of his presidency—it defined it throughout. This can be seen as an indictment of Obama's strategy, or a defense—or, to some extent, both. Just as Obama's economic policy was initially dominated by the need to recover from an emergency inherited by his predecessor, so too did inherited conditions determine the course he set in world affairs. The Bush administration had let loose a chaotic failed state in the Middle East at the cost of thousands of American casualties and hundreds of billions of dollars while diminishing America's standing throughout the world. Obama's task required a corrective effort, a restoration of the (usually sober) internationalist traditions that had defined American policy for decades, from the end of World War II to Bush.

It is easier to make a provisional judgment of domestic policy than foreign policy. The Truman administration's strategy of containing the Soviet Union absorbed bitter criticism from left and right, and its full success could only be judged four decades later, when the Soviet bloc crumbled (confounding predictions of the hawks who demanded aggressive rollback as the only solution) without starting World War III (as anti–Cold War doves claimed it would). Numerous heavy-handed American interventions in the developing world seemed to yield short-term success while seeding resentment and blowback whose costs would not become fully apparent for years to come. Still, a rough judgment can be cautiously ventured. Unlike his approach to domestic policy and politics, Obama's foreign policy was not transformative. Obama slowed the bleeding of the Bush years but never fully stanched it. This negative quality of Obama's foreign policy strategy—the way in which his non-Bushness overshadowed any positive characteristics—provides the key to understanding both its virtues and its limits.

As he rocketed onto the national stage as a first-term senator, Obama needed to present himself as a plausibly seasoned statesman. Two moments in the campaign turned into fodder for his opponents to cast him as a naïf unsuited to the responsibilities of leading the free world. During a Democratic presidential debate in July 2007, a questioner asked the candidates if, in their first year as president, they would meet without preconditions with the leaders of Iran, Syria, Venezuela, Cuba, and North Korea. Obama immediately and unequivocally replied that he would. His opponent, Hillary Clinton, seized upon this promise as "irresponsible and frankly naïve," the gross mistake of an undereducated rookie.

Obama's response was, indeed, almost certainly a political gaffe. Diplomats have a process for determining when a president meets face-to-face with a foreign head of state. After the debate, the Obama campaign proceeded to insist that their candidate had actually meant that he would merely *consider* such meetings rather than commit to them without conditions. As president, Obama did not follow through on the pledge he had made spontaneously onstage. But the reasoning he used to justify his promise proved to be a harbinger: "The notion that somehow not talking to countries is punishment to them, which has been the guiding diplomatic principle of this administration, is ridiculous."

The second moment took place during another debate the next year, this one pitting Obama, now the Democratic nominee, against Republican John McCain. Asked whether he would pursue Al Qaeda terrorists into Pakistan even if it meant invading that country's sovereignty, Obama replied that he would. McCain immediately pounced. "Senator Obama likes to talk loudly," he shot back, contempt dripping from every word. "In fact, he said he wants to announce that he's going to attack Pakistan. Remarkable."

Those debate confrontations prefigured crucial elements of Obama's approach as president. He widened the contours of America's diplomacy with its adversaries, eventually producing breakthrough agreements with Iran and Cuba, two of the countries he was asked about in 2007. He also extended the parameters of American military power against Al Qaeda, expanding the use of air strikes, and sending Navy SEALs into Pakistan to kill Osama bin Laden. In comparison to his predecessor, Obama made American policy more dovish, but not unequivocally so.

In reality, Obama's promise was not to abandon the war against Al Qaeda that his predecessor had launched, but to refocus it instead. The Bush administration had allowed the widespread use of torture upon detainees, and the origin of the methods it selected hinted at its ineffectiveness. Intelligence agencies used Cold War–era resistance training against torture used by totalitarian regimes, and simply borrowed the same techniques they had been trained to resist, such as sleep deprivation, extreme cold, stress positions, and waterboarding. Since those torture methods had been devised not to collect intelligence but to extract (often false) confessions for propaganda purposes, it was not surprising that investigators later found these methods ineffective. Making things worse, the 2004 exposure of widespread torture at Abu Ghraib prison in Iraq provided a boon of anti-American propaganda in the Muslim world. Two days after taking the oath of office, Obama signed an executive order ending torture and the secret prisons in which it had taken place.

The 2011 departure of American combat troops from Iraq after more than eight years of intermittent success in suppressing civil war, and consistent failure in creating the conditions for a stable government, fulfilled a key Obama campaign promise, though the decision was made less by him than by the Iraqi parliament. (Lawmakers in Baghdad, tired of the occupation, refused to grant legal protections and immunities to American soldiers, a necessary protection to prevent those soldiers from being sent to Iraqi prisons.) Conceivably, Obama might have succeeded in persuading Iraq to allow American soldiers to remain. But the Shiite majority was not willing to accommodate the Sunni minority that had oppressed it for decades under Saddam Hussein's Baathist dictatorship. Absent such a willingness, it was clear that the country would remain mired in turmoil as Sunnis revolted against Baghdad. Once the Bush administration had blown the lid off Iraq, there was no way to force it back down, and Obama concluded that American occupation could suppress the violence but could not create the conditions for internal peace. Maintaining the occupation therefore served no long-term purpose.

America's failure in Iraq reverberated throughout the region for years after Bush's initial intervention. In 2011, rebels in Libya took up arms against that country's longtime dictator Muammar Qaddafi, and nearly drove him from power. But even as his government disintegrated around him, Qaddafi rallied loyal militias, who struck back, beating and killing peaceful protesters. In Benghazi, a port city on the Mediterranean, his militias cornered the rebels and threatened to slaughter the residents "like rats." The rebels appealed to NATO for protection against a massive pending atrocity, and U.S. military advisers proposed to Obama to enforce a "no-fly zone," in which NATO would shoot down any Libyan military aircraft. Obama rejected this as a half measure that would not prevent a massacre, and instead approved an even more ambitious plan: a bombing campaign against Qaddafi that would allow the rebels to win.

In its immediate objective, the bombing campaign succeeded. The NATO coalition, which had fractured over the Iraq War, pulled together to conduct round-the-clock strikes against Qaddafi's militias. The rebels rolled those troops back and then drove the dictator from power. From that initial success, however, conditions deteriorated quickly. American efforts to train and fund democratic forces in the chaotic new state failed. (It was in the post-intervention chaos that radical mobs overran an American compound and murdered four diplomats.) The intervention in Libya prevented a humanitarian catastrophe, but it failed to bring democracy or even stability. Unlike the Bush invasion of Iraq, a war of choice that occurred on Washington's timetable, Obama's administration did not have in Libya the luxury of time to plan its occupation and transition to a new regime. Still, even accounting for the hurried conditions it couldn't avoid, the administration's planning in Libya clearly failed. Whether Libya stabilizes in the years to come or disintegrates into a terror-exporting failed state will determine how heavily history weighs this failure.

Also in 2011, a similar episode began to unfold in Syria. Protests rocked the iron grip of Bashar al-Assad, a dictator whose regime, inherited from his father, had clung to power for decades through brutality and fear. This time, lacking confidence that his administration could identify rebels to entrust with American weapons and training without fear that they might turn their guns against the United States, Obama reached a different conclusion. Faced with terrible options, the safest route, from the standpoint of the United States, was to minimize the risk of a disastrous entanglement—while also foregoing any chance to spare Syrians the horrors of an unending war.

It is impossible to know what intelligence was available to Obama, and in turn whether the administration's restraint proved correct, or whether an early investment in aid to Syrian rebels might have yielded a better outcome. It is certain that the actual outcome, while succeeding at keeping American troops out of another deadly and expensive war, was disastrous. The Syrian civil war threw that country into unspeakable horror, set off a refugee crisis as civilians fled to safety, and gave space for ISIS, a terrorist organization whose barbarism boggles the imagination, to take root.

The merits of Obama's choices will be debated for years. What seems indisputable is that he bungled by threatening to intervene if al-Assad used chemical warfare on his people, which he called a "red line."

After Bashar al-Assad used chemical weapons, and the administration did not attack, his credibility with allies abroad took a significant hit.

What is also indisputable is that the administration failed to carry out a comprehensive response to the disintegration of states across the Middle East. The causes of instability in the Middle East run backward for centuries. The map, crafted up by colonial European powers, is composed largely of arbitrary states, drawn with ample straight lines on maps by distant rulers without regard to tribal or sectarian divisions. Those states, held together by fear and force, started to fall apart under Obama's watch. The post-2003 Middle East has only presented American policy makers with options ranging from bad to worse. No state in the region has produced either durable political majorities that support moderate democracy or any peaceful formula that would allow rival factions to coexist harmoniously. Peace has required repressive governments, and the alternative to peace has invariably been chaos. Nothing Obama did caused the unraveling, but nothing he did seemed to be able to resolve it, either. At best the administration found itself attempting to contain the fallout.

The rise of ISIS during Obama's term created a frightening new source of capricious terrorist violence, which was in turn the source of bitter recriminations spawned by the administration's inability to eradicate the threat. It is notable, however, that Republican critics failed to devise any alternative strategies that differed from the administration's except around the margins. Donald Trump, the party's nominee, proposed to "bomb the shit out of ISIS," without explaining what targets he would strike that had not already been attacked. Trump is known for his bombast, but even mainstream Republicans failed to describe credible alternatives. Presidential candidates like Marco Rubio and Ted Cruz proposed a mix of special forces on the ground, no-fly zones, targeted air strikes against identified ISIS positions, organizing friendly local Sunni militias where they presented themselves, and intelligence-gathering—all strategies Obama pursued; Republican candidates simply expressed those same ideas in forceful, action-hero language. None of those aiming for the GOP nomination dared endorse alternatives like a large-scale ground occupation or indiscriminate bombing of cities held by ISIS, out of the correct belief that such actions would produce a backlash among the local population and expand ISIS's base of support.

Philip Gordon of the Council on Foreign Relations, who advised the administration on the Middle East, argued in 2015 that the United States lacked the power to steer the region to a better outcome. "In Iraq, the U.S. intervened and occupied, and the result was a costly disaster," he wrote. "In Libya, the U.S. intervened and did not occupy, and the result was a costly disaster. In Syria, the U.S. neither intervened nor occupied, and the result is a costly disaster." Undoubtedly, Syria and Libya cannot be counted as achievements for the administration. How heavily these failures ought to weigh against Obama's record depends on the unknowable question of whether an alternative strategy might have worked. They were, at best, disasters he failed to avert, and episodes unlikely to be admired or emulated by a future president.

The withdrawal from Iraq served an immediate purpose of sparing American soldiers from the horror of endless carnage in service of a political goal— reconciliation between Iraq's Sunni and Shia—that lay mostly out of their control. But it also fed into a larger strategic imperative. Obama's course correction—not only on Iraq and torture, but also with regard to his country's general respect for diplomacy and international institutions—tangibly rebuilt America's standing abroad. The Bush administration had badly tarnished the image of the United States. A 2007 Pew survey found that, over the preceding half decade, favorable views of America had dropped in 26 of the 33 countries for which PEW could compare public opinion. Obama's presidency reversed the tide of anti-Americanism. By 2015, Pew surveys found that favorability had climbed 14 percentage points in the United Kingdom, 20 points in Germany, and more than 30 points in France. The trend could be seen not just in Western Europe—where the Bush administration had ostentatiously thumbed its nose—but elsewhere, too: approval had risen 10 points in China, 20 points in Turkey, more than 30 in Indonesia.

Obviously, popularity isn't everything. But "soft power" always undergirded the core of American strength across the globe, and widespread admiration for America's system of government, prosperity, culture, and technological know-how is an essential element of American leadership. Public resentment abroad of the United States encourages anti-American demagogues and makes it difficult for sympathetic leaders to build close diplomatic, military, and economic ties with Washington. Sympathetic opinion has the opposite effect.

An example of how this increased sympathy paid off was seen in 2014, when in response to demonstrations in neighboring Ukraine in favor of Western-style democracy, Russia began a stealth invasion. Pro-Russian demonstrators and militiamen wearing plainclothes infiltrated Crimea, part of Ukrainian territory, and ultimately pried it loose. It was an imperial land grab of the sort Russia had done for centuries, but the duplicity with which it was undertaken revealed an important weakness. Vladimir Putin didn't simply march in columns of soldiers, as previous Russian and Soviet dictators had done to neighboring lands; instead, because he was trying to wage a contest of political legitimacy against the United States, he needed the pretense of "organic" local demonstrations and the nonviolent transfer of power. Putin fancied himself the leader of a competing bloc of autocracies that, fattened by oil and gas wealth, could challenge the United States for regional supremacy. But while he did succeed in seizing chunks of Ukrainian territory, and Obama's refusal to challenge Russia's aggression fed into the Republican narrative of weakness, history has shown that American presidents have always hesitated to challenge Russia militarily in its own sphere of influence—which is why figures like Eisenhower, Johnson, and Reagan allowed the Soviets to crush Hungary, Czechoslovakia, and Poland, respectively, when people in those countries attempted to assert their independence. And Obama's reaction to the assault on Ukraine was hardly impotent: a 2014 United Nations resolution confirmed Russia's isolation, with one hundred countries condemning Russia's annexation of neighboring territory, and just eleven opposing the UN action. Sanctions imposed by the United States and the European Union threw Russia's economy into a deep recession, draining the source of Putin's influence. Far from being drawn into Russia's orbit, Eastern Europe drew closer to the West. Whatever immediate gains Putin extracted came at a deep price of isolation and impoverishment.

Obama had other ideas for how he might use soft power as a weapon. A few months into his presidency, he explained how this strategy might work in an interview with *Newsweek* in which he made the case for reaching out to negotiate with Iran. Why extend a hand to an aggressive regime ruled by religious extremists that had sponsored terrorism and brutalized its own people? Obama explained that doing so would undercut Iran's ability to portray itself as the helpless victim of American bullying. "I assure you, I'm not naïve about the difficulties of a process like this," he added. "If it doesn't work, the fact that we have tried will strengthen our position in mobilizing the international community, and Iran will have isolated itself, as opposed to a perception that it seeks to advance that somehow it's being victimized by a U.S. government that doesn't respect Iran's sovereignty."

The same logic ran through much of Obama's diplomacy. He would listen to adversaries, and take seriously their complaints. Sometimes these complaints were well-founded: The United States had for decades propped up congenial dictators in Latin America and the Middle East; Muslims harbored resentment against Western invaders dating back to the Crusades. Obama acknowledged this painful history, including during a high-profile 2009 speech in Cairo, in which he conceded, "The fear and anger that it provoked was understandable, but in some cases, it led us to act contrary to our traditions and our ideals," and highlighted American support for a coup against a democratic Iranian government in 1953.

Republicans attacked such concessions as an "apology tour"—a groveling attempt to appease America's enemies—or, perhaps worse, evidence that the president secretly agreed with them. Mitt Romney, laying the groundwork for his presidential candidacy, titled his 2010 campaign book *No Apology,* anticipating at the time that Obama's alleged habit of apologizing for American misdeeds would supply his most potent cam-

paign theme. But those Republicans failed to acknowledge that Obama combined his concession of America's
inconsistency in applying its ideals with a rousing defense of the ideals themselves.

The administration's December 2014 opening of
diplomatic relations with Cuba was an attempt both to
demonstrate American soft power and to increase it.
The United States had suspended relations with Cuba
since its communist revolution. But in four and a half
decades, neither the diplomatic freeze-out nor the related economic embargo had shown any sign of accom-
plishing its intended effect of weakening the despotic
Castro regime. The Obama administration argued that
it stood a better chance to advance democratic values by
engaging with Cuba's government, oppressive though
it might be.

The domestic debate over the Cuba opening followed the pattern of many of the administration's negotiations with hostile regimes. Conservatives insisted
that acknowledging any legitimacy to the enemy's
point of view weakened the American position. "It
is just another concession to a tyranny by the Obama
administration," thundered Rubio, in response to the
announcement, "rather than a defense of every universal and inalienable right that our country was founded
on and stands for." But Obama believed demonstrat-

ing flexibility could build American credibility and strengthen its hand. "The focus has been for so many years on the U.S. policy toward Cuba, not on the record of Cuba," José Miguel Vivanco, the director of the Latin America program at Human Rights Watch, told the *New York Times*. "This puts the U.S. government and the Obama administration in a very different position with much more credibility when it comes to talking about democracy and human rights." Within a year, numerous Republican elected officials were undertaking visits of their own or supporting bipartisan legislation to end the economic embargo.

Obama's Cairo speech was widely seen as an effort to drain the poison from American relations with the Muslim world, and the historical and abstract dimensions of the first African-American president reaching out to a faith his domestic opponents had falsely accused him of secretly holding captured most of the attention. There was, however, one passage from that speech that, while more narrowly tailored and less than poetic, carried weight that would become much clearer years later. "Any nation—including Iran—should have the right to access peaceful nuclear power if it complies with its responsibilities under the Nuclear Non-Proliferation Treaty," he said. "That commitment is at the core of the treaty, and it must be kept for all who fully abide by it."

In fact, one of the first issues to seize Obama's attention as a U.S. senator was the spread of nuclear weapons. The end of the Cold War had left the world with a vast nuclear stockpile throughout a Soviet Union that was splintering into breakaway republics, and whose government was disintegrating and beset by corruption. The Bush administration had reacted to 9/11 by defining the terrorist threat in the broadest possible terms—so broad that it included Saddam Hussein's secular Baathist dictatorship. But the threat that compelled many foreign policy experts was the prospect that nuclear material might fall into terrorist hands. The potential damage Al Qaeda could inflict with a nuclear device—or even a "dirty bomb," which uses a conventional explosive to scatter radioactive material in a city—would dwarf the scale of 9/11.

As a freshman senator, Obama cosponsored a bill with Richard Lugar, an Indiana Republican and foreign policy moderate, to strengthen efforts to lock down nuclear material worldwide. As president, Obama downplayed the danger of conventional terrorist attacks, while ratcheting up warnings about the danger of a nuclear terrorist attack. His agenda followed that calculation. He invested diplomatic resources in nuclear security—undramatic, high-value bureaucratic grunt work. His administration persuaded former Soviet republics like Ukraine and Belarus to surrender their stockpiles of highly enriched uranium, triumphs that almost no Americans would hear about, but which minimized the odds of catastrophe. (Minimizing or preventing disasters has been a recurrent theme of the administration's work—accompanied by the inherent lack of credit that comes with indistinguishable success.) In December 2010, in the wake of the Republican midterm landslide, the administration pushed successfully for Senate ratification of the New START Treaty with Russia, a pact that committed both countries to reduce their nuclear stockpiles. Conservative Republicans opposed the deal, following a pattern of right-wing suspicion of any negotiation with a hostile foreign power. Texas Republican senator John Cornyn lambasted the treaty for sending "a message of timidity"; South Carolina senator Jim DeMint called it "appeasement."

But the treaty won strong support from whatever remained of the old moderate Republican foreign policy establishment. Former president George H. W. Bush and five former Republican secretaries of state endorsed the pact, as did moderate Republicans in the

Senate like Lugar and Tennessee senator Bob Corker. Here, too, as was the case with many of his domestic policies, the fault lines over Obama's foreign policy followed a familiar pattern: Obama had borrowed ideas and programs from the moderate wing of the Republican Party, only for conservatives to react by purging those very things from their party canon. (In the subsequent election, a right-wing primary challenger toppled Lugar, whom conservatives had come to despise in large part due to his having worked with Obama.)

The central nuclear proliferation threat faced by the Obama administration was Iran. Though it was somewhat overshadowed by the Iraq War catastrophe, the Bush administration had also countenanced a debacle of nontrivial size one country over, where Iran had furiously raced to construct a nuclear weapons program. By the time Obama took office, Iran had nearly 4,000 working centrifuges and an additional 1,600 installed, and had produced 171 kilos of low-enriched uranium. The Bush administration had hardly supported Iran's nuclear program, obviously. The problem was that its hard-line stance, refusing to negotiate and threatening military strikes without taking action, had failed to do anything to stop Iran's race for the bomb. Other countries showed little interest in supporting American sanctions.

The Obama administration instead followed a dual-track strategy that perfectly embodied the president's conception of approaching adversaries. He opened negotiations with Iran, which gave the United States the moral leverage with the international community to win dramatically stronger economic sanctions against Iran with the passage of a United Nations Security Council resolution in 2010 sanctioning Tehran for violating the Nuclear Non-Proliferation Treaty. Impressively, the sanctions gained support even from China and Russia, hardly American allies. Republican critics proclaimed their certainty that Obama's strategy of using leverage to force Iran to the negotiating table stood no chance of success. "The serious choice now before the Administration," argued a 2011 *Wall Street Journal* editorial, "is between military strikes and more of the same"—the latter of which would result in Iran obtaining a nuclear weapon "within a year," which meant by 2012.

Instead, the strategy worked. The severity of those sanctions forced Iran to make deep concessions, and ultimately to surrender the guts of the nuclear program it had been racing to assemble. Under the agreement, Iran surrendered 14,000 of its 20,000 centrifuges—including all its most advanced models—and 97 percent of its enriched uranium. What remained would not allow Iran to come anywhere close to weaponizing enough material to build a nuclear bomb, but simply allowed it to save face by claiming to be pursuing a nuclear program for peaceful purposes. While no country would allow utterly unlimited inspections—which would mean inspectors could barge into any Iranian security meeting or leader's home at any moment, day or night—inspectors gained wide latitude to monitor any suspected nuclear site. By 2016, international weapons inspectors announced that Iran had complied with the terms of the agreement ahead of schedule, having shipped 98 percent of its nuclear fuel abroad, ended all uranium enrichment, and filled its heavy-water reactor at Arak with concrete. That year, former Israeli defense minister Moshe Yalon declared Iran's nuclear capability had been "frozen in light of the deal signed" and, as a result, "does not constitute an immediate, existential threat for Israel."

The agreement was backed up by an innovative form of United Nations sanctions designed by Obama's diplomats. The normal hang-up with restoring sanctions upon a country that's violated the terms of international law is that the UN Security Council is a slow, divided organ that has trouble taking any action, especially because Russia and China tend to use their veto power to thwart American policy. The Iran deal flipped the normal dynamic. If the United States, or any country on the Security Council, alleges that Iran has violated the terms of the deal, sanctions automatically go back into effect, unless a majority of the council votes to suspend them. This made the creaky, often-dysfunctional tool of UN sanctions suddenly swift and efficient.

The Iran deal won acclaim among a wide array of foreign policy experts. Lugar along with former Georgia senator and arms control expert Sam Nunn wrote, "this agreement makes it far less likely that the Iranians will acquire a nuclear weapon over the next 15 years." Right-wing Israeli prime minister Benjamin Netanyahu denounced the deal in apocalyptic terms, but numerous hard-headed members of Israel's security establishment endorsed its terms. Even R. Nicholas Burns, George W. Bush's pragmatic lead negotiator on Iran, conceded, "this has been a successful effort." Historian Robert Dallek called it "the most significant international accord since the 1978 Camp David agreement."

While its main goal in the agreement was to stop a radical Iranian regime from obtaining nuclear weapons, the Obama administration believed the deal might bring an even more important change eventually. By reducing confrontation with the West and opening

Iran's economy to the world, the diplomatic initiative might, eventually, empower Iranian moderates (who favored the agreement) at the expense of radicals (who opposed it). This would be a long-term change that will not be apparent for many years, if it materializes at all.

The Iran agreement was notable for its structure as well as its substance. The administration had to craft a diplomatic agreement in the face of a Congress implacably hostile to any serious negotiation with the enemy, making a formal treaty, which would have required sixty-seven votes to pass the Senate, impossible. Instead, Obama creatively used his executive powers to advance his goals. Rather than passing a law lifting sanctions on Iran—another impossibility, given the Republican Congress—Obama used his executive power to waive sanctions (a power Congress had already delegated). It then dangled the promise of such a move as its leverage in the negotiations.

This was the same method the administration had used to forge the Paris climate agreement. Obama employed executive action (in the case of Paris, through the Environmental Protection Agency and other departments), and used the promise of such actions to make a diplomatic agreement. Harvard law professor Jack Goldsmith, who had served as assistant attorney general in the second Bush administration (and resigned to protest its torture policies) credited these treaties for forging a new kind of presidential authority that still honored the administration's respect for both the Constitution and international law. "[T]he Obama team made singular innovations by cobbling together tools that significantly expanded the President's power to make international agreements without Congress' consent, and sometimes in the face of clear congressional opposition," wrote Goldsmith in 2016. "These new tools do not add up to a revolution in international law or presidential power. But in the aggregate they are significant advances in both and will mark the Obama administration's defining contribution in this area."

Aside from the Iran deal, Obama's foreign policy was not transformational. It was, for the most part, corrective. Obama replaced an ideological administration that thrashed wildly about with one of calm, patient pragmatism. The lack of sweeping doctrinal flair deprived the administration of the memorable drama that is often required to imprint a president's view of the world upon public consciousness. Obama never created a Monroe Doctrine or Rooseveltian Big Stick to emblazon his ideas. Obama had set out to execute a "pivot to Asia," the administration's catchphrase for an overarching plan to dial back Washington's all-consuming obsession with the Middle East and redirect its attention to East Asia, where India and China loomed as future superpowers. Obama managed his relations with India and China well, especially on climate change, where he negotiated breakthrough treaties of historic importance. But the "pivot" that seemed so sensible in the abstract never quite came off.

Obama's speechwriter Ben Rhodes told the *New Yorker* at one point, "If you were to boil it all down to a bumper sticker, it's 'Wind down these two wars, reestablish American standing and leadership in the world, and focus on a broader set of priorities, from Asia and the global economy to a nuclear-nonproliferation regime.'" What this tells us (aside from the fact that Rhodes has an unrealistic idea of how much text can fit onto a bumper sticker) is that the administration never managed to devise a simple rule to guide every foreign policy decision. But Obama's inability to boil his approach down to a fender decal, or a single all-purpose doctrine, was also a source of strength. Obama made case-by-case judgments on the basis of careful evidence. He succeeded mostly in increments and the avoidance of error. "Like George H. W. Bush and Bill Clinton, Obama will likely pass on to his successor an overall foreign policy agenda and national power position in better shape than when he entered office, ones that the next administration can build on to improve things further," concludes Gideon Rose, editor of *Foreign Affairs*. "Given how many administrations fail even that limited test, such an accomplishment is worthy of praise rather than the contempt the administration's foreign policy often receives."

Rose's assessment hardly amounts to effusive praise. His list of presidents who strengthen their country's position in the world includes three of the last four occupants of the Oval Office, pointedly excluding only George W. Bush. Not being George W. Bush may not qualify as the pinnacle of historic achievement, but it certainly beats the alternative.

If any single thing can burnish Obama's foreign policy legacy more than the contrast with the president who came before him, it would be the contrast with the one who came after. Donald Trump's foreign policy agenda during his campaign had even less detail than his domestic agenda, but the impulses guiding it could be understood well enough. He stood for sweeping animosity against other countries in general and Muslim ones in particular. He threatened to extort NATO allies for money, repeatedly praised or denied Russian aggression, promised to restore the use of torture, and urged the United States to use its military power to seize natural resources abroad. It was difficult to imagine just how this would work out, but the options seemed to range from bad to disastrous on a historic scale.

In general, history does not hold presidents responsible for the decisions of other presidents, yet comparisons are inevitable. Just as George W. Bush made Bill Clinton's foreign policy (which during its time was subject to complaint across the political spectrum) look better in hindsight, so too will Trump make Americans and the world deepen their appreciation of the virtues of the forty-fourth president.

Chapter 6
The Inevitability of Disappointment

At some point for most of Barack Obama's supporters, the euphoria of his historic election gave way to a moment of disillusionment, perhaps even regret. That moment arrived for some on December 7, 2008, when Obama announced that conservative evangelical pastor Rick Warren would speak at his inauguration. "Abominable," fumed John Aravosis on AmericaBlog. "Obama's 'inclusiveness' mantra always seems to head only in one direction—an excuse to scorn progressives and embrace the Right," seethed *Salon*'s Glenn Greenwald. On MSNBC, Rachel Maddow rode the story almost nightly: "I think the problem is getting larger for Barack Obama." Negative thirty-four days into the start of the Obama presidency, the honeymoon was over.

If it is hard to believe that Obama's presidency has amounted to a historic success, and has fulfilled most of his policy goals, that is because Obama's supporters have experienced it as a continuous disappointment, frequently spiking onto outright panic, punctuated only by brief moments of joyous relief. "We are all incredibly frustrated," Justin Ruben, MoveOn's executive director, told the *Washington Post* in 2011. "I'm disappointed in Obama," complained Steve Jobs, according to Walter Isaacson's biography. Even Shepard Fairey, the artist who designed the famous "HOPE" poster of Barack Obama in 2008, quickly grew disillusioned. In 2015, *Esquire* asked Fairey if he thinks Obama has lived up to his poster. "Not even close," Fairey said. "Obama has had a really tough time, but there have been a lot of things that he's compromised on that I never would have expected."

In October 2010, a poll from Pew and *National Journal* surveyed the electorate as to how much the Congress had accomplished. This was the Congress that had passed the biggest fiscal stimulus in history, the Affordable Care Act, and the biggest financial reforms since the New Deal, among other things. Asked if the Congress had achieved more than other recent Congresses, just one-third of

Democrats—*Democrats*—agreed, while 60 percent offered that the Congress had achieved the same as or less than other recent Congresses.

A wave of critics from the left cast Obama as helpless before the forces of reaction, or even complicit with them. *Buyer's Remorse,* a 2016 book by the liberal cable television host Bill Press, flays Obama for selling out his supporters. ("Instead of recognizing their burning desire for strong progressive leadership, Obama tried to be a 'post-partisan' president.") Thomas Frank's *Listen, Liberal,* published that same year, arrived at the same conclusion, that Obama had merely continued a regime of economic dominance by the rich and powerful. Also that year, *Democracy in Black,* by Princeton African-American studies professor Eddie Glaude Jr., applied the critique to race. "Obama sold black America the snake oil of hope and change," he argues. "The reality, amid the thick fog of unmet expectations, is that very little has changed in this country. In fact, things have gotten worse." Bernie Sanders—who supplied a glowing testimonial for Press's book—borrowed versions of this critique for his surprisingly popular campaign. Sanders told supporters it was "too late for establishment politics," his term for the political style employed by Obama as well as Hillary Clinton, which

Sanders and his supporters believed had accomplished pathetically little.

While Obama's supporters may view him more sympathetically, they have tended to adopt an apologetic tone rather than a boastful one, blaming Republicans for his shortcomings rather than crediting his success. As the comedian Chris Rock put it in 2011, "I'm like everybody, I want more action." In a 2015 *Harper's* cover story assessing Obama's legacy, headlined, "What Went Wrong," Yale University professor David Bromwich noted that the Obama supporters he came across retreated quickly to the defense that his failure lay in factors out of his control. "Obama's warmest defenders have insisted, against the weight of his own words, that such hopes were absurd and unreal—often giving as evidence some such conversation stopper as 'this is a center-right country' or 'the American people are racist,'" Bromwich recorded. This defense of the president cast him as a sympathetic victim, rather than a figure of notable success. (The critics simply blamed Obama for his failures.) That his record was one of general failure constituted a generally accepted premise.

The yawning chasm between the scale of Obama's achievements and the mood of his supporters presents one of the mysteries of the era. Its resolution also helps us understand how to judge the Obama presidency.

What would a successful presidency even look like? Would Democrats recognize one if they saw it?

In 1993, Bill Clinton, less than four months into his hopeful presidency, launched a blistering attack upon a villain hardly any Americans had ever contemplated: the private student loan industry. Clinton's administration was looking at ways of making college more affordable, and lenders provided the most obvious target.

The student loan system was set up so that students who needed money for college would go to banks to borrow. Since the 1960s, the federal government had guaranteed the loans, so that if a student defaulted on her payments, Washington would pay it back. This managed to get a lot of tuition dollars into students' hands, but it also created billions of dollars in profits for the banks, who were risking nothing: if a student made all their payments, the bank would make money on the deal, and if the student couldn't make the payments, the federal government would lose. The profits were privatized, and the risk was socialized.

One of Clinton's first proposals was to cut out the middlemen altogether. The largest single entity that profited off the operation was Sallie Mae, a privately owned bank whose business was supplied and underwritten by Washington, the purest incarnation of corporate welfare. If the federal government wanted to make college loans more affordable, Clinton concluded, it could simply lend the money itself. On May 11, the still-youthful president ventured to Fenton High School, in suburban Chicago, to denounce the vampiric industry in a populist flourish. "No sooner had I even mentioned changing this system than Congress was deluged with lobbyists," Clinton told his audience. "The biggest organization, Sallie Mae, alone, that's supposed to be in the business of helping you get money to go to college, has already hired seven of the most powerful lobbyists in Washington to try to stop this process from changing."

The struggle dragged on for more than a year, ultimately ending in a compromise. Rather than completely killing off the college lending boondoggle, direct loans would get about half the market share of the loan program, with the banks getting the rest. Clinton had settled for half a loaf, but it was a major achievement, saving billions for taxpayers.

The saga of Clinton's fight against the private lenders is worth a brief reconsideration here because it provides an example of what an ordinary, medium-sized political success looks like—or what it used to look like, before Obama's rush of momentous accomplishments recalibrated the scale. The achievement was important enough that journalist Steven Waldman devoted a whole book, *The Bill,* to chronicling the drama, in which Clinton had taken on one of the most powerful and greediest lobbies in Washington, and fought it to a draw.

The episode is also worth a second glance because the story continued into the Obama years. Following their half defeat in 1994, the private lenders gradually gained the upper hand. The banks grabbed more and more of the market share, enlisting colleges to sign exclusive agreements that would funnel all their students in need of loans their way, shutting out Clinton's direct-lending program despite the lower interest rates it could offer. "Direct lending has just become one lender among thousands, and it is still struggling to be relevant," gloated one bank lobbyist. "Some five hundred colleges have stopped participating [with direct lending] because of shoddy management and financial losses," jeered conservative activist Stephen Moore.

But it turned out something other than the magic of the free enterprise system accounted for the banks' success in beating back their competition from Washington. In 2007, a major scandal came to light, exposing the systemic use of bribes to entice colleges to enlist their students with the banks. Lenders plied college loan officers with meals, cruises, and other gifts. Some of the loan officers accepted stock offers from the lenders to whom they supplied clients. Columbia's director of undergraduate financial aid bought stock in Student Loan Xpress—which became one of that school's preferred lenders—for $1 per share and sold it two years later for $10 per share. Some lenders offered millions to the universities to drop out of the direct-lending program. The Bush administration's Department of Education failed to detect any of this widespread wrongdoing. One of its key officials assigned to oversee the program owned more than $100,000 in stock from one of the lenders he was supposed to be regulating.

Obama, following Clinton's example, sought to eliminate the expensive and now demonstrably corrupt private lending program. His efforts languished in Congress. Republicans, nearly unanimous in opposition to every Obama proposal, denounced it in their usual florid terms. Republican senator Lamar Alexander, his party's leader on education policy, called Obama's plan "Soviet-style." A handful of Democrats whose states contained major student lenders dragged their feet, complaining in a letter that eliminating the private loans could "could put jobs at risk." (This was true, as far as it goes, but since any government program employs somebody, this logic would justify keeping even the most wasteful giveaway in place in order to protect jobs.) Pinned down on other fronts—trying to shepherd transformative legislation on health care and climate change while pulling the economy out of the economic crisis—Obama's college lending reform languished in obscurity and appeared headed for a quiet demise.

But then the saga took an unexpected turn in March, at a time when Democrats in Congress had struggled to rouse health care reform from its deathbed via the budget reconciliation maneuver. Some of the changes the House demanded made subsidies for health care more generous, which cost the government more money. Congress's rules require that a reconciliation bill reduce the budget deficit. Thus Democrats needed to find a way to offset those costs, or it couldn't pass the reconciliation bill, which meant it couldn't pass a health care bill.

There happened to be a big pot of savings sitting around: Obama's direct-lending plan. The Congressional Budget Office estimated that direct lending would save the federal government $61 billion over a decade, just by cutting out the profits siphoned off by the middleman. Obama could plow some of those savings into lower rates for students and use the rest to reduce the deficit. And so, moving quickly in those frantic, desperate days, Congress simply added Obama's college lending reform to the reconciliation bill that passed as part of health care reform. Since the measure was included in a bill that could not be filibustered, Congress could pass it with a majority vote, allowing for the defection of a handful of pro-bank Democrats.

The whole thing happened so quickly—and in the shadow of the biggest social policy reform in decades—that hardly anybody noticed. But there it was, a small add-on to the Affordable Care Act—technically, the law was called the Health Care and Education Reconciliation Act of 2010—that wiped out one of the most notorious giveaways in the federal budget in one fell swoop.

A reform of this scale may have earned a chapter in the history of an ordinary presidency. It amounted to a footnote in Obama's. The full-scale switch to direct lending amounted to a major accomplishment of its own right, but also an episode that epitomized the gap between the imprint Obama has left on the federal government and the public's awareness thereof. The administration's domestic legacy has ranged far wider than acknowledged, in part because its major dramas overshadowed a number of smaller ones.

The theme binding together these reforms is that they undertook the politically difficult work of putting the government on the side of the public interest in the face of opposition from narrow interests that benefit from the status quo. An old political science truism holds that, on issues where the public pays little attention, small groups who care about the issue a great deal can shape the outcome to their favor, even at the expense of the broader good. In a number of unglamorous ways, some of them overlooked or even unnoticed, the Obama administration wrenched the weight of the government back toward the public interest.

Much of this work is the bread-and-butter of a Democratic presidential administration: judicial appointments, administrative reforms, medium-sized legislation. An incomplete list* would include directing the Federal Communications Commission to require Net neutrality (which prohibits broadband providers from controlling Internet content); An end to the ban on openly gay military service; A doubling of the income limit of workers automatically eligible for overtime pay; a crackdown on abusive for-profit colleges; legislation banning hidden credit card fees and

---

* The administration and its supporters often claim the legalization of same-sex marriage as an achievement, but that change, resulting from the 2015 *Obergefell* Supreme Court ruling, was a judicial act. Two Obama-appointed justices joined the majority, but the liberal justices they replaced would probably have ruled the same way. For that reason I don't count the ruling as an Obama accomplishment.

deceptive practices; the most aggressively pro-labor re-definition of workers' rights in four decades thanks to his appointees to the National Labor Relations Board; and a revamp of immigration enforcement, to emphasize dangerous criminals over unauthorized migrants. Many of these reforms required acrimonious fights in Congress and aroused deep opposition from lobbyists. They fleshed out Obama's promise to restore balance to a government that had come to operate on behalf of wealthy and self-interested insiders. And then there were two other major fights that rose well above the ordinary policy grind, and reshaped the face of major institutions in American life: public education and the financial industry.

In July 2010, Obama appeared at the Washington Convention Center to speak before the National Urban League. In that speech, which came after the stimulus, after the bank restructuring plan, and after health care reform, the president revealed what he saw as his administration's most significant achievement. "Now, over the past 18 months, the single most important thing we've done," he announced, ". . . is to launch an initiative called 'Race to the Top.'"

That Race to the Top amounted to Obama's most important measure is a hard case to make, and it's impossible to know if he actually believed it, or merely wanted to use hyperbole to draw attention to an overlooked accomplishment. But, of all the things Obama's administration has done, Race to the Top—a pot of money the administration used to lure states to reform their schools—is surely the one with the largest gap between perception and reality. It happened suddenly, with little buildup, and made barely a ripple in the national debate. The impact will take years to properly understand, but it has clearly been profound.

Education is an issue that national candidates have always talked about a lot because voters care about it a lot, and because education is the most essential mechanism for training future citizens and workers. But it's not an issue they've *done* a great deal about, because education is overwhelmingly financed and directed by state and local governments. And this atomization is itself a problem: it has produced huge inequalities between rich and poor states and, especially, rich and poor districts; and it has discouraged innovation, because there is little means to track and measure different approaches within such an atomized system. Most schools simply muddle through doing things more or less as they have always been done. The imbalance between the scale of the educational system's importance to the nation's social and economic future, and the political system's ability to direct it, has frustrated generations of presidents of both parties.

Experts in health care and tax policy and the like have spent decades studying and refining proposals. In education, experts are trying to figure out what works. Much of the job of reform is focused not on imposing worked-out solutions, but on creating the conditions that would allow those solutions to be discovered, and then replicated. In the years leading right up to Obama's election there was great excitement centered on findings about teacher impact, which varies enormously, not merely from district to district but within schools. Research has found that the best teachers can teach their average student a grade and a half's worth of material, while the least effective teachers can advance their students about half a year's worth. Much of the education reform movement has therefore concentrated its energies on finding ways to increase the supply of the most effective teachers, and either train up or allow principals to replace the least effective ones.

This effort placed education reformers onto treacherous ground with many members of the teachers' unions. The union movement has historically protected teachers from the abusive labor conditions they faced in the early parts of the twentieth century. But its protections have also treated teachers as a mass of undifferentiated, replaceable parts. Union contracts require that teachers be paid according to their length of service, with little possibility of rewarding excellent performance, and make it difficult or impossible to fire teachers except in the cases of the most gross negligence (and in some cases, not even then). Those contracts have thus made it impossible to do the thing teacher-effectiveness research considers most necessary: make a practical distinction between individual teachers based on their performance. Expressing the solidarity that is the core spirit of the labor movement, unions tended to treat any criticism of the least effective teachers as an attack on all teachers. The resulting dynamic—unions and the reform movement coming to view each other with a distrust that blossomed into outright loathing—has had the curious effect of making Democratic supporters of education reform unusually reticent about their beliefs. Why alienate a group that includes some of their staunchest supporters and most dedicated campaign volunteers?

And so Obama has carried out his education agenda with a lack of fanfare bordering on secrecy. Back in 2006, then a freshman senator, he introduced the Innovation Districts for School Improvement Act. Rather than handing grants to all the school districts, or to some select group determined in advance, the act would use the grant money as a prize, rewarding districts that establish data systems to track student progress and create more flexible contracts that allow principals greater autonomy to reward, retrain, or dismiss a given teacher's performance. With a Congress controlled by pro-union Democrats, and a White House still occupied by an anti-domestic-spending Republican, Obama's bill had no chance to pass, but his sponsorship of the bill indicates the importance he placed on education reform from the outset of his time on the national stage.

After starting his presidential campaign, Obama took a much more taciturn approach to education policy, to the point where neither pro-reform Democrats nor pro-union Democrats knew which camp he would favor once in office. The answer came quickly and quietly. In the course of crafting the stimulus, Obama inserted a $4.3 billion grant modeled after the bill he had proposed as a senator. The funds would serve as reward money for a nationwide contest, this time measured state by state. Any state that chose to enter would submit a plan explaining how it planned to overhaul its educational policy. The applications, called "Race to the Top," would be judged along four criteria: adopting rigorous standards and assessments; recruiting, evaluating, and retaining effective teachers;

building data systems to measure learning; and turning around low-performing schools.

Many Democrats allied with the unions would ordinarily oppose any major reform initiative. Indeed, David Obey, chairman of the House Appropriations Committee, scoffed at Obama's proposal. But it was thrown into an emergency bill that Democrats dared not kill or even delay, at the peak of Obama's political honeymoon. It also mollified its critics by coming alongside a much larger $100 billion grant to prevent states, whose budgets had collapsed in the wake of the recession, from laying off teachers. There was only one brief moment when a sweeping education reform could have passed; the Obama administration seized it. In the years that followed, Race to the Top and the wave of experimentation it unleashed became the subject of bitter acrimony from teachers' unions. It would soon be hard to imagine how it passed so quickly and uncontroversially. Indeed, Race to the Top is the one policy where the Republican accusation of government by stealth—passing a major policy change without extensive review or debate—rings true: the reform was tucked into a massive emergency bill with little debate. The grants received hardly any public attention before Obama signed the stimulus. The phrase "Race to the

Top" did not appear in the *New York Times* in conjunction with the program until four days after Obama signed it into law.

Structuring the program as competitive grants was an ingenious way around the problem of local control, which had long stymied educational reform. Obama was not imposing regulations upon districts, or even states. No state had to enter the contest if it didn't want to. And since states had to vouchsafe their plans to reform their schools in order to enter the contest, the prize money had an impact vastly out of proportion to its cost. More states would enter the contest (and impose reform programs as their entry requirement) than would win. The relatively small amount of prize money, some one-half of one percent of the stimulus, would leverage reform on a sweeping scale. All in all, thirty-four states overhauled their education policy in response to the contest. Education secretary Arne Duncan warned that states that did not allow, or artificially capped, public charter schools would put their application for funds at risk.

"The contest for the stimulus money," wrote Steven Brill in *Class Warfare,* a history of the school reform fight, "became a call to arms for a snowballing network of education reforms across the country—an unlikely army of non-traditional urban school chiefs, charter school leaders, researchers at think-tanks who were producing data about how teaching counted more than anything else, philanthropists and hedge-fund billionaires who ate up the data, fed-up parents, and a growing corps of unconventional Democratic politicians." Washington, D.C., schools chancellor Michelle Rhee won a breakthrough new contract, raising teachers' annual average base pay by $14,000, providing an additional $20,000–30,000 in annual performance bonuses to the most successful of them, as well as allowing principals to replace ineffective teachers (without effectively guaranteeing them a teaching job somewhere, as was the case under the old contract). In New York, the state legislature, which had resisted unsettling the status quo, was forced to lift New York City's cap on charter schools—some of which had produced extraordinary gains in its poorest neighborhoods. New York schools chancellor Joel Klein told Brill, "This is a bend in history's arc, caused by the Race."

In 2015, William Howell of the University of Chicago measured the impact of Race to the Top and found it had been a transformative one. Starting with a list of thirty-three different reform policies (like measuring teacher effectiveness and allowing charter schools) he found that, in the seven years before Race to the Top, states enacted just 10 percent of them. From 2009 to

2014, they enacted 68 percent of them. Howell found that even states that did not win grants had dramatically increased their adoption of reforms, a measure of how effectively the program leveraged a small amount of funding into sweeping change. "The surge of post-2009 policy activity constitutes a major accomplishment for the Obama administration," concluded Howell. "With a relatively small amount of money, little formal constitutional authority in education, and without the power to unilaterally impose his will upon state governments, President Obama managed to jump-start policy processes that had languished for years in state governments around the country."

After the funding for Race to the Top expired, the administration discovered another way to encourage reform—this time without spending any money at all. In 2001, the Bush administration had signed an education law called "No Child Left Behind," which called for every student in America to reach a defined level of academic proficiency. The goals were aspirational rather than realistic, and the measurements quite blunt: they relied entirely on test results, holding every district to the same standard. Obama-era education reforms used test results to account for no more than half the criteria for measuring teachers, and the tests were calibrated to students' baseline level, so that schools could be deemed successful for enticing improvement out of low-achieving students in areas of high poverty. In fact, the administration used waivers from No Child Left Behind's harsh punishments the way it used Race to the Top bonus funds—as an incentive to coax states to implement better systems for measuring and rewarding effective schools and teachers.

The administration's encouragement to the reform movement scrambled the normal trench lines in ways that none of the participants knew fully how to handle. Just as Obama was hesitant to alienate a core constituency, union leaders refrained from directly attacking a president who retained high general popularity with their members. Instead they directed their ire at Secretary Duncan, as though he were some rogue agent implementing a radical agenda of school reform behind the president's back. Many Republicans who had sympathy with the reform movement were too invested in all-out opposition to Obama to complicate their line of attack by praising his education policies. In many states, teachers' unions wound up donating to Republican candidates. Neither the unions nor the Republicans have had much interest in publicizing the strange-bedfellows alliance, but it makes a certain sense. The traditional conservative Republican educational prescription emphasizes local control. Allowing schools to stay the course, unmolested by central authorities, conveniently allows the unions to maintain their traditional influence. "President Obama and other liberals still cling to the belief that, despite nearly half a century of failure, Washington can 'fix' education," scoffed Lindsey Burke, an analyst for the Heritage Foundation. Pro-union liberals have attacked education reform from a slightly different premise, insisting that educational progress is possible, but only if the root causes of poverty are solved first. The left-wing *Nation* editorialized, "[E]ducation policy must be devised in concert with health reform, poverty alleviation initiatives and economic development in order to address the roots of failure in the most depressed areas." (Of course, Obama's program has also done a great deal for health care, poverty alleviation, and economic development.) Coming from opposite ends, the left-wing and right-wing critiques of the reform movement share a fatalistic premise, convinced that more effective methods of education cannot be designed, tested, and spread.

But reasons for optimism abound. The education reform movement is still in the early stages, but charter school attendance grew rapidly, and some charter schools have shown the possibility for spectacular results. Charter schools, unlike private schools, cannot select their student body; they must take all comers, and if applications outstrip openings, as often happens, admit students by random lottery. Programs like the Success Academy and the KIPP schools have yielded spectacular academic gains among low-income students. A landmark 2015 study by Stanford's Center for Research on Education Outcomes carefully compared urban students in charter schools with students who had similar characteristics (family income, percentage of English language learners, and special education students) who attended traditional neighborhood-based schools. The charter students outperformed their similar peers by an average of 40 additional learning days a year in math, and 28 additional learning days in reading. No single model for education had been discovered, and definitive evaluation of student performance takes years to track, since the end goal is to help those students find career and life success. But an era of stagnation had given way to one of ferment, experimentation, and progress.

While almost nobody saw the financial meltdown coming, in retrospect it was a virtual inevitability. Huge segments of finance had moved into new, lightly regulated investment vehicles that used complex structures to bury massive risks. Much of the industry's investments required housing prices to stay afloat in perpetuity. The housing market had formed a bubble, as many analysts saw at the time, but no regulators had the primary task of protecting consumers from the subprime loans that banks were shoveling out the door. When the housing bubble popped, huge segments of Wall Street collapsed, as though the foundations beneath it had disintegrated.

As the financial crisis gave way to a bailout and then a recession, the public's mind ran toward punishment as recourse—Americans had suffered, and somebody had to pay. That punitive impulse hurt Obama badly in 2009 when he had to make the case for fiscal stimulus, when the public believed, despite the conclusions of most economists, that the government had to cut its spending. But in 2010 the president set out to reform the financial sector, and here the still-simmering anger worked in his favor.

Reforming finance was never going to be a politically simple matter. When financial irresponsibility has not triggered an economic meltdown, ordinary people care little about financial regulatory policy. Even during economic convulsions, the vast majority of those who pay close attention to the issue are those with substantial money at stake, and they mostly want regulators to leave them alone. The previous major wave of regulation of the heart of the financial industry had occurred decades before Obama was born, during the Great Depression, amid the last bout of ferocious public anger at Wall Street.

What's more, most of the industry delusionally viewed itself as the victim of bad luck, rather than its own misdeeds. Even the cataclysmic collapse of the world economy could not budge the titans of finance from thinking of themselves as the great and deservedly rewarded minds driving American prosperity. All the more so because of this wild ego inflation, the public backlash against their misbehavior frightened them, the angry crowd seen as a homicidal collective subjecting innocent Wall Street to irrational bloodlust And so, while much of the industry accepted the inevitability of some reregulation, it hardly rolled over, instead rallying Republicans to oppose the bill from the outside, and lobbying moderate Democrats from the inside.

The result of this push-and-pull between populist anger and the lobbyists' mastery of the Washington game was the most significant financial regulatory reform in three-quarters of a century. The summer 2010 legislation, named after its major cosponsors, Connecticut senator Chris Dodd and Massachusetts's Barney Frank, lacks the poetic elegance of a simple, silver-bullet solution. Instead it imposed a wide array of complicated reforms:

It created new exchanges where swaps—a kind of investment that trades expected cash flows from one thing for cash flows from another—must be traded. The exchanges brought out into the open a vast realm of activity that had been conducted privately. Forcing the prices out into the open already cut the banks' revenues on this business by more than a third by 2014—reflecting a reduced opportunity to make money on the basis of inside information.

It imposed the "Volcker Rule," which separated out proprietary trading—another high-risk form of investment—from normal banking. The rule had been proposed by former Federal Reserve chairman Paul Volcker, against fierce industry opposition, in order to limit chances for bad investments to contaminate the safer kind. When the rule first passed in its sketched-out form, nearly everybody expected the industry to shoot it full of loopholes. Instead it survived in strong form: Goldman Sachs, Bank of America, Morgan Stanley, and Citigroup all shut down their departments that had invested the firm's money in risky outside ventures. Concluded business writer Kevin Roose in *New York* magazine in 2013, "That's exactly what was supposed to happen—a transfer of risk away from too-big-to-fail, FDIC-backed banks to parts of the industry that could absorb losses more cleanly."

It created a new agency, the Consumer Financial Protection Bureau. Initially dreamed up by Elizabeth Warren, then a Harvard professor, the bureau filled a yawning gap in the architecture of the regulatory state: it would police banks to ensure they did not exploit their customers—a chronic problem in a product whose complexity made even the economically sophisticated vulnerable to fine print and hidden charges. Republicans fought the agency's creation desperately, even refusing to confirm any director at all unless Obama would agree to severely curtail its powers. (The administration eventually installed a director, Rich Cordray, after Senate Democrats threatened to eliminate the filibuster rule entirely, forcing Republicans to relent.) The agency has performed as its advocates hoped—cracking down on billions of dollars of scams by mortgage lenders and banks. It created national regulations on payday lenders, which furnish short-term, high-interest loans to strapped low-income customers, many of whom used to wind up paying ruinously high interest rates. It authorized the Securities and Exchange Commission to require stockbrokers and portfolio managers to follow their customers' "fiduciary interest"—which is a technical way of saying their advice has to be designed in the best interest of the customer. (That may sound obvious, but brokers have often unloaded what they know to be bad stocks onto their clients in order to make money for their firm.) And it allowed customers to file class-action lawsuits against financial firms for misconduct. (Technically, the right to sue existed before, but financial firms inserted language into contracts signing away that right, leading to case after case of financial fraud for which customers had no recourse. With a stroke of a pen, the agency shifted billions of dollars from large banks to ordinary savers.) These pro-consumer reforms have enraged the Wall Street lobby.

Perhaps most important, and certainly most controversial, the law created a mechanism to prevent a future dilemma where a huge firm required a bailout in order to prevent its losses from melting down the entire economy. Firms labeled "systemically important"—that is, so big that their failure would threaten the entire system—had to keep higher levels of capital to ensure against their losses. And the government now had the authority, which it lacked in 2008, to take those firms over, rather than just write them a giant check. That meant that if a firm had to be taken over, the shareholders would lose everything—an incentive that encourages these firms not to take excessive risks.

Republican critics of the Dodd-Frank law fixated on this last provision as the center of their attacks, but the debate over financial reform placed them in a perilous spot. They opposed reform, in keeping with their opposition to bigger government in general and anything Obama wanted in particular. Opposing reform also gave Republicans access to the largest source of campaign donations—after giving somewhat more to Democrats in 2008, the financial industry lurched overwhelmingly toward the Republican Party after Obama took office. Boehner called the bill "killing an ant with a nuclear weapon"—an overreaction to a relatively minor problem. Jeb Hensarling, the ranking Republican on the House Financial Services Committee, said that his party's "answer" was "more vigorous enforcement of our existing fraud and consumer protection laws" and "to end taxpayer bailouts." The Republicans opposed new regulations on the finance industry. They instead proposed supposedly stronger enforcement of existing rules (despite their long-standing efforts to starve the SEC's enforcement budget) and refusing to bail out any companies in the future (an appealing position to take, until a firm is actually about to collapse and drag the rest of the economy down with it).

But opposing reform did not sit well with the public. Republican message consultant Frank Luntz explained in a memo to fellow members of his party that, given the state of public opinion, "the status quo is not an option." Rather than position themselves as advocates of deregulation, Luntz advised Republicans to label the reforms a "Big Bailout Bill," and to argue, "The legislation is filled with lobbyist loopholes that exclude certain wealthy, powerful industries from regulations." The legislation did not create bailouts—it ensured that firms whose failure could trigger a broader collapse would bear the brunt of their own failure, rather than offloading the cost onto taxpayers. The disingenuous argument meant that putatively anti-business Republicans echoed the same themes of completely earnest critics from Obama's left, who feared that he had given up a once-in-a-lifetime chance to cut Wall Street down to size. And since the legislation was so fiendishly complex, and the industry's scheming so fresh in the public mind, the most cynical interpretations of the law became the most plausible ones. Wall Street, it was proclaimed, had secretly prevailed—or it would when the fine print was written behind closed doors. It was easy to believe that the industry had outwitted (or co-opted) its would-be regulators, and difficult to believe that Washington had imposed fundamental change upon it against its will.

Yet, in the years since the law's passage, a mounting body of evidence has proved that this very thing happened. Opponents of the bill charged that firms deemed systemically important under Dodd-Frank—that is, too big to fail—were receiving special treatment from the government. As the influential liberal financial journalist Mike Konczal found, the opposite proved to be the case. Firms lobbied Washington *not* to be designated systemically important—the costs of the new requirements the law imposed on too-big-to-fail firms exceeded any benefit. What's more, the Government Accountability Office found that Dodd-Frank had eliminated a major advantage big banks had previously enjoyed. Before the law passed, the biggest firms were perceived by lenders as safer bets, since it was reasonable to expect they would be bailed out in the event of a collapse. They were thus able to borrow money at lower rates than smaller firms (whom investors expected the government would let die). After Dodd-Frank's passage, the difference in interest rates disappeared. Dodd-Frank was not helping the biggest firms, as the cynics suggested.

The law has not turned Wall Street into a barren wasteland, but it altered the landscape profoundly. "Four years after the Dodd-Frank financial law became reality, Washington's regulatory machine is altering Wall Street in fundamental ways," the news pages of the *Wall Street Journal* concluded. "Banks are selling off profitable business lines, pulling back from the short-term funding market, cutting ties with businesses that could attract extra regulatory scrutiny, and building up defenses to help weather future crises. While profits are up as firms slash costs and reduce funds set aside to cover future losses, their traditional profit engine—trading—is showing signs of weakening as banks step away from some activity amid regulatory pressure." Just as the law's authors hoped, banks were focusing on banking, and abandoning high-risk investments.

Liberal policy wonks steeped in the regulatory debate have reached the same conclusion. "There is no question that many of the highest-risk activities, which happened to be the most profitable activities for Wall Street, are now at least reduced and often totally gone," Dennis Kelleher, chief executive of Better Markets, a progressive organization advocating tighter restrictions on finance, told *Politico*'s Ben White. "They've had to exit hedge funds and private equity funds and they sold off any business with 'proprietary trading' on the door." The industry has recovered from the depths of the financial crisis, but at a far more modest trajectory. Finance accounted for 10 percent of new jobs in New York City during the go-go 1990s recovery. As of 2015, it accounted for less than 1 percent. In 2015, some financial institutions simply sold off their massive banking operations. Before the financial crisis, financial firms accounted for a staggering 30 percent of all corporate profits in the United States. By 2015, that share had fallen to 17 percent. The financial industry, swollen beyond any reasonable scale, has been cut down to size.

The new Republican administration came into office vowing to repeal the Dodd-Frank reforms. Indeed, the shocking news of Trump's victory caused major Wall Street stocks to soar 9–10% immediately, on the belief these firms would receive more lax regulation. But Obama's array of financial regulations represent one aspect of his legacy that Trump and his Republican allies had little capacity to destroy. They could use a budget reconciliation bill to make changes exclusively related to taxes and spending. (They could use such a bill to zero out the subsidies needed to make Obamacare affordable, for instance.) But to wipe Dodd-Frank off the books would require them to gain the sixty votes needed to overcome a filibuster, a nearly impossible task in a Senate with forty-eight Democrats, or to abolish the filibuster permanently, a move many Republicans oppose (and which would require fifty of them to carry out).

The Trump administration can, and almost certainly will, refuse to enforce the law as intended. But this is the standard approach by a Republican presidency toward regulations they don't approve of but lack the votes to overturn. Republican administrations inevitably refuse to enforce labor law, environmental regulations, workplace protections, and so on. Dodd-Frank will fall into the same category. And when a Democrat (or perhaps a moderate Republican in a chastened future party) returns to 1600 Pennsylvania Avenue, without having to wait or hope for congressional approval, the legacy of these reforms will be renewed.

In the wake of the crisis, progressives dreamed of repeating Franklin Roosevelt's epic leveling of Wall Street's power. For decades after the New Deal, finance was a boring profession, until it emerged in the 1980s as a center of staggering wealth and risk. Obama's reforms have not restored Wall Street to the way it was, when Gordon Gekko was an unimaginable character. They did land a powerful blow against out-of-control finance, whose impact will be felt far into the future. "Most of the industry was violently opposed to the new rules," political scientist J. Nicholas Ziegler, who studied the law's passage, told financial reporter James Surowiecki. "But a combination of small but very engaged advocacy groups and gutsy regulators made sure they got through." Government worked. The good guys won.

In August 2011, the liberal author and psychology professor Drew Westen wrote a *New York Times* essay explaining what, for many liberals, was already a self-evident truism: that the Obama administration had failed. Rather than bending the arc of history toward justice, observed Westen, the president "has broken that arc and has likely bent it backward for at least a generation." Westen blamed Obama's failure on his centrist instincts, and mourned that his refusal to lead the public allowed the Republican rhetorical fixation with deficits to dominate the political agenda instead. "Had the president chosen to bend the arc of history," Westen lamented, "he would have told the public the story of the destruction wrought by the dismantling of the New Deal regulations that had protected them for more than half a century."

Around the same time, *New York Times* columnist Thomas Friedman expressed his displeasure with Obama in roughly the opposite terms. Friedman touted the possibility of a third-party movement, called Americans Elect. The main peculiarity of Friedman's argument was the triviality of his substantive disagreement with the administration. On virtually every issue, Obama was supporting policies Friedman demanded: short-term stimulus, long-term deficit reduction through a mix of taxes and entitlement cuts, clean energy, education reform, and social liberalism. Where Westen flayed Obama for his willingness to compromise with Republicans on a long-term deficit agreement, Friedman heartily agreed with it. He advocated for a third-party candidate anyway, because such a figure, he wrote, "would have offered a grand bargain on the deficit two years ago, not on the eve of a Treasury default." He agreed with Obama's plan, in other words, but argued for a new party because he disagreed with his *legislative sequencing*.

When we see such a disconnect between the depth of the grievances against Obama and the shallowness of their substance, we have to conclude that some other dynamic is at work. Whatever economic policy errors Obama made do not suffice to explain the depth of the reaction he engendered. The liberal dissatisfaction with Obama tells us more about the liberals than it does about Obama.

One premise held in common by critics from Obama's left, like Westen, and critics from Obama's right, like Friedman, is that the president has the sole responsibility for policy outcomes at the federal level. The "Westens" demand that he use his rhetoric to summon a populist wave that overpowers the resistance of Republican opponents, and the "Friedmans" demand that he use his negotiating skills to lure them into compromising away their theological opposition to higher taxes. Despite their differing goals, they share a belief that Obama has within him the power to impose his will upon the legislative branch.

Passing a law requires the agreement of the House and Senate along with the president—a fact known to high school civics class students, but often forgotten by political commentators. Popular culture shares the same bias for viewing all political stories through the lens of presidential drama. (Aaron Sorkin's film *The American President* and his acclaimed series *The West Wing* both imagined Washington as a fantasy realm revolving around the president, who was capable of crafting a speech so compelling that, with the aid of a well-chosen background score, it could transform the landscape instantaneously.)

But Congress does not view itself as a mere appendage to the presidency. Members of the legislative branch have interests that often diverge from the president's, not to mention healthy egos. Congressional diffidence grows out of a tradition peculiar to American history. Unlike the parliamentary systems found in most other democracies, where the majority is elected on a unified platform, the separated powers in a presidential system establish the legislature and the executive as coequal branches. During the twentieth century, the Republican Party had strong moderate and even progressive northern wings to balance its conservatives, while the Democrats had a large, conservative white southern wing to balance its liberals. Defections across partisan lines occurred with natural frequency. After the civil rights movement drove white conservatives out of the Democratic Party, the two coalitions gradually sorted themselves into cohesive blocs. But the old barons of Congress, reared in an age when Lyndon Johnson might rely heavily on northern Republicans to pass civil rights laws, or scores of Democrats would support Ronald Reagan's budget, clung to their habits.

Even during its initial, two-year period of Democratic control, Congress ostentatiously (and nearly immediately) announced its independence from the new president. Shortly after Obama took office, Senate majority leader Harry Reid stated, "I don't work for him." Even House Ways and Means chairman Charlie Rangel, whose Harlem constituents danced in the streets after Obama's election, sniffed at Obama's plan to raise taxes on the rich, "I have to study it but I really don't take president's recommendations that seriously." "Recommendation" is a pregnant term, indicating the conviction by the baron of the House Ways and Means Committee that a president might submit a suggestion, as any adviser might, but the job of crafting laws belongs to him. Some welcome mat.

While the Democratic Party has grown more ideologically homogeneous during the twenty-first century, it has retained divisions, especially in its economic base. Unlike European socialist parties, which can rely solely on the power of labor, the Democratic Party requires significant support from business along with groups that sometimes feud with business, like unions, environmentalists, and consumer groups. That often-ungainly coalition can serve as an advantage, allowing Democrats to take into account a wide scope of economic interests. On the other hand, the Republican Party's more uniform economic base, consisting of businesses and wealthy individuals with no labor or environmental support to speak of, inevitably produces policies favoring a narrow sliver of the population. But the uniformity helps Republicans in Congress pull together.

The Democrats' economic divisions were on clear display from the outset. Just a month after Obama took the oath of office, North Dakota Democrat Kent Conrad, then the Democratic chairman of the Senate Budget Committee, gave an interview expressing deep reservations about the president's budget proposals. Conrad said that he objected to a provision to limit tax deductions for high-income earners. He likewise opposed Obama's plan to limit subsidies to farmers who earn $500,000 per year. Conrad insisted his main objection to Obama's plan was that it failed to reduce the long-term deficit deeply enough, notwithstanding his own opposition to these two Obama deficit reduction proposals. Nebraska senator Ben Nelson gainsaid Obama's plan to reform college lending by cutting out payments to private lenders. All politics are local: North Dakota has lots of farmers, and one of the most lucrative private college lenders had its headquarters in Lincoln, Nebraska. And so it went down a good portion of the line, short-term constituent or donor concerns trumping greater support for the president of their own party.

The influence of business over the party agenda is a problem no Democratic president has ever fully escaped. There is no evidence that Obama has ever shared left-wing goals like eviscerating the financial industry or soaking the rich with punitive taxes, but even if he secretly desired those ends, the economic makeup of his party base would prevent it. As noted earlier, Obama did proclaim his support for a health care reform that included a "public option"—a government-run plan that would compete head-to-head against private insurers on the exchanges he would create. The insurance industry, which went along with health care reform only grudgingly (and even financed attack ads against the law at times), deemed a public option completely unacceptable. Several Democrats in the Senate with close ties to the insurance industry made elimination of the public option a condition of their support for reform.

Most liberal health care experts considered the public option a helpful feature, but not a crucial one—if properly designed, the public option would give consumers more options and increase pressure on insurers to hold down prices. Indeed, political scientist Jacob Hacker, who designed the public option, endorsed the Senate bill even after it was stripped out.

For many liberal activists, however, the public option's absence doomed health care reform. "If Barack Obama's health care plan gets changed to exclude a public option like Medicare, then it is not health care reform," insisted Howard Dean. "Legislation rises and falls on whether the American public is allowed to choose a universally available public option or not." (It's worth recalling that Dean's own health care plan in his 2004 presidential campaign did not include a public option.)

The saga of the public plan revealed elements of the congenital liberal failure to accept some of the normal features of legislative give-and-take. There was the habit of imputing all outcomes to the president personally. The *Huffington Post*'s Dan Froomkin, for instance, insisted in 2009 that Obama either "will come out with a strong bill" or "will come out of it having given away the store." The choice would reflect on the president's character. "Is the real Obama being serially co-opted by his aides in there? Or is the real Obama at heart a conflict-averse facilitator, rather than a leader?" he asked, neglecting to even consider the possibility that Congress might have limited his options.

Liberals are correct in their belief that business interests often sit in tension with liberal goals. But some of the opposition to Obama embraced a more extreme assumption that business interests are *completely incompatible* with the public interest. That more radical belief animated some of the left-wing opposition to Obama. Widely read bloggers like Markos Moulitsas and Marcy Wheeler, not to mention Keith Olbermann, the then-influential MSNBC talk show host, denounced bills in Congress as a bailout for the health insurance industry. The sometimes pernicious influence of business upon the Obama agenda produced spasms of rage that did not arise out of any considered public philosophy of the left. It is true that increasing access to private health insurance benefits the insurance industry, just as increasing access to food benefits the agriculture industry and building more infrastructure benefits the construction industry. Opposing health care reform solely to deny customers to the insurance industry made no sense from a liberal standpoint, or even a socialist standpoint. Instead, it reflected a kind of infantile rejection of the compromises inherent in governing. The historian Arthur Schlesinger Jr., writing in 1949, assailed liberal idealists who were abandoning Truman for the millennial promises of Henry Wallace and his Progressive Party. Schlesinger defined this impulse as a "fear . . . of making concrete decisions and being held to account for concrete consequences." The attraction of protesting the status quo might lure liberals, but the realities of exercising power would invariably repulse them.

This reflexive disgust with governing arose not only on the left of the Democratic Party but also at its center. Marshall Ganz, the liberal grassroots organizer, lamented in the *Los Angeles Times* in 2010, "Abandoning the 'transformational' model of his presidential campaign, Obama has tried to govern as a 'transactional' leader." Jon Stewart put it in even more anguished terms, expressing his disappointment that politics itself did not change under Obama: "He ran on this idea that the system and the methodology are corrupt. It felt like the country was upset enough that he had the momentum needed to reevaluate how business is done. Instead, when he got elected, he acted as though the system is so entrenched that it has to be managed." (Note that this complaint was diametrical to the complaint that Obama was *too aloof* from the practical horse-trading to have success in Congress, in supposed contrast to the legendary wheeler-dealer Lyndon Johnson, for whom many of Obama's liberal critics pined.)

This is a deep-rooted feature of the liberal style of politics. It expresses itself as a persistent desire to improve not just policy but politics itself. Since conservatives are focused only on *dismantling* the domestic functions of government, the great movements to *reform* politics have all come from the left. Progressivism developed a century ago out of a desire to cleanse politics of bosses and transactionalism. Some liberals attribute their disappointment in Obama to the excessive hopes he raised about representing better, cleaner, more uplifting politics. But the euphoria surrounding Obama's election, while it exceeded that of previous presidents, was hardly a completely unique phenomenon. Bill Clinton was the Man from Hope, touring the country with Al Gore and promising the renewing spirit of a younger generation. Jimmy Carter frequently pledged, "I will never lie to you," and moved the 1976 Democratic convention hall to tears. Liberals found the experience of Barack Obama's presidency mostly dissatisfying because they find power itself discomfiting. They can be happy with the *idea* of a Democratic president—indeed, dancing-in-the-streets delirious—but not with the real thing. The various theories of disconsolate liberals all suffer from a failure to compare Obama with any plausible baseline. Instead they compare Obama with an imaginary president—either an imaginary Obama or a fantasy version of a past president.

Back in February 2008, during the heat of the Democratic primary contest between Obama and Hillary Clinton, machinist union president Tom Buffenbarger had unleashed a rip-roaring endorsement of Clinton combined with an even rip-roaring-er assault on her young opponent. "I've got news for all the latte-drinking, Prius-driving, Birkenstock-wearing, trust fund babies crowding in to hear him speak!" he'd shouted. "This guy won't last a round against the Republican attack machine. He's a poet, not a fighter."

By 2011, with Obama in the depths of his debt ceiling ransom debacle, members of his party began to recall Buffenbarger's indictment as prophetic. Olbermann replayed the clip from three and a half years earlier on his MSNBC program, calling the union leader "Nostradamus." By then a broader "buyers' remorse" had set in among the party faithful. They had nominated the wrong candidate, saddling themselves with a weakling helpless in the face of Republican attacks. HBO's Bill Maher professed Hillary Clinton would have been a better president because "[s]he knows how to deal with difficult men."

Often the viewpoint resorted to scatological explanations. The former Clinton White House adviser James Carville told reporters, "If Hillary gave up one of her balls and gave it to Obama, he'd have two." Matthew Dickinson, a presidential scholar at Middlebury College, was slightly more subtle when he wrote in *Salon*, "If I heard it once this past week, I heard it a thousand times: You were duped by Obama's rhetoric—the whole 'hopey-changey' thing. . . . It's time to elect someone who can play hardball, who understands how to be ruthless, who will be a real . . . uh . . . tough negotiator in office."

The newfound appreciation for Hillary Clinton's persona as hero of the working class drew upon memories of rapid economic growth during the Bill Clinton administration, fused them with Hillary's beer-chugging outreach to white working-class Democrats, and produced a powerful mythos of the Clintons as butt-kicking heroes of the people.

The retrospective embrace of the Clintons helped underscore how deep the liberal tendency runs to idealize the past in contrast with the present. Indeed, the chief political adviser for Hillary Clinton's 2008 campaign, Mark Penn, wrote periodic columns throughout Obama's presidency urging Obama to give up on health care reform, make nice to businesses, and stop taxing the rich. And recall what happened when the Clinton administration proposed an economic stimulus shortly after taking office. Bill Clinton had campaigned promising a stimulus bill to alleviate widespread economic pain, with unemployment at 7.5 percent at the start of his term. Like Obama, Clinton needed a handful of Republican senators to pass it (Obama needed two Republican votes to break a filibuster, Clinton three). Clinton's proposed stimulus was $19.5 billion. Unable to break a Republican filibuster, Clinton offered to pare it down to $15.4 billion. Republicans killed it anyway, creating an image of a Clinton administration in disarray.

Certainly, the circumstances faced by Clinton were different. (For one thing, the recession was far less deep and passed its worst point shortly after he took office, making the case for stimulus less urgent.) Still, nothing in this episode suggests Clinton possessed any special communicative or legislative skill that would have enabled him or his wife, had either held office in 2009, to pass a larger stimulus than the $787 billion bill Obama signed.

Certainly Bill Clinton's election, following a dozen years of Republican presidencies, ushered in buoyant hopes of renewal. But liberals experienced his presidency as immediate and almost continuous deflation and cynicism. Clinton did enjoy one major triumph in his first year, when he passed a budget bill that raised the top tax rate, expanded the Earned Income Tax Credit, created a new national-service program for graduates, and reformed other parts of the budget. This was the progressive apogee of the Clinton administration. Liberals at the time viewed it as a sad half measure. Its focus lay on deficit reduction, not public investment, and each iteration of the legislation that worked its way through the congressional machinery emerged less inspiring than the last. "The Senate's machinations on President Clinton's budget plan have left many Democratic House members feeling angry and betrayed," noted a *New York Times* editorial.

The rest of Clinton's first two years consisted of a demoralizing procession of debacles and retreats.

A series of Clinton appointments—Lani Guinier, Zoë Baird—came under conservative fire and were withdrawn in a panic. He steered his agenda toward right-of-center goals, like the North American Free Trade Agreement and a crime bill, serving only to alienate his liberal allies without dampening hysterical attacks from conservatives and the business lobby. Health care reform collapsed entirely, in part because liberals refused to support a compromise final measure. Six months into Clinton's presidency, after he had abandoned his effort to integrate gays into the military, then–*New York Times* columnist Bob Herbert summarized what had already settled as the liberal narrative: "The disappointment and disillusionment with President Clinton are widespread. . . . He doesn't seem to understand that much of the disappointment and disillusionment is because he tries so hard to be liked by everyone." Hardly anybody contested that portrait.

After Republicans swept the midterm elections, Clinton moved further rightward. He famously declared that "the era of big government is over" and brought in reptilian operator Dick Morris—not yet the right-wing conspiracy-monger seen on Fox News these days, but distinctly right of center—as his chief political adviser. He signed a welfare reform bill containing such draconian provisions that several liberals resigned from his administration in protest.

Clinton, according to his contemporaneous liberal critics, turns out to have suffered from the same pliability and pathological eagerness to please the opposition that liberals diagnosed in Obama. But here is a funny thing. If we move back in time toward the last Democratic president before Clinton—Jimmy Carter—we find the same pattern of liberal despondency asserting itself again.

In fact, the liberal failures of Obama and Clinton are but tiny potholes next to the vast gulch of failure that was the Carter presidency. Today Carter is remembered as a president anchored in liberal values, a revision of history both conservatives and Carter himself are happy to leave uncorrected. But the truth is that Carter's domestic agenda carried only small bits of liberalism, and those small bits (a consumer protection agency, tax reform) met with total failure in the Democratic Congress. Carter's policy accomplishments tilted right of center—he deregulated the airline and trucking industries and cut the capital gains tax. Most infuriatingly to liberals, Carter refused to push for comprehensive health care reform. A Carter adviser later recalled that the president "did not see health care as every citizen's right, nor did he think the government has an obligation to provide it."

Carter's post-presidency commitment to moral action was hardly evident while he was in office. After James Fallows departed the Carter administration, where he worked as a speechwriter, he wrote a damning 1979 story in *The Atlantic* titled "The Passionless Presidency." Ted Kennedy challenged Carter during the 1980 primaries and came close to unseating him. During the general election, progressive Republican John Anderson waged a third-party bid that won some of the liberal anti-Carter vote. The *Times*'s editorial board captured the liberal view of the era when it relayed the joke of a voter with a gun to his head who was asked to choose between Carter and Ronald Reagan and replied, "Shoot." *The New Republic*, in a 1980 editorial endorsing third-party candidate Anderson, concluded Carter "has failed by both the general standards of competent administration and the special standards of the liberal agenda."

The last Democratic president before Carter also had a turn as object of liberal fantasy and stand-in. Lyndon Johnson came to epitomize the ability, allegedly absent in the forty-fourth president, to bend Congress to his will. As one political reporter noted wistfully in 2011,

"Unlike Obama, he knew how to work the system." True, Johnson did pass sweeping domestic legislation during his first two years, when he enjoyed enormous margins in both chambers. But after his party suffered setbacks during the 1966 midterm elections, Johnson's agenda ground to a halt—suggesting either that his magical ability to cajole Congress had left him, or that Congress always had minds of its own, and Johnson could pass lots of laws only when he had enough minds predisposed to agree with him.

The Obama-era veneration of Johnson must have evoked dark laughter among the progressive activists who drove LBJ from the race and held violent protests against his successor, Hubert H. Humphrey, a liberal stalwart who had extended the New Deal and pushed his party to adopt civil rights. (The famous demonstrations in Chicago in 1968 were, of course, directed not at Richard Nixon or even Johnson but at Humphrey, who was further stalked by angry crowds on the campaign trail until the election.)

But what about John F. Kennedy, the liberal icon? Kennedy's reputation benefited from a halo of martyrdom, deepened by liberals' rage against Johnson, which retroactively cast Kennedy as far more progressive than he actually was. In reality, Kennedy's domestic agenda slogged painfully through a Congress controlled by a coalition of Republicans and conservative southern Democrats. He campaigned promising federal aid for education and health insurance for the elderly but didn't get around to passing either one. The most agonizing struggles came on Kennedy's civil rights agenda. His soaring campaign promises quickly grew entangled in a series of bargains with Jim Crow Democrats that liberals justifiably saw as corrupt. Kennedy understood he lacked the votes in Congress to push the civil rights legislation he promised. When Freedom Riders traveled into the Deep South to test the meager protections in place, Kennedy pressured them to call it off, then struck a deal to have them arrested (to avert the likely alternative that white supremacists would kill the riders).

Trying to jump-start a domestic agenda that conservative southern Democrats had bottled up, Kennedy placated James Eastland, a powerful Jim Crow senator from Mississippi, by nominating the arch-segregationist judge William Harold Cox to the federal bench. Civil rights leaders viewed Kennedy's machinations with something less than unbridled gratitude. Rev. Martin Luther King Jr. said that Kennedy "vacillated" on civil rights. When he set up a meeting with civil rights activists, Kennedy was surprised to be "scorched by anger," as G. Calvin Mackenzie and Robert Weisbrot wrote in a recent history of the 1960s.

Harry Truman has become the patron saint of dispirited Democrats, the fighting populist whose example is invariably cited in glum contrast to whatever bumbling congenital compromiser happens to hold office at any given time. In fact, liberals spent the entire Truman presidency in a state of near-constant despair. Republicans took control of Congress in the 1946 elections and bottled up Truman's domestic agenda, rendering him powerless to expand the New Deal, which liberals had hoped he would after the war had ended. Liberal columnist Max Lerner decried Truman's mania for "cooperation" and his eagerness "to blink [past] the real social cleavage and struggles," attributing this pathological eagerness to avoid conflict to his "middle-class mentality." (Some contemporary critics reached the same psychoanalysis of Obama, substituting his bi-racial background as the cause.) *The New Republic*'s Richard Strout lamented how "little evidence he has shown of being able to lift up and inspire the masses." The historian Richard Pells has written that in the eyes of liberals at the time, "the president remained an incorrigible mediocrity." The *Nation* called him a "weak, baffled, angry man."

An exception to this trend, but only a partial exception, is Franklin Roosevelt, the most esteemed of the historical Democratic president-saints. Roosevelt is hard to compare to anybody, because his achievements (helping pull the country out of the Great Depression and win World War II) were so enormous, and his failures so large as well (court-packing, interning Japanese-Americans). But even his triumphs, gleaming monuments to liberalism when viewed from the historical distance, appear, at closer inspection, to be riddled with the same tribulations, reversals, compromises, dysfunctions, and failures as any other.

Drew Westen, among others, fixated upon Roosevelt as the ultimate counterexample to Obama:

> In similar circumstances, Franklin D. Roosevelt offered Americans a promise to use the power of his office to make their lives better and to keep trying until he got it right. Beginning in his first inaugural address, and in the fireside chats that followed, he explained how the crash had happened, and he minced no words about those who had caused it. He promised to do something no president had done before: to use the resources of the United States to put Americans directly to work, building the infrastructure we still rely on today. He swore to keep the people who had caused the

crisis out of the halls of power, and he made good on that promise. In a 1936 speech at Madison Square Garden, he thundered, "Never before in all our history have these forces been so united against one candidate as they stand today. They are unanimous in their hate for me—and I welcome their hatred."

This version of the Roosevelt legend is mostly false. Roosevelt did not run for office promising to boost deficit spending in order to stimulate the economy. He ran a campaign lacerating Herbert Hoover for his allegedly irresponsibly high deficits, then immediately passed an austerity budget in his first year. Roosevelt did come around to Keynesian stimulus, but he never seemed to understand it, and in 1937 he reversed himself again by cutting spending, helping plunge the economy into a second depression eventually mitigated only by war spending. Roosevelt, unlike Obama, benefited from having taken office after the depths of the recession had settled in, rather than just before the economy plunged into an abyss.

Modern liberals like to believe that Roosevelt, perhaps through his famous fireside chats, taught Americans the efficacy of government spending in order to combat mass unemployment. In fact, he utterly failed to convince Americans to support fiscal stimulus. A 1935 Gallup poll asked, "Do you think it necessary at this time to balance the budget and start reducing the national debt?" Seventy percent of the public answered in the affirmative. Even after Roosevelt's sweeping 1936 reelection, another poll yielded 65 percent agreeing that a balanced budget was necessary.

FDR's 1936 speech denouncing "economic royalists" represented just a brief populist turn of his rhetoric. Usually he tried to placate business. When he refused to empower a government panel charged with enforcing labor rights, a liberal senator complained, "The New Deal is being strangled in the house of its friends." Roosevelt constantly feared his work-relief programs would create a permanent class of dependents, so he made them stingy. He kept the least able workers out of federal programs, and thus "placed them at the mercy of state governments, badly equipped to handle them and often indifferent to their plight," recalled historian William Leuchtenburg. Even his greatest triumphs were shot through with compromise. Social Security offered meager benefits (which were expanded under subsequent administrations), was financed by a regressive tax, and, to placate southern Democrats, was carefully tailored to exclude domestic workers and other black-dominated professions.

Compared with other Democratic presidents, Roosevelt enjoyed relatively friendly relations with liberals, but there nonetheless existed a left opposition during his time, mostly of socialists and communists, who criticized him relentlessly. Progressive senator Burton Wheeler complained that FDR, "for all his fine talk, really preferred conservatives to progressives." And actually, the Roosevelt era had the same pattern we see today, of liberals angry with the administration's compromises, and the administration angry in turn at the liberals. In 1935, Roosevelt adviser Rexford Tugwell groused of the liberals, "They complain incessantly that the administration is moving into the conservative camp, but do nothing to keep it from going there."

Princeton professor and activist Cornel West, a vituperative Obama critic, reached even further back into history for a comparison with which to disfavor the subject of his bitter disappointment. "You would think that we needed somebody—a Lincoln-like figure who could revive some democratic spirit and democratic possibility," he told Thomas Frank. "You have to be able to speak to those divisions in such a way that, like FDR, like Lincoln, you're able to somehow pull out the best of who we are, given the divisions. You don't try to act as if we have no divisions and we're just an American family."

The Lincoln of West's imagination, then, was a figure who would never "act as if we have no divisions and we're just an American family." This is the same Lincoln who, in his inaugural address—delivered after seven states *had already seceded from the Union*—declared, "We are not enemies, but friends. We must not be enemies. Though passion may have strained, it must not break our bonds of affection."

In fact, the real Lincoln was a carefully calculating politician, always careful not to step too far ahead of public opinion. Progressives distrusted and even loathed Lincoln with an intensity that exceeds West's own distrust of Obama. In 1862, William Lloyd Garrison called the Great Emancipator "nothing better than a wet rag." Frederick Douglass lambasted him for "allowing himself to be . . . the miserable tool of traitors and rebels."

It is not as if the criticisms of Lincoln were always wrong. In his time, Lincoln was a politician, not the saint of historical memory. He carefully tended his political capital, compromising repeatedly with advocates of slavery in order to maintain his war coalition. Even the Emancipation Proclamation was cautiously framed as a war measure, rather than an attack on slavery, and it withheld freedom from slaves in Union states. Nor were his political calculations always shrewd. Lincoln saddled his army with incompetent generals for years. Fearing for his reelection prospects, he replaced his abolitionist vice president, Hannibal Hamlin, a committed opponent of slavery, with Andrew Johnson, a proslavery southern Democrat. When Johnson assumed the presidency following Lincoln's assassination, he fervently obstructed efforts to safeguard rights for freed slaves, making his appointment by Lincoln one of the most consequential (and avoidable) errors in history. Lincoln was "a pretty sad man, because he could not do all he wanted to do . . . and nobody can," concluded one student of his presidency, in 1940. That student was Franklin Roosevelt—who, like every figure to hold the office, had been shorn of any illusion of presidential omnipotence.

All this is to say that eight years of almost continuous disappointment and dismay (or, perhaps, at best, grudging acceptance) reflect an absence of any plausible standard. When liberals judge Obama, or any president, they measure him against a baseline of something very close to perfection. Their desired president enjoys political success without being a politician. When they do try to summon a historical example of a great president, they summon a fantasy. In 2014, the left-wing Georgetown historian (and dismayed Obama enthusiast) Michael Kazin mourned the president's "ineptitude," which contrasted against the great presidents of the past, like Roosevelt and Lincoln, among others, whose success was owed to the fact that "both admirers and detractors knew exactly what they stood for." This not only inverts the facts of those historical presidents whose constant trimming and equivocation drove their own supporters mad—it inverts the very process of how progress works. Victory is never clean or total. As with every president in history, Obama's achievements were not merely limited and compromised by circumstances beyond his control, but he also compounded his difficulties with errors of strategy. Being president is hard, and Obama has not done the job perfectly. His supporters, however, displayed a consistent inability to measure his successes and failures against a realistic comparison.

The left, in particular, yearns for a climactic triumph over the massed forces of reaction and wealth. Left-wing dissatisfaction produced splinter candidates in 1948 (Henry Wallace, to whom progressive voters disillusioned with Harry Truman flocked) and 2000 (Ralph Nader, whose vote total in Florida outstripped George W. Bush's winning margin in the state many times over). Liberal dissatisfaction played a major, and likely decisive, role in Richard Nixon's 1968 victory over Humphrey. Despair is the liberals' default state.

The American state of the present day has a dramatically more progressive cast than it did a half century ago, and it had a more progressive cast a half century ago than it did fifty years before, and on and on. Yet the progressives who produced these victories have lived them as deflating failures. They have made the same errors of perception time and again.

"It's naive to think you're going to change American policy by compromising on a lot of stuff," complained *Rolling Stone* editor Jann Wenner. That happens to get historical reality almost perfectly backward. Presidents change policy *almost exclusively* through compromise. Seen through the prism of ideological purity, the history of American liberalism from emancipation (which left millions of former slaves in slavelike conditions) to Social Security (a piddling pension initially denied to 40 percent of the workforce) to Medicare (designed to placate the doctor and insurance lobbies) is a history of sellouts. Only with the perspective of history, and often a series of incremental improvements, do such things acquire the sheen of idealistic grandeur. That clarity will emerge over time, as Obama's supporters embrace an appreciation that largely eluded them during his.

Chapter 7
Obama's America

When Obama stood in Grant Park, Chicago, on November 4, 2008, to speak to the country as president-elect for the first time, his election appeared to represent something more than just the repudiation of a failed Bush presidency, more also than just the election of the first president who was not white and male. It represented a generational upheaval. Among voters more than forty-five years old, the new president had actually lost; younger voters had accounted for his entire victory margin. Indeed, the youngest cohort—voters under thirty—supplied most of his cushion, supporting Obama by a staggering margin of more than two to one.

A generational divide of this size had not appeared before, at least not in the era in which exit polling exists. (In 2000, Al Gore, who won a narrow plurality of the vote, carried voters over sixty by four points. Obama, who won by a comfortable seven-point margin, performed a net eight percentage points worse than Gore among the oldest voters.) In every election since 1972—when George McGovern lost by half a dozen points among the young, while getting slaughtered by thirty-plus points among every older cohort—age had played barely any role. The young and old moved between the two parties more or less in tandem. Now it seemed a new America had arrived, and the new president seemed to embody it. He walked onto the stage, aside a glamorous and beautiful wife, with two school-aged daughters, the youngest, Sasha, nestling her head against her father's elbow. Obama looked youthful—more closely resembling the twenty-eight-year-old who had made national news for the first time when he won the presidency of the *Harvard Law Review* than he would the gray-haired man at the end of his second term. In so many ways, the young, dark-skinned, urban president-elect was the incarnation of his disproportionately youthful, city-dwelling, minority, college-educated supporters.

To Republicans, this cast a bleak vision of a future that might be slipping away from them. The 2008 election and the collapse of the Bush administration's program at home and abroad created a widespread belief that the GOP would have to alter its policies. Even much of the right accepted this premise. "Republicans," wrote conservative Ramesh Ponnuru in *Time* a few weeks after Obama's victory, "will have to devise an agenda that speaks to a country where more people feel the bite of payroll taxes than income taxes, where health-care costs eat up raises even in good times, where the length of the daily commute is a bigger irritant than are earmarks." Instead of moving toward the center, though, the Republican Party lurched even more sharply rightward. By doing so, it gained a temporary tactical advantage, but may have solidified Obama's majority coalition.

On January 10, 2009, eleven days before Obama's inauguration, House Republicans met to plan their strategy for the new term, in which Democrats would control the presidency as well as both houses of Congress. A PowerPoint presentation boiled down their strategy to its essence. "If the goal of the majority is to govern, what is the purpose of the minority?" one slide asked. "The purpose of the minority is to become the majority."

While this was presented as a simple axiomatic truth, in reality, the Republican Party was embarking on a strategy without any modern precedent in American history. Most Americans have had the sense that the parties are supposed to work together—that governing is the job of all elected representatives, not just those in the president's party. It would become clear during Obama's presidency that the basis for this tradition had disappeared.

The American political system during the twentieth century had a peculiar character, compared to the tight-knit party systems operating in most democracies, but which Americans took for granted. Bipartisanship evolved into a hallowed tradition, understood almost as a form of civic virtue. Conservative Democrats might block their own president's policies and work closely with a Republican president, while moderate or liberal Republicans would do the opposite. Both Democrats and Republicans recruited Dwight Eisenhower to run as their presidential candidate in 1952, believing, reasonably enough, that his moderate views would fit about as well in one party as the other. Republicans in Congress overwhelmingly supported Lyndon Johnson's 1964 Civil Rights Act, allowing the bill to survive mass defections by southern Democrats. Ronald Reagan worked closely with conservative Democrats to enact his 1981 tax cut.

The political scientists Keith Poole and Howard

Rosenthal have developed a system for measuring the ideology of members of Congress and their parties. They found that northern Democrats occupied about the same ideological space from the early 1960s through the present day—that Kennedy and Johnson Democrats from north of the Mason-Dixon Line had the same vision of the role of government as Obama Democrats. But after 1964, white southern Democrats went into a long, slow, terminal decline, and their departure pushed the Democrats somewhat to the left of center. The Republican Party underwent a much more dramatic change. From the early 1960s to the present day, Republicans in the House moved four times as far to the right as their Democratic counterparts moved to the left. The conservative movement, which began this period as a small minority faction within the GOP, took it over completely—a radical transformation. During the 1950s, conservatives maintained a bitterly hostile relationship to the party's leadership and its president, Dwight Eisenhower. They rejected the Republican Party's postwar acceptance of the enhanced role of government in economic life created by the New Deal, and its foreign policy of containing rather than destroying communism abroad. William F. Buckley, the most important intellectual among the fringe, dismissed Eisenhower as "undaunted by principle, unchained to any coherent ideas as to the nature of man and society, uncommitted to any estimate of the nature or potential of the enemy."

Conservatives tended to see every extension of government, even small ones, as the looming extinction of freedom. Economist Milton Friedman compared John F. Kennedy's program to fascism. In the early 1960s, Ronald Reagan warned that if Medicare passed, the government would inevitably force doctors to live in cities where they did not want to, and future generations would no longer know "what it once was like in America when men were free." (Conservatives continue to tout that speech today as if it has proved prescient.)

Certainly, mainstream Republicans of this era sometimes opposed new government programs, or disagreed with Democrats about their design or scope. But the conservatives utterly rejected the idea that their party should be about simply accepting a smaller or better-run version of the same model endorsed by the Democrats. This was because they didn't actually care about the design of government policies—they opposed big government on principle, because they believed it inherently impinged upon freedom. Friedman once wrote, "freedom in economic arrangements is itself a component of freedom broadly understood, so economic freedom is an end in itself." Barry Goldwater, the political leader of the conservative movement, declared:

> I have little interest in streamlining government or in making it more efficient, for I mean to reduce its size. I do not undertake to promote welfare, for I propose to extend freedom. My aim is not to pass laws, but to repeal them. It is not to inaugurate new programs, but to cancel old ones that do violence to the Constitution, or that have failed their purpose, or that impose on the people an unwarranted financial burden. I will not attempt to discover whether legislation is "needed" before I have first determined whether it is constitutionally permissible. And if I should later be attacked for neglecting my constituents' "interests" I shall reply that I was informed that their main interest is liberty and that in that cause I am doing the very best I can.

Their distrust of the social and political elite made conservatives prone to paranoia. Senator Joseph McCarthy enthralled conservatives by describing lurid communist conspiracies that eventually extended to Eisenhower himself. In 1964, *None Dare Call It Treason,* a book by the conservative author and Republican activist John Stormer, alleging "a conspiratorial plan to destroy the United States into which foreign aid, planned inflation, distortion of treaty-making powers and disarmament all fit," eventually sold 7 million copies.

One of the most persistent sources of conservative paranoia concerned their own marginalization within the party. It was self-evident to them that the Republican Party would always win national elections if it moved to the right, rather than promote "a Dime Store New Deal," as Goldwater contemptuously described Eisenhower's moderate policies. The right-wing activist Phyllis Schlafly wrote a tract, *A Choice Not an Echo*, arguing "there is no way Republicans can possibly lose as long as we have a presidential candidate who campaigns on the issues." However, the party had been thwarted by "a small group of secret kingmakers, using hidden persuaders and psychological warfare techniques, [who] manipulated the Republican National Convention to nominate candidates who would sidestep or suppress the key issues." Schlafly's book, like Stormer's, also developed into a key organizing tool for the Goldwater campaign in 1964.

The mainstream of the party, believing that allowing conservatives to control the party would court political annihilation, did not give up without a fight. Moderates at the GOP convention in 1964 proposed a resolution condemning extremism of all varieties. Goldwater supporters voted it down, their position echoed by the candidate's famous declaration that "extremism in the defense of liberty is no vice" and that "moderation in the pursuit of justice is no virtue." Many moderates stalked out of the convention, including centrist George Romney and his teenage son, Mitt. Governor Romney subsequently penned a twelve-page letter to Goldwater explaining why he had not endorsed him. When conservatives defeated moderate California senator Thomas Kuchel, the Senate's second-ranking Republican, Kuchel lashed out at what he called a "fanatical neo-fascist political cult" in the grips of a "strange mixture of corrosive hatred and sickening fear."

Goldwater suffered an overwhelming defeat in 1964, but his supporters did not see his loss as an indictment of their theory that a true conservative could never lose. And, as it happened, the conservative hope that they could turn the party more right-wing and still win was not as irrational as it appeared in the wake of Goldwater's defeat. As noted earlier, the conservative strategy, articulated by movement theorists like William Rusher, publisher of *National Review,* was to add to Republican ranks the tens of millions of conservative voters in the white South who had shunned the GOP since the time of Lincoln. The timing for this shift was opportune: the former Confederacy's historic attachment to the Democratic Party, shaken loose by Harry Truman's embrace of civil rights, started an irrevocable break after the 1964 Civil Rights Act, which Goldwater had opposed. In the ranks of southern Democrats alienated by their party's embrace of civil rights the Republican Party would find a vast new trove of conservatives who would supply the votes for its new, much more conservative identity.

Despite the initial setback in 1964, the party's new conservative course soon began to bear fruit. The 1966 midterm elections revealed a public moving steadily rightward, and the Republicans were poised to exploit this shift. White America had come to see the Democratic Party's domestic agenda as a transfer of resources from the white middle class to the black poor. Violent crime shot upward, starting in the 1960s, a trend that continued into the 1990s. Whites fled cities for the suburbs, and many of them came to associate African-Americans with welfare, which became a synecdoche for laziness and unearned entitlement. Ronald Reagan regaled audiences with stories about a "welfare queen" driving a Cadillac, or a "strapping young buck" who used food stamps to buy steak while "you were waiting in line to buy hamburger." In 1985, Stanley Greenberg, then a political scientist and later a close adviser to Bill Clinton, immersed himself in Macomb County, a blue-collar Detroit suburb where whites had abandoned the Democratic Party in droves. He found that the so-called Reagan Democrats there understood politics almost entirely in racial terms, translating any Democratic appeal to economic justice as taking their money to subsidize the black underclass.

Simultaneously, conservatives steadily gained ground within the Republican Party. Republicans won five of the next six presidential elections, interrupted only by a single, narrow defeat in 1976 in the wake of the Watergate scandal. Nevertheless, the full triumph of conservatism within the Republican Party took decades to complete. Nixon cut a marginally less offensive profile than Eisenhower, from a conservative standpoint, but still offended the right by expanding regulation, negotiating détente with communist China and the Soviets, and even proposing a universal health care plan (which Democrats opposed as insufficiently liberal). The turning point came when Reagan, an old fighter from the Goldwater movement, won two presidential elections, signifying the right's triumph within the GOP.

Reagan's triumph confounded pundits, who initially treated him as another Goldwater, marching the party off the cliff to the right. Conservatives could look back on this period as vindication for their original belief that staunch conservatism, rather than moderation, offered their path to success. When Reagan's successor, George Bush, lost in 1992, Republicans largely concluded that his deviation from the conservative faith—a 1990 budget deal in which he submitted to a small tax increase in return for hundreds of billions of dollars in spending cuts—had done him in.

In the meantime, generations of conservative activists slowly replaced the old-line party apparatus. The movement had identified conservatism with Republicanism so thoroughly that no competing power center was left standing. Republican moderates in the 1950s and 1960s had drawn ideas from mainstream organizations such as the Ripon Society, Republican Advance, and the Committee for Economic Development, and center-right publications such as the *New York Herald Tribune, Confluence,* and *Advance.* By the 1980s, those were all dead or in steep decline, and the conservative movement controlled every media outlet and think tank with influence over the GOP. No competing ideological tradition or political strategy had any public legitimacy within the party. Reaganism (and the ideal of conservative purity that his acolytes believed, somewhat exaggeratedly, he followed unswervingly) was the standard of perfection agreed upon by all sides. The political habits built during this long period would shape the Republican response to Obama.

Beginning in 1968, Republicans enjoyed a national political terrain favorable to their party. But for a party to hold a natural majority does not mean it always wins; short-term circumstances can play an enormous role. Think of the two conditions affecting elections as akin to climate and weather: in any given part of the world, the climate might be growing warmer over the years, but the weather could easily undergo a cold snap at some given point.

In 1992, Bill Clinton interrupted the long period of Republican presidential success. He accomplished this by taking advantage of a presidency that had grown unpopular during the 1991 recession, and by adapting his message to the conservative tenor of the times. The governor of a southern state, Clinton presented a national persona (primarily in his support of welfare reform and a severe crime bill) that soothed white fears about the party's support for African-Americans. (That

Clinton was able to do this while maintaining deep support from black voters displayed both his political skill and the pragmatic tradition of the African-American electorate.) Clinton's identity as a "New Democrat" (as he put it) displayed his recognition that the old Democrats had lost their majority.

But in 2002, journalist John Judis and demographer Ruy Teixeira noticed a deeper trend in the electorate that had largely escaped detection. The Republican Party had come increasingly to depend on the support of one constituency, white voters without a college degree, and this constituency was steadily shrinking as a share of the electorate. College-educated white voters, once reliably Republican, had turned more Democratic. Combined with racial minorities—another traditional Democratic bloc—which were growing as a result of immigration, the outlines of a winning coalition had come into view. Their book, *The Emerging Democratic Coalition*, initially drew more ridicule than support. Partly this was because the timing of its publication, right after the post-9/11 patriotic upsurge that had given Republicans a sharp boost, seemingly repudiating Judis and Teixeira. But the 9/11 effect eventually melted away in the Bush administration's failed occupation of Iraq, and their argument became harder and harder to dismiss. Whites without a college degree cast more than 60 percent of the votes in the 1980 presidential election. By 2012 their share had fallen to 36 percent. The Republicans had built a majority upon the foundation of a populist appeal to blue-collar whites and had failed to notice that the foundation was shrinking beneath its feet. The white population was growing—and is continuing to grow—more educated and secular, and friendlier to the Democratic worldview. Meanwhile, the white share of the electorate has been shrinking by two percentage points every four years.

Judis and Teixeira sketched out a vision of a Democratic coalition that would dominate in urban areas, universities, and tech centers. They singled out Colorado, Nevada, and Arizona, with skyrocketing Latino populations, and Virginia and North Carolina, with their influx of college-educated whites, as the most fertile ground for the expanding Democratic base. Obama's two victories followed that blueprint. Campaign reporters cast the election as a triumph of Obama's inspirational message and cutting-edge organization, but above all his impressive win reflected simple demography. One measure of how thoroughly the electorate had changed by the time of Obama's election was that, if college-educated whites, working-class whites, and minorities had cast the same proportion of the votes in 1988 as they did in 2008, Michael Dukakis—the prototypically hapless 1980s Democrat, who lost forty states—would have triumphed (just barely, but he would have won). By 2020, nonwhite voters should rise to a third of the electorate. By 2040, or perhaps shortly after, nonwhites will outnumber whites.

The rising cohort of Democratic voters held assumptions about the world that would have seemed alien, and even radical, a generation before. Obama's youngest supporters—the "millennial generation," born between the early 1980s and the early 2000s—included far fewer whites than earlier generations. What's more, its white voters displayed distinctly more liberal views, including on the crucial questions of racial identity. The youngest cohort of whites is far less likely than the oldest cohort to believe that white people face discrimination, and far less likely to be upset at "the idea of a Latino person being president of the United States." Their proclivities may portend a full-scale sea change in American politics.

Not all of these changes have helped Obama's party. A long-standing pattern of American politics is that older people, who have deeper roots in their communities, vote at higher rates. The gap is especially large during midterm elections, which lack the blaring publicity generated by presidential races. Historically, age made relatively little difference in voting behavior. But in the Obama era, the generational split handed conservatives a huge advantage in midterm elections; when young voters stay home in nonpresidential years, the electorate now swings heavily Republican. That fact has driven enormous Republican gains in congressional races, state legislatures, and other down-ballot races.

A second quality of the new Obama coalition hurt the party even more: Democrats have grown increasingly concentrated geographically. As Obama built increasingly huge majorities in urban centers, the party declined in small towns. As a result, Democrats, tightly packed into urban districts, tend to "waste" many of their votes in legislative races. House Democrats won more votes in 2012, but Republicans easily held their majority of the chamber. This was because Republicans win suburban districts with 55 percent or 60 percent of the vote, while Democrats pile up 80 percent or 90 percent of support in their city districts. In many states, Republicans have used their majorities to draw districts designed to deepen their geographic advantages. In Ohio, which Obama carried in 2012 by 3 percent, the Republican-controlled legislature drew a map in which 12 of the 16 House districts supported Romney. In Michigan, where Obama defeated Romney by 9.5 percent, 9 of the 14 House districts supported

Romney. In some of these cases, the GOP's advantages compounded each other. The disproportionately older and whiter voters who showed up during the midterms elected Republican officials in state legislative positions, and they used their legislative control to give their party favorable districts in Congress.

The party's dependence on rural voters intensified in 2016. One unexpected result of this was that Republicans gained an advantage in the Electoral College, which Trump won despite having lost the national vote. Trump turned out enough voters in small towns and the Rust Belt to flip previously Democratic states like Michigan, Pennsylvania, and Wisconsin. Meanwhile, fast-growing states with high minority populations—Texas, Arizona, and Georgia—all moved closer to the Democrats, just not quite enough to flip them from red to blue just yet. It was a trend with ominous portents for a Republican party growing ever more dependent upon drawing every last drop of support from a shrinking portion of the country.

More than four decades ago, political scientists Lloyd Free and Hadley Cantril identified the core of Americans' political thinking as a blend of symbolic conservatism and operational liberalism. Most Americans, that is, oppose big government in the abstract but favor it in the particular. They oppose "regulation" and "spending," but favor, say, enforcement of clean-air laws and Social Security. The push and pull between these contradictory beliefs has defined most of the domestic political conflicts over the last century. Public support for most of the particulars of government has stopped Republicans from rolling back the advances of the New Deal, but suspicion with "big government" has made Democratic attempts to advance the role of the state rare and politically painful.

This tension continues to define the beliefs of American voters. Among the 2012 electorate, more voters identified themselves as conservative (35 percent) than liberal (25 percent), and more said the government is already doing too much that should be left to the private sector (51 percent) than asserted that the government ought to be doing more to solve problems (44 percent). But this is not the case with younger voters. By a 59 percent to 37 percent margin, voters under thirty said the government should do more to solve problems. And 33 percent of voters under thirty identified themselves as liberal, as against 26 percent who called themselves conservative—which is remarkable, since conservatives have long outnumbered liberals among the electorate as a whole, requiring Democrats to dominate among moderate voters.

What all this suggests is that we may soon see a

political landscape that will appear from the perspective of today and virtually all of American history as unrecognizably liberal. Democrats today must amass huge majorities of moderate voters in order to overcome conservatives' numerical advantage over liberals. They must carefully wrap any proposal for activist government within the strictures of limited government, which is why Bill Clinton declared the era of big government to be over, and Obama promised not to raise taxes for 99 percent of Americans. It's entirely possible that, by the time today's twenty-somethings have reached middle age, these sorts of limits will cease to apply.

Obviously, such a future hinges on the generational patterns of the last two election cycles persisting. A long-standing piece of folk wisdom says that people inevitably grow more conservative as they age. That is not necessarily true. In reality, voters tend to acquire voting habits early on, and hold them throughout their life. A Pew survey that tracked the behavior of different generations through time found that early choices persist for decades. Voters who came of age during the Roosevelt administration voted Democratic at a heavier rate throughout their life than voters who came of age during the Eisenhower administration. Hillary Clinton lacked the cultural connection with younger voters enjoyed by Obama, a much younger and hipper politician. But she still won voters under the age of thirty by nearly a 20-point margin, and prevailed among voters between thirty and forty-five by 8 points. The political cast of the young is likely to remain a Democratic-leaning force for decades to come.

The growth of Obama's coalition did not go ignored by Republicans. The political transformation his election seemed to augur unnerved them deeply. In the waning days of the 2012 election, a Republican strategist told journalist Ron Brownstein, "This is the last time anyone will try to do this"—"this" being a presidential campaign that tries to assemble a majority almost entirely through white votes. Conservatives saw the waters rising all around them.

Yet the psychology of decline does not always operate in a straightforward, rational way. A strategy of managing slow decay is unpleasant, and history is replete with instances of leaders who persuaded themselves of the opposite of the obvious conclusion. Rather than adjust themselves to their slowly weakening position, they chose instead to stage a decisive confrontation. If the terms of the fight grow more unfavorable with every passing year, well, all the more reason to have the fight sooner. Such was the thought process of the antebellum southern states, sizing up the growing population and industrial might of the North. It was also the thinking of the leaders of Austria-Hungary, watching their empire deteriorate and deciding they needed a decisive war with Serbia to save themselves.

At varying levels of conscious and subconscious thought, this is also the reasoning that drove Republicans in the Obama era. Surveying the landscape, they concluded that they must strike quickly and decisively at the opposition before all hope is lost. Jim DeMint wrote a book in 2012 titled *Now or Never: Saving America from Economic Collapse.* DeMint, who the next year left the Senate to take the presidency of the Heritage Foundation, painted a haunting picture: "Republican supporters will continue to decrease every year as more Americans become dependent on the government. Dependent voters will naturally elect even big-government progressives who will continue to smother economic growth and spend America deeper into debt. The 2012 election may be the last opportunity for Republicans."

Paul Ryan, then-chairman of the House Budget Committee, wrote a document that was not merely a fiscal blueprint but a sweeping vision statement that he called "The Roadmap," which warned, "America is approaching a 'tipping point' beyond which the Nation will be unable to change course." Arthur Brooks, the president of the conservative American Enterprise Institute and a high-profile presence on the Republican intellectual scene, wrote a 2010 book titled *The Battle,* urging conservatives to treat the struggle for economic libertarianism as a "culture war" between capitalism and socialism, in which compromise was impossible. Time was running short, Brooks pleaded in apocalyptic tones. The "real core" of what he called Obama's socialistic supporters was voters under thirty. "It is the future of our country," he wrote. "And this group has exhibited a frightening openness to statism in the age of Obama." Peter Wehner, a former deputy to Karl Rove and conservative opinion writer, sadly conveyed his observation that conservatives "believe that America is at an inflection point. That we are about to enter into the land of no return." This paranoia bled from the fringes all the way into the party's prestigious centers. Even a blue-blood like Jeb Bush declared in 2015, "I think the left wants slow growth because that means people are more dependent upon government."

The right's doomsday mood and vision breathed new life into an important stream of far-right thought: the ideology developed by Ayn Rand. A Russian émigré whose affluent family suffered persecution at the hands of the Bolsheviks, Rand constructed a worldview that turned the ideology of her Bolshevik tormentors upside down. Recapitulating the methodology of the Marxists she so despised, Rand believed that politics boiled down to a struggle between two opposing economic classes, in her vision one that created all wealth (the makers), and the other that stole it (the takers). Rand identified the producer class and the parasite class as the opposite of how the Marxists did: the producers were the capitalists, the parasites the workers. "The man at the top of the intellectual pyramid contributes the most to all those below him, but gets nothing except his material payment, receiving no intellectual bonus from others to add to the value of his time. The man at the bottom who, left to himself, would starve in his hopeless ineptitude, contributes nothing to those above him, but receives the bonus of all of their brains," explained John Galt, protagonist of Rand's novel *Atlas Shrugged*, giving voice to its author's beliefs. (Rand, a screenwriter and author, articulated her ideas mainly through fiction.)

Rand's ideas provided the formative worldview for generations of conservative thinkers. One of them was Ryan, who told a group of Rand followers in 2005 that her ideas were "the reason I got involved in public service" and said in 2009, "we are right now living in an Ayn Rand novel, metaphorically speaking." Rand's ideas gained a new vogue during the Obama era, as conservatives saw in the new president the first signs of the attack on wealth and the inevitable social and economic disintegration Rand had depicted. In a 2011 speech before the American Enterprise Institute, Ryan fused Randian thought with the party's fresh terror that Obama's supporters threatened to permanently overtake them. "The tipping point represents two dangers," he announced: "first, long-term economic decline as the number of makers diminishes [and] the number of takers grows . . . Second, gradual moral-political decline as dependency and passivity weaken the nation's character." In Wehner's endorsement of Stanley Greenberg's findings he concludes that his fellow Republicans believe "[t]hat demographic trends are all troubling and that the 'takers' in America will soon outnumber the 'givers.'"

The hysterical response to Obama's presidency did not just bubble up from the inflamed grass roots. It filtered down as well from the party's intellectual elite, whose ideas had prepared them to conclude that the only response to Obama entailed an all-out class struggle. Republican leaders at the beginning of 2009 understood, in a way minority parties had not understood before, that total opposition to Obama served not only their policy goals but also their political interest.

Republicans in Congress did not announce publicly
that their strategy was to deny the administration support for any of its initiatives. They generally maintained
in public that the administration was to blame for their
lack of support. But a wide array of evidence supports
the conclusion that the party followed a conscious plan
of mass opposition. On the evening of his inauguration,
journalist Robert Draper later reported, more than a
dozen Republicans in both chambers met to plot how
the party would respond to Obama. They affirmed the
message of the House Republican meeting ten days
before—they would open fights on every front. "We've
gotta challenge them on every single bill and challenge
them on every single campaign," House chief deputy
Republican whip Kevin McCarthy told the group.

Vice President Joe Biden, who had cultivated deep
social ties to his fellow senators during his six terms
of service, claimed that seven Republican senators told
him they had to promise to support their party leadership on every procedural vote, or else be stripped
of their chairmanships. Biden's report of private con-
versations cannot be verified, and he obviously has an
interest in playing up Republican partisanship. But at
least one Republican senator more or less confirmed
Biden's account. "If [Obama] was for it, we had to be

against it," Ohio's George Voinovich said, after retiring in 2010. Biden's report would also explain a curious anomaly from 2009, when moderate Republican senator Olympia Snowe voted for health care reform in the Senate Finance Committee, then went on to vote against the bill when it came to the floor. (The latter vote was procedural; the former was not.)

The old Washington folk wisdom held that the opposition party had to tread carefully. If it opposed the president too harshly, or was seen as reflexively partisan, voters would hesitate to trust them with power again. This seems to be more of a comforting fable, useful for encouraging responsible behavior, than a realistic analysis. Mitch McConnell, the Republican Senate leader, explained in 2010 the importance of maintaining unified Republican opposition to health care reform: "It was absolutely critical that everybody be together because if the proponents of the bill were able to say it was bipartisan, it tended to convey to the public that this is O.K., they must have figured it out." The next year, McConnell reiterated his point, telling *The Atlantic*, "We worked very hard to keep our fingerprints off of these proposals. Because we thought—correctly, I think—that the only way the American people would know that a great debate was going on was if the measures were not bipartisan. When you hang the 'bipartisan' tag on something, the perception is that differences have been worked out, and there's a broad agreement that that's the way forward."

McConnell's logic was very shrewd, echoing the previously mentioned findings of John Hibbing and Elizabeth Theiss-Morse. McConnell knew that most Americans have little time to follow the intricacies of the policy debate, and instead take their cues from indirect signals. Bipartisan agreement provides one such important signal. If the two parties seem to agree on a bill, it implies the idea is broadly acceptable and moderate. If they disagree, it sends a signal that something with the bill is wrong. Even many pundits who follow politics for a living tended to fall back on the same reasoning, albeit in more sophisticated form. Self-identified centrists in Washington tend to assume that the sensible position lies halfway between whatever the two parties are saying at any given moment. "The middle is often the commonsensical place to be," explained ABC News commentator Cokie Roberts. "The notion that one side is right and one side is wrong is generally, as one finds in life, not the case." They conclude, as a matter of course, that if the two parties cannot agree, they are equally to blame. It is striking how little support moderate opinion leaders gave Obama throughout his presidency, even when he endorsed their preferred policies, as he often did. The centrist establishment's most urgent priority remained long-term deficit reduction, and the centrists urged both parties to compromise in pursuit of this goal—Republicans would have to yield on their opposition to new taxes, and Democrats on their reluctance to reduce spending on retirement programs. When Obama and his allies did exactly this, however, centrists were forced to ignore it—after all, if they sided with one of the parties, they wouldn't be "nonpartisan" anymore!

Obama made several attempts to forge a debt compromise with Republicans—offering concessions publicly on some occasions, or behind closed doors on others. All these attempts failed because Republicans refused to give in on higher tax revenue. After Obama publicly endorsed a mix of revenue increases and cuts to Social Security, the New York Times's David Brooks wrote a column accusing him of "declin[ing] to come up with a proposal to address the problem." When Senate Democrats offered a plan to mix spending cuts and higher revenue, the centrist Washington Post editorial page dismissed it as a "non-starter." Technically, this was true—Republicans rejected these proposals, unilaterally making them a political nonstarter. So even though the Post editorial page itself had in the past explicitly endorsed the very policy ideas the Democrats were proposing, they dismissed Democrat support for them as useless on the grounds that Republicans wouldn't support them. Republicans were therefore able to block any bipartisanship in the knowledge that liberal pundits might oppose them, but conservatives would take their side, and centrists would apportion blame on both sides regardless.

The most important benefit of the Republican strategy was that voters tend to care less about process than results. Political scientists have found over and over that voters tend to hold the incumbent party responsible for conditions, the most important of which is the state of the economy, but studies have also shown that voters can project their feelings of support or lack thereof onto matters that politicians have nothing to do with, such as weather conditions or the record of the local football team. What's more, at a national level, the electorate does not split the credit or the blame between Congress and the president—they tend to hold the president almost solely responsible. This does not hold true of voters alone. Again, the pundits frequently employ the same logic. Ron Fournier conceded that Obama had agreed to compromise on the budget and Republicans had not, but insisted Obama shared the blame anyway. "President Obama makes a credible case that he has reached farther toward compromise than House Republicans," he wrote in the *National Journal*. "But knowing who's at fault doesn't fix the problem. To loosely quote Billy Joel: You may be right, Mr. President, but this is crazy." Even by 2016, when Senate Republicans immediately followed the death of Supreme Court justice Antonin Scalia by announcing they would block any replacement, however moderate or well qualified, some reporters continued to lay the blame equally. Obama "can't even get Senate Republicans to give him a hearing," said CBS reporter Norah O'Donnell. "Most Republicans won't even meet with Judge [Merrick] Garland. Does that say something about President Obama's inability to reach across the aisle?"

The most successful application of the Republican strategy came in 2011, when they threatened not to lift the debt ceiling. The episode left them with a double victory. The dysfunction in Washington, and the possibility that Congress might set off a potential global economic meltdown, justifiably shook the public's faith in the recovery. Consumer confidence dropped steeply that summer, and Obama's approval ratings dropped along with it. Gleefully, Republicans learned that they could inflict immediate harm on the American economy and the blame would accrue to Obama—which

would, of course, improve their own electoral prospects. (It was in the wake of the debt ceiling scare
that Obama's reelection prospects were most deeply
imperiled.) Additionally, by refusing to compromise,
they forced Obama to accept budget sequestration. The
resulting slowness of the recovery gave the GOP better
odds of defeating Obama and his congressional allies.

In 2012, Greg Walden, chairman of the House Republicans' campaign arm, explained why he expected
members of his party to hold their majority, despite its
almost completely dysfunctional governance: "this is
an election that is a referendum on the president's policies." If Walden's claim was to be taken at face value,
and there was no reason not to do so, he was arguing
that voters would not hold the House GOP's performance against it. Instead, they would reward or punish
House Republicans as a kind of reverse indicator of
Obama's policies. The worse they felt Obama had performed, the more seats they would award Republicans.
The leaders of the House had grown aware they had
no incentive to govern well, and certainly not to help
speed along the recovery. Their incentive ran the opposite way.

As early as the fall of 2008, anti-Obama passions
among conservative voters had started to run ahead

of the party leadership. In the waning weeks of the 2008 election, crowds at Republican events had grown rabid, leaving John McCain, the putative head of the party ticket, visibly discomfited. By that point, the emotional center of the GOP had fallen to his running mate, former Alaska governor Sarah Palin, who captured the anti-resentment enveloping the right. At the time of her appearance, Palin presented an electrifying, novel profile: she spoke not like a politician but like an average person, and perhaps knew hardly any more about public policy than one, but conveyed righteous indignation at the increasingly likely possibility that this young, unfamiliar man from Chicago might soon inhabit the Oval Office. The McCain campaign was hesitant to exploit white racial fears, but Palin shook loose from the campaign—"going rogue," as alarmed McCain staffers put it—and launched fiery, unauthorized attacks on Obama's background and alleged lack of patriotism.

The appearance of Palin prefigured a recurrent pattern during the Obama era. The leadership of the opposition passed out of the hands of the formal heads of the opposing party—first McCain, then Mitch McConnell and John Boehner—and into a series of angry populist figures. Palin, Joe the Plumber, Glenn Beck, Herman Cain, and Donald Trump all captured a belief that Obama was not just wrong but dangerous, an alien figure, arising quickly from circumstances that appeared suspicious and seemed to cover some dark origin-secret that could be traced back to a Marxist puppet master from his youth, or perhaps even to Kenya. Stanley Kurtz, a longtime writer for *National Review*, published a 2010 book, *Radical-in-Chief: Barack Obama and the Untold Story of American Socialism*, alleging that the president concealed a far-left agenda. *Gangster Government: Barack Obama and the New Washington Thugocracy*, by *Washington Examiner* columnist David Freddoso, and *The Roots of Obama's Rage*, by Heritage Foundation fellow and *Forbes* columnist Dinesh D'Souza, fleshed out these themes.

In a polarized age, it has become normal for partisans to bitterly resent presidents of the opposing party. But the opposition to Obama had an unusually fervent cast. Dark, atavistic fears haunted the minds of Republican voters. A 2009 survey found that conservative Republicans, about a fifth of the country, did not believe that Obama was merely misguided, or cynical, or even corrupt, but that his agenda was "purposely designed to fail." As the report concluded, "Our groups showed that they explicitly believe [Obama] is purposely and ruthlessly executing a hidden agenda to weaken and ultimately destroy the foundations of our country."

Their belief held that, under the guise of promoting a recovery, Obama was deliberately fomenting economic collapse in order to expand government power. "I do not want economic collapse," the popular conservative radio host Rush Limbaugh explained in 2009. "The problem is this administration has no interest in it stopping right now."

Similar kinds of conspiracy theories about the Bush administration could be found on the left. The difference is that the far left remained largely isolated from the political mainstream, much as the far right had been before Goldwater. The right-wing takeover of the GOP had brought the paranoid style into control of a major party.

Republican leaders could not repudiate even the most transparently absurd conspiracy theories circulating among their supporters. In a 2011 interview between NBC's David Gregory and Eric Cantor, the House majority whip repeatedly danced around the question of whether the state of Hawaii had created a fake birth certificate in order to conceal the president's secret, foreign birth. The exchange was both representative and revealing:

GREGORY: There are elements of this country who question the president's citizenship, who think that it—his birth certificate is inauthentic. Will you call that what it is, which is crazy talk?

CANTOR: David, you know, I mean, a lot of that has been an, an issue sort of generated by not only the media, but others in the country. Most Americans really are beyond that, and they want us to focus. . . .

GREGORY: Right. Is somebody [who] brings that up just engaging in crazy talk?

CANTOR: Well, David, I, I don't think it's, it's nice to call anyone crazy, OK?

GREGORY: All right. Is it a legitimate or an illegitimate issue?

CANTOR: And—so I don't think it's an issue that we need to address at all. I think we need to focus on . . .

GREGORY: All right. His citizenship should never be questioned, in your judgment. Is that what you're saying?

CANTOR: It is, it is not an issue that even needs to be on the policy-making table right now whatsoever.

Obama's reelection forced Republicans to recalibrate in a way that his first election did not. After 2012, the Republican Party established a committee to reexamine its operations. The ensuing report tiptoed carefully around most of the party's ideological problems. It did, however, hint that its harsh antigovernment message and identification with the business class left many Americans with the sense Republicans did not care about them. While generally avoiding policy recommendations, it urged the passage of immigration reform, to give Republicans a chance to court the increasingly Democratic Latino vote. And indeed, as Obama's second term opened, even many staunchly conservative Republicans—like Ryan, Boehner, and Rubio—pushed the party to pass immigration reform and clear the issue off the table in advance of the 2016 election.

There was, however, a flaw in the plan. The flaw was that it is not easy to ferociously incite your supporters into a state of terror against the president and then turn around and pragmatically cut deals with that same president. A mutually reinforcing cycle had taken hold, in which Republicans helped convince their voters that Obama represented a fundamental and unprecedented threat to freedom, and the conservative base pushed its leaders to oppose the president on those terms. Republican leaders found it immensely difficult to compromise with the president even on those occasions when their self-interest dictated doing so, because a large segment of their voters could not imagine that normal rules of politics applied during the Obama era: that the two parties had divergent but occasionally overlapping interests that could be mediated through negotiation. There is no negotiating with a president who sits at the heart of a subversive plot.

Conservative activists blocked the party leadership from any compromise on immigration. They likewise forced Republicans in Congress to shut down the federal government. The movement's ideological cadres demanded that the party stand by its agenda of reducing taxes in a way that disproportionately benefit a small percentage of the highest earners; eliminating coverage for millions of Obamacare beneficiaries; opposing the minimum wage; and other stances with limited appeal to the broader electorate. But by the end of Obama's presidency, Republican elites discovered that the fury they had harnessed against the president's policies had raged completely beyond their control.

In 2011, Donald Trump, a figure from the world of tabloid gossip and reality television, appeared on the Obama-era political scene. Before this time, Trump had regularly floated the possibility that he would run for president, but he invariably decided not to follow through, and his political profile was an ever-mutating hodgepodge, sometimes endorsing liberal ideas like single-payer insurance and higher taxes for the rich, and other times embracing bigotry or standard right-wing tropes. The conspiratorial ferment over Obama's citizenship attracted Trump, who insisted a treacherous scheme was afoot and promised to send investigators to uncover the "real" story. It seemed to amount to nothing more than his latest outrageous publicity stunt—with one small exception. The next year, Mitt Romney, after sewing up his party's nomination, met with Trump and accepted his public endorsement, gripping hands and smiling like old friends. Why would a putatively mainstream figure go out of his way to associate himself with a controversial crank peddling a transparently bogus conspiracy theory? Because Trump's racialized paranoia turned out to represent a deep core of the conservative vote Romney needed—far deeper, perhaps, than any Republicans were willing to admit, and perhaps even deeper than Romney realized at the time.

Conservatives had a fable about their takeover of the Republican Party, one that in its countless retellings over the decades had come to be accepted by them as a timeless truth. The story began with William F. Buckley, who had publicly broken ranks with some of the most irrational and bigoted elements of the right—anti-Semites, and followers of the John Birch Society, the latter of which not only opposed Dwight Eisenhower (as Buckley himself did) but considered him a communist agent. Buckley "upheld the honor of the mainstream conservative movement," wrote *Wall Street Journal* columnist Bret Stephens in 2016, and so, even though liberals accused conservatives of pandering to racism, "the accusation rang hollow because the evidence for it was so tendentious." Having purged itself of bigotry, the fable went, the conservative movement then took over the Republican Party with appeals to the small-government beliefs of the majority of the public. Yes, they conceded, Goldwater had opposed the 1964 Civil Rights Act, but this was a minor slipup caused by his excessive zeal for the Constitution. As discussed in the first chapter, this perspective held that American passion for limited government accounted for conservatism's appeal—if anybody was exploiting race, conservatives insisted, it was the Democrats, with their "tribal" appeals to "special interests."

This willful delusion persisted through the Obama era—indeed, the pervasive racialized fear mongering on the right made it more necessary for Republicans to insist that conservatives' ideas had inspired the right-wing uprising against the first black president. Charles Krauthammer lauded what he called "a popular reaction, identified with the Tea Party but in reality far more widespread, calling for a more restrictive vision of government more consistent with the Founders' intent." Yuval Levin agreed: "the Tea Party has also been intensely focused on recovering the U.S. Constitution, and especially its limits on government power." But any close attention to what Tea Party activists actually said and believed would have dispelled this comforting fantasy. Theda Skocpol, a Harvard sociologist, conducted a detailed study of Tea Party activists and discovered that they saw themselves beset by parasitic Democrats. "Along with illegal immigrants," she wrote, "low-income Americans and young people loom large as illegitimate consumers of public benefits and services." The Tea Party activists also felt gripped with "anxieties about racial, ethnic, and generational changes in American society." Stanley Greenberg held extensive focus group discussions with Tea Party voters in 2013 in North Carolina, Virginia, and Colorado, and described their worldview in detail. Their most intense belief held that Obama had used the power of expanded government to build a majority voting coalition of racial minorities, those on welfare and food stamps, those soon to be legalized via immigration reform, those getting free health care, and the like. They were "very conscious of being white in a country with growing minorities." Abstract libertarian theories about the role of government did not interest them. They wanted to keep in place government programs that benefited people like them, shut down border crossings, and roll back social change.

The truth is that, even in its most erudite forms, conservatism was never the haven of race-blind idealism its adherents liked to imagine. (Even the sainted Buckley, who supposedly cleansed the movement of ugly bigotry, had endorsed segregation, and then, a quarter century after it was outlawed in the American South, defended apartheid in South Africa.) Trump's astonishing success in the Republican primaries blew to smithereens decades of conservative self-delusion. Here was a demagogue whose appeal barely intersected with the right's abstract ideas about the role of the state. Rather than attack government for being unworkable or too large and proposing to shrink it, as good Reagan Republicans customarily do, he attacked it for being allegedly run by morons and promised to solve all problems by having it be run by his own great business genius. Trump promised to protect every cent of Social Security and Medicare. He cravenly exploited the bigotry of the Republican electorate, even mocking their gullibility. ("I could stand in the middle of Fifth Avenue and shoot somebody and I wouldn't lose any voters," he boasted at one point.) Trump's appeal stripped away the illusions about just what made so many Americans pull the Republican lever for so long. "If Trump were to become the president, the Republican nominee, or even a failed candidate with strong conservative support," editorialized *National Review* in January 2016, well before Trump's nomination seemed inevitable, "what would that say about conservatives?" Brett Stephens lamented in the *Wall Street Journal,* "It would be terrible to think that the left was right about the right all these years." By conservatives' own logic, Trump's nomination proved exactly that.

Trump's rampage through the Republican primaries also demonstrated something else. It revealed that the grassroots Republican fury at Obama was not premised on any abstract vision of "constitutionalism"—indeed, it didn't have anything to do with any particular actions Obama had taken. Obama did not provoke a backlash by passing health care reform or other measures, nor did he fail to consummate possible deals with the Republican Party. Trump revealed how little the party base cares about governing philosophy—Trump's crude attacks on Obama, even though they were rooted in an absurd conspiracy theory, or perhaps exactly for this reason, were enough to establish his tribal loyalties. The revulsion of Obama by the party base was a racialized backlash, rooted more in the president's identity than his policies, and despite the hand-wringing of his centrist critics, no different set of policies could have avoided it.

Worst of all, from the Republican point of view, Trump blew away whatever faint remaining hopes the party nurtured of healing its reputation. Trump was the very incarnation of every value abhorrent to the Obama coalition, the anti-Obama incarnate—loud, impulsive, ignorant, intolerant, backward-looking. Trump's racism, misogyny, and contempt for expertise offended college-educated voters, racial minorities, and feminists, among others. And the America that saw itself in Trump's vision rather than Obama's was dying off. In its desperation to stop Obama, the conservatives had signed their own demographic death warrant.

Yes, Trump did win the Electoral College. In the wake of his triumph, jubilant Republicans boasted that the country had rejected Obama at last. Paul Ryan called Trump's election "a repudiation of the status quo of failed liberal progressive policies" and "a mandate"—a bizarre description of an election in which his party finished second in the national vote.

In reality, Clinton failed to carry the Electoral College for a combination of reasons attributable largely to her personal image, rather than her association with the popular incumbent. Her poor decision to use a private email server received more news coverage than all policy issues combined, creating for her an image of indelible untrustworthiness that made many voters rule her out. Clinton was unable to overcome simultaneous attacks by Russian intelligence, which stole emails of her allies and leaked them selectively in order to generate negative coverage in the American media, and the FBI, whose director made an extraordinary intervention in the race's final days to return the server issue to the forefront of the debate. Polls showed that voters considered her less honest and trustworthy than an opponent who was literally facing trial for fraud.

Republicans claimed Trump had won a mandate, which they could use to launch frenetic attacks upon the Obama legacy, not because they had any confidence that their ideas commanded the sustained support of the public, but because they knew that they did not. For eight years, Obama had filled them with the growing dread that the young president and his often-young supporters represented the future of a diversifying country alien to their own values. Trump's surprise victory gave them a last-gasp chance to stave off defeat.

But it would come at a terrible long-term price. Any chance the party could distance itself from the brand damage of its association with America's most famous bigot disappeared when his presidency became inevitable. Trump will leave a deep imprint on the psyche of young Americans, who mostly loathe him, and especially on immigrant communities, who associate him indelibly with nativist hate. In 1994, Republican Pete Wilson won the governorship in California by railing against illegal immigrants from Mexico. His state had supported Republicans in every presidential election from 1968 through 1988, and in 1992, Bill Clinton had won just 46% of the vote in a three-way race. California has tilted overwhelmingly Democratic since. Trump seems to have taken Wilson's immigrant-demonization strategy as a model rather than a cautionary tale, but his party will face the consequences. Fifty years from now, there will be Latinos and Asian-Americans who, asked why they vote Democratic, give Trump's name as an answer.

Conservative Republicans won power, but they lost the future, and they also lost the argument. The triumph of a blustering, cartoonishly dishonest and manifestly anti-intellectual candidate was a forceful display of the party's retreat from seriousness. Their critique of Obama's program amounted to doomsaying predictions that had failed to come to pass. Their alternative was a retread of failed policies and free market aphorisms sold to the public through bombastic slogan-eering and social resentment. Trump is the poisoned chalice of a failed ideology. Obama, not Trump, is destined to supply the model for American governance in the decades to come.

The GOP has not been able to escape the political identity it carved for itself in reaction to 1960s liberalism—an identity that appealed to a country consisting mostly of blue-collar whites, but which has alienated the emerging majority. The Obama presidency completed the tectonic shifts that had begun in the 1960s. The civil rights movement drove southern whites out of the Democratic Party and into the GOP. It turned the Republicans into the party of blue-collar white America, and Democrats into the party of racially liberal (mostly college-educated) whites and racial minorities. It allowed Republicans to move sharply right, and to build a majority that dominated national politics for a quarter century. But the Obama era revealed a new world in which the parties' identities, forged during this era, had hardened but their fortunes had reversed. Fittingly, many of Obama's policies borrowed from and updated the moderate Republicanism that its old party had forsaken. Obamacare copied the success Mitt Romney, the lineal heir to the moderate Republican tradition, had achieved with health care reform in Massachusetts. Obama's climate plan used a law passed under Nixon, and enjoyed the support of moderate Republican environmental regulators. His foreign policy embraced the ideas and frequently enjoyed the support of mainstream Republican foreign policy veterans. Obama had, in essence, turned the ethos of the banished moderate and liberal Republican wing—with its support for civil rights and openness to well-designed, market-friendly public solutions to social problems—into a highly effective blueprint for Democratic governance.

The Obama presidency was able not only to advance the interests of its new and growing coalition, but also to represent its values: humane, pragmatic, open to evidence and science, and welcoming to outsiders and diverse perspectives. Obama presented a new vision of America, to the world and to itself. And he had, to a degree hardly anybody recognized at the time, made his vision of a new America real.

Many Americans, those sympathetic to Obama's aims as well as those opposed, spent his presidency believing he had largely failed. But this conclusion rested on the premise that Obama had undertaken to bring about a revolution, or a post-racial society, or the banishment of all political disagreement—none of which he had ever actually promised. What had Obama promised? To unleash structural transformation in American health care and education, to bring down the country's carbon dioxide emissions, and to spare the economy from another depression. He had likewise promised thoughtful, honest governance—a "no drama" president, whose style embodied the famous Rudyard Kipling poem "If":

> *If you can keep your head when all about you*
> *Are losing theirs and blaming it on you,*
> *If you can trust yourself when all men doubt you,*
> *But make allowance for their doubting too . . .*

In 2008, sixty-nine and a half million Americans voted to entrust the presidency to Barack Obama. Many believed in him deeply, even fervently. Their faith was vindicated.

Acknowledgments

I am not always right. But Barack Obama is a subject
I believe I got right, right from the beginning. I concluded early on in Obama's presidential campaign that
he possessed a keen mind, oratorical gifts, and just the
right combination of idealism and skeptical, analytic
thinking to identify the best methods to achieve those
goals. I spent Obama's first campaign and two terms
first as an opinion journalist at *The New Republic* and
then at *New York* magazine, laying out this case as it
unspooled day by day. I criticized him when I felt he
deserved it, but mostly I found myself defending and
admiring what I concluded early on was an exceptional
and historic presidency.

The decision to turn this journalistic narrative into
a coherent book-length argument was the product of
several minds: this book's editor, Geoffrey Shandler,

my agent, Gail Ross, and my friend and former editor, Franklin Foer. It incorporates more than eight years' worth of writing I did in collaboration with my talented colleagues and editors at both magazines, including, but not limited to, Frank, Chris Orr, Jonathan Cohn, Michael Crowley, Rachel Morris, Greg Veis, Richard Just, Noam Scheiber, Ryan Lizza, David Haskell, Ben Williams, Adam Moss, Adam Pasick, Noreen Malone, and Jebediah Reed. The number of people who influenced my thinking on the subject, some of them by sharpening it with challenging critiques, is far too great to list.

Writing this book took me away from my family many nights and weekends. I hope my children read this one day, and if they do, that they consider the sacrifice worthwhile. Robin, Joanna, and Benjy, and Mom, Dad, and Daniel, I owe everything to you.

About the Author

Jonathan Chait is a political columnist for *New York* magazine. He was previously a senior editor at *The New Republic* and has also written for the *Los Angeles Times,* the *New York Times,* the *Wall Street Journal,* and *The Atlantic.* He has been featured throughout the media, including appearances on NPR, MSNBC, Fox News, CNN, HBO, *The Colbert Report, Talk of the Nation,* C-SPAN, *Hardball,* and on talk radio in every major city in America. He lives in Washington, D.C.